Inventory Accounting

Inventory Accounting

A COMPREHENSIVE GUIDE

Steven M. Bragg

John Wiley & Sons, Inc.

For general information on our other products and services, or technical support, please
contact our Customer Care Department within the United States at 800-762-2974, outside
the United States at 317-572-3993, or fax 317-572-4002.

Wiley also publishes its books in a variety of electronic formats. Some content that appears in print may not be available in electronic books.

Library of Congress Cataloging-in-Publication Data:
Bragg, Steven M.
  Inventory accounting : a comprehensive guide / Steven M. Bragg.
    p. cm.
  Includes bibliographical references and index.
  ISBN 0-471-35642-5 (cloth)
  1. Inventories—Accounting. 2. Inventory control. I. Title.
HF5681.S8B73 2005
657'.72—dc22

                                                              2004019939

Printed in the United States of America

10 9 8 7 6 5 4 3 2 1

Dedication

Once again, to Victoria. If a warehouse looked like your room, the fire marshall would shut it down.

Contents

Preface

The accountant can find answers to almost any inventory-related question in this book. Within the general area of inventory accounting systems, it addresses data entry for inventory transactions, tracking inventory through different types of manufacturing environments, key control points and related fraud problems, several dozen inventory-related measurements, several inventory report formats, and budgeting for inventory. A large part of the book also covers inventory valuation, including many cost layering systems, the lower of cost or market rule, overhead calculations, joint and by-product costing, and the management of obsolete inventory issues. There are also several chapters devoted to special topics, including IRS inventory rules, counting procedures, best practices related to inventory, transfer pricing, and inventory terminology. Thus, *Inventory Accounting* not only includes answers to the basic inventory valuation questions, but also provides the accountant with a great deal of additional information related to controls, budgeting, data collection, fraud, and inventory management.

The first six chapters cover the general subject area of inventory accounting systems. Chapter 1 describes the application of bar coding, wireless data transmission, radio frequency identification, document imaging, and electronic data interchange to the collection of inventory data. Chapter 2 addresses the flow of inventory through a basic manufacturing system, as well as through a manufacturing resources planning system and a just-in-time system. Chapter 3 describes 68 possible inventory controls in such areas as in-transit inventory, inventory storage, obsolete inventory, and inventory transactions. As a logical follow-up to Chapter 3, Chapter 4 discusses 18 types of fraud that involve inventory in some manner. Chapter 5 includes 32 measurements, 3 forms, and 7 reports that can be used to determine the status of inventory levels and related systems. Chapter 6 discusses the budgeting process to be used for the raw materials, work-in-process, and finished goods inventories.

The next six chapters cover the general subject area of inventory valuation. Chapter 7 describes how to use several inventory cost layering systems: the first-in, first-out (FIFO), last-in, first-out (LIFO), dollar value LIFO, link-chain, and weighted average methods. Chapter 8 describes the lower of cost or market rule and how to apply it. Chapter 9 addresses the contents of overhead cost pools and how to apply those costs to inventory (including the use of activity-based costing). Chapter 10 covers various cost allocation and pricing methodologies for inventory designated as joint products or by-products, while Chapter 11 reveals how to locate, dispose of, and account for obsolete inventory. Chapter 12 contains a summary of those journal entries that are most commonly used by the inventory accountant.

The final four chapters and an appendix address special inventory topics. Chapter 13 is a direct extract of that portion of the Internal Revenue Code related to inventory, with integrated commentary by the author. Chapter 14 discusses how to create an inventory tracking system and conduct both periodic physical counts and cycle counts. Chapter 15 lists best practices clustered into the general areas of inventory purchasing, receiving and shipping, storage, picking, production, transactions, and quantity management. Chapter 16 describes the need for transfer pricing and compares the applicability of six transfer pricing methods. Finally, Appendix A contains definitions for more than 150 inventory-related terms.

Inventory Accounting is intended to be an expansive compendium of inventory-related information for the accountant. It is extremely useful not only for handling basic inventory transactions, but also as a source of information for improving inventory control systems, measuring inventory performance, and reducing a company's investment in inventory. Enjoy!

Steven M. Bragg
Centennial, Colorado
August 2004

About the Author

Steven Bragg, CPA, CMA, CIA, CPIM, has been the chief financial officer or controller of four companies, as well as a consulting manager at Ernst & Young and auditor at Deloitte & Touche. He received a master's degree in finance from Bentley College, an MBA from Babson College, and a Bachelor's degree in Economics from the University of Maine. He has been the two-time president of the 10,000-member Colorado Mountain Club, is an avid alpine skier and mountain biker, and is a certified master diver. Mr. Bragg resides in Centennial, Colorado. He has published the following books through John Wiley & Sons:

Accounting and Finance for Your Small Business

Accounting Best Practices

Accounting Reference Desktop

Billing and Collections Best Practices

Business Ratios and Formulas

Controller's Guide to Costing

Controller's Guide to Planning and Controlling Operations

Controller's Guide: Roles and Responsibilities for the New Controller

Controllership

Cost Accounting

Design and Maintenance of Accounting Manuals

Essentials of Payroll

Financial Analysis

GAAP Implementation Guide

Inventory Best Practices

Just-in-Time Accounting

Managing Explosive Corporate Growth

Outsourcing

Payroll Accounting

Sales and Operations for Your Small Business

The Controller's Function

The New CFO Financial Leadership Manual

The Ultimate Accountants' Reference

Also:

Advanced Accounting Systems (Institute of Internal Auditors)
Run the Rockies (CMC Press)

1

Inventory Data Collection[1]

1-1 Introduction

The classical view of inventory data collection is that of employees filling out forms of various kinds throughout the warehouse and production areas, which are then forwarded to a central data entry location, where hordes of clerks keypunch the data into a central computer database. Although this was a reasonably accurate view of the situation in the past, the types of systems available for collecting information are now more efficient and effective. These systems were developed because of a growing recognition that traditional data collection methods require a great deal of employee time that could be better spent on value-added tasks. Also, having a secondary data entry step increases the likelihood of keypunching errors, which can be completely avoided by some of the data collection methods discussed in this chapter.

Some of the data systems that can be used to collect inventory information are shown in Exhibit 1-1. They lie along a continuum that begins with loosely formatted data, such as that found on a faxed document, and ends with perfectly formatted data that can be directly entered into a computer system without alteration, such as electronic data interchange (EDI) transactions or transactions entered through an electronic form. A special case is document imaging, which can be tightly coupled to a company's computer systems or maintained as a freestanding system with no linkages at all. Accordingly, it is surrounded by a larger box in the exhibit, indicating the range within the exhibit that it can occupy. Based on the information in the exhibit, it is evident that an inventory accountant should recommend installation of the systems noted in the upper right-hand corner because they provide the best means for collecting the highest-quality costing information that can be injected directly into a company's central database of costing information.

This chapter discusses the more advanced data collection techniques noted in Exhibit 1-1, as well as a pair of more specialized methods that apply only to the

---

[1]Several sections of this chapter were adapted with permission from Chapter 4 of Bragg, *Cost Accounting: A Comprehensive Guide*, John Wiley & Sons, 2001.

Exhibit 1-1 *Characteristics of Data Collection Systems*

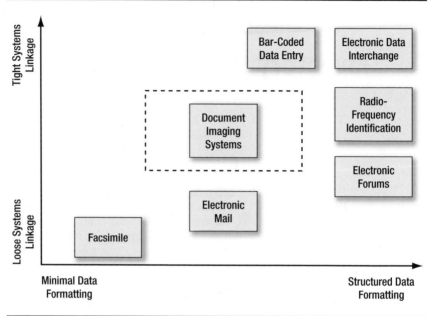

picking function: voice picking and pick-to-light. It also notes how to use back-flushing to avoid most inventory transactions.

1-2   Bar Coding

Let us say that Company Alpha wants to track the progress of a product through every step of its production process. Being a technologically advanced organization, it has installed data entry keypads at each of its workstations. One of these products is assigned the part number AD-546-798. The operator of each workstation is required to enter the part number using a keypad, followed by the number of units completed. The inventory accountant uses this information to determine the progress of work-in-process batches as they move through the plant. However, the part number is so meaningless that 3 of the 10 workstation operators enter the information incorrectly by transposing numbers. The 546 part of the number is in the same row on the keypad as the 798 portion of the number, so transpositions are difficult to avoid. This error results in unreadable reports that the inventory accountant must manually correct by going to the shop floor and tracking each job by hand.

Obviously, data entry inaccuracy is a big problem in this instance. In the real world, it is an enormous issue because employees are asked to enter data into computer systems even if they are not properly trained in data entry. The author recently observed a situation where a workforce whose primary language was not English, and which also experienced an annual turnover rate of greater than 200%, was asked to enter production data into a warehouse database; the results were continuing inventory record inaccuracy levels of 50% or greater despite weekly cycle counts. In short, the human element of data entry can cause considerable difficulty in ensuring that accurate data is entered into a computer database. This problem can be resolved through the use of bar codes.

A bar code is a set of alternating parallel bars and spaces of different widths that signify letters, numbers, and other characters. When scanned by a laser beam attached to a computer chip containing a decoding algorithm, this cluster of bars and spaces is converted to an alphanumeric character. Several algorithms result in different types of bar codes. One of the most popular is Code 39, which contains both letters and numbers (i.e., is alphanumeric) and is heavily used in manufacturing. Another is Interleaved 2 of 5, which contains only numeric characters; this bar code is most commonly found in the automotive, warehousing, and baggage handling industries. Yet another variation is the universal product code (UPC), which is primarily found in supermarkets and in the retailing industry. Whatever the method used, all of these bar codes can be generated within a company by entering the required characters into a computer, which converts them to the needed bar code format and sends them to a printer. A laser printer is recommended because it yields a higher-resolution bar code, although inkjet printers are close in comparative levels of resolution. Dot-matrix printers are not recommended for bar code printing because of their much lower resolution levels.

Whatever the type of bar code used, the subsequent processing steps are the same. A bar code is manufactured at the point of use, typically by a special application printer that only produces bar codes. The bar code is typically a self-adhesive one that is affixed to the item to be tracked; this procedure can be automated if the volume of activity warrants investment in such machinery. Then the item being tracked moves through whatever process is occurring and is scanned at fixed points in the process. This scanning can be conducted by a person with a handheld scanner or by an automated scanning station. The scanner extracts information for the bar code and feeds it directly into the computer database.

There are several types of scanners, and the choice of model depends on the application. The main categories of scanners are as follows:

- *Light pen.* This is the least expensive type, requiring a user to manually drag the scanning device across the bar code. It has a low success rate and may require several scans before an accurate scan is completed. It is most commonly used for low-volume applications where the speed of scanning is not important and where low cost is the determining factor of use.
- *Handheld scanner.* This device contains a motor that rapidly sends a series of laser scans across a bar code, resulting in a much faster scan. It can also be used with bar codes printed with relatively poor resolution. This scanner can be used with a direct wire linkage to a computer or through radio transmission to a local radio receiver, thereby allowing roving use of the device. A handheld scanner is several times more expensive than a light pen, and radio-frequency scanners usually cost several thousand dollars each.

■ *Stationary fixed-beam scanner.* This device is not intended for manual use. Instead, it is fixed in place at a point past which items are moved, such as on a conveyor belt. The scanner must achieve success on a single scan of any passing bar code or no read will result. To handle this situation, the conveyor belt must be equipped with a shunting gate so that the unscanned items are pushed to one side, allowing machine operators to move them back through the scanning station for a second attempt.

■ *Stationary moving-beam scanner.* This device is the same as a stationary fixed-beam scanner except that it is equipped with a motor that sends a series of scans over each bar code, ensuring a high percentage of successful scans. This type of scanner is more expensive than the fixed-beam variety, but its added cost can be offset against the reduced (or eliminated) need for a shunting gate and the manual labor associated with it.

Bar coding is tailor-made for inventory transactions. For example, an inventory identification number is often randomly assigned to a component or product and so has no meaning to the person entering it into the computer system for a transaction. This situation leads to inaccurate data entry. To avoid this problem, bar codes can be attached to all inventory items, which are then scanned as part of any inventory move transaction.

Another inventory-related use of bar codes is shop floor control. As a job works its way through the production area, some companies require the production staff to extract information from a routing sheet attached to the job and enter it into a local data entry terminal. This information tells the production control staff where the job is located in the production process and can also be used by the accounting staff to determine the costs that each job has compiled thus far. It is possible for the data entry person to enter this identification incorrectly, so bar codes can be added to the routing sheet in place of written identification information. The data entry person then scans the bar codes into the local data entry terminal instead of making a typed entry.

Clearly, there are many uses for bar coding. It is ideal for situations where the risk of data entry error is high and is also useful when a company wants to use automation to avoid manual data entry. However, there is a cost associated with the purchase and implementation of bar code printing and scanning equipment, so the inventory accountant should first calculate the costs and benefits associated with the use of this equipment before proceeding to an actual installation.

1-3   Wireless Data Transmission

When a transaction is entered into a computer terminal, it travels through a wire or fiber-optic cable to a database for storage. Unfortunately, this data entry method requires one to walk to a fixed terminal location in order to enter data, which is not always possible for employees who collect data as they travel through a facility.

The answer to this problem is to obtain a terminal that sends wireless transmissions to a receiver that in turn is directly linked to a database. This allows data entry to take place virtually anywhere. This mode of data entry has improved rapidly, and several types of portable terminals have been developed. One is the radio-frequency bar code scanner, which is an integrated liquid crystal display, keyboard, and scanner. It is frequently used in warehouses, where cycle counters can enter quantity changes on the spot rather than write them down, walk to a terminal, enter the data, and then walk back to the counting area. Another terminal is the wireless Palm computer (and several knockoff versions thereof), which one can enter information into with a stylus and then send it to a Web site, from which it is sent as an electronic message to a company's database. Yet another variation is a portable computer linked to a cellular phone; a modem connection is made through the phone, which transmits data over a phone line to the company, where it is converted to a digital signal and sent to the corporate database.

Wireless applications are directly applicable to inventory transactions. For example, a major problem with any inventory system is that the warehouse staff conducts a transaction and then must find a computer terminal in which to enter the information. This may involve a long walk, so there is some risk that the worker will forget some of the information to be entered or entirely miss making the entry. Radio-frequency bar code scanners avoid this problem because they are readily available for use no matter where the worker travels within a facility. The information is scanned or punched into the portable unit, and the transaction is immediately sent to the central computer database for updating.

Also, any manager who wants to ensure a high level of inventory accuracy must send an employee into the warehouse to confirm that the inventory quantities listed in the computer are the same as those on the shelves. The trouble is that the cycle counter must plod through the warehouse with a thick sheaf of inventory reports, locate the item to be counted in the report, find it on the shelf, write down any corrections, go back to the terminal, and enter any changes. Clearly, this is a time-consuming process. A better approach is to use a radio-frequency bar code scanner to scan the part number of the item on the shelf, scan the bar code for the item's warehouse location, have the scanner immediately reveal whether there is a counting discrepancy by accessing the central database, and then making a correction on the spot.

Assuming a high level of staff training, the adoption of a wireless system combined with bar-coded transactions can push a company's inventory transaction error rate to well under 1%. Also, given the reduced amount of time required to enter transactions, one can count on the labor capacity of the warehouse staff to increase substantially.

1-4   Radio Frequency Identification (RFID)

A major problem with any manually operated inventory system is the vast number of transactions required to track receipts into the warehouse, moves between bins, issuances to the shop floor, returns from the floor, scrap, and so on. Every time someone creates a transaction, there is a chance of incorrect data being entered, resulting in a cumulative variance that can be quite large by the time a stock item has wended its way through all possible transactions. Incorrect inventory information leads to a host of other problems, such as stockouts, incorrect purchasing quantities, and a seriously inaccurate cost of goods sold. Although bar coding applications can resolve these problems, bar codes can be destroyed in some environments, are too difficult to read, or require too much staff time to locate for scanning purposes.

One way to avoid these transactional errors is to use the new RFID technology. Although only recently formulated,[2] the technology has already been adopted by Wal-Mart, which should ensure a rapid rollout in at least the retail industry. The basic RFID concept has been around for years—attach a tiny transmitter to each product, which then sends a unique encoded product identification number to a reader device. The cost of these transmitter tags has dropped to about 10 cents (depending on their level of complexity and power source), which begins to make it a cost-effective alternative for some applications. Growing use of the technology will likely reduce the cost further.

When a tagged inventory item is passed near a reader device, the reader emits a signal, which powers up the tag, allowing it to emit its unique product identification number. In order to read a large number of tags, the reader turns on each tag in sequence, reads it, and turns off the tag, thereby preventing confusion with repetitive reads. The tag information is then logged into the inventory tracking system, indicating an inventory move past the point where the reader was located.

The most likely implementation scenario for RFID is to first roll it out within the warehouse and manufacturing areas of a company, using it to track entire pallet loads (good for receiving and inventory control transactions) and then implementing it for smaller tracking units, such as cases (good for picking, cycle counts, and shipment transactions) or even individual items (most applicable for work-in-process inventory or retail applications). This implementation approach allows for a progressively increasing investment in the technology as a company gradually learns about its applicability.

A major advantage of RFID is its ability to provide inventory count information without any manual transaction keypunching. This eliminates the need for manual receiving, inventory move, and issuance transactions. It can also provide real-time information about the precise location of all inventory, which can assist with locating missing inventory, arranging cycle counts, and auditing stock. If issued to suppliers, this information tells them precisely how much inventory is currently on hand, so they can more accurately determine when to deliver more stock to the company.

An additional capability of RFID is the activation of an alarm if a tagged item is shifted off the company premises. Another possibility is the use of a more expensive self-powered tag (currently costing about $15 each) that can actively relay its precise location in relation to a fixed overhead positioning unit. The latest tag technology also allows one to rewrite the information stored on a tag many times, which

---

[2]The RFID standards can be found at *www.epcglobalinc.org*.

brings up the possibility of adding data regarding the progress of a unit through various workstations in the production area. Yet another option is to track trailers in a storage area by affixing a single self-powered unit to each one, thereby solving the problem of where specific inventory batches are located. Finally, RFID can be used as an error-prevention device to ensure that goods intended for a specific customer are not loaded onto the wrong truck.

One problem with RFID is the possibility of radio interference, which can be a major problem in heavy manufacturing environments. As a general rule, if wiring in the warehouse and shop area must already be shielded in order to ensure proper data transmission, then RFID may not work. If this potential exists, then be sure to conduct extensive transmission testing in all areas where inventory may be tracked to ensure that radio interference will not be an issue. Another problem is that certain products, such as steel or fluids, obviously cannot be tagged. Yet another issue is that no suppliers have yet developed a complete turnkey RFID solution, so companies are still forced to use consultants to cobble together a disparate set of components into a working system. Given the difficulty of setting up these systems and the introductory level of much of the technology, it is impossible to install even a simple system for under $100,000, with large multisite installations costing well into the millions.

1-5   Document Imaging

The assumption in most organizations is that a paper document must be manually transcribed into a computer database. However, an alternative to this labor-intensive approach is to simply insert the document into a scanner and punch an indexing number into an attached computer terminal, thereby converting the document directly into a digitized form and making it easily accessible from any linked computer terminal throughout the company.

The basic structure of this document imaging system is shown in Exhibit 1-2, which illustrates several ways to input documents into a computer, the most common being the use of a scanner. When a document has been converted to a digital format by this means, it still cannot be stored in the computer database because there would be no way to retrieve it. Consequently, one or more indexing numbers must be punched in. For example, these could be the unique number assigned to the scanned document, the name of the customer, the date, or any other information allowing a user to readily access the document again. The key issue is to ensure that the document is not lost in the database.

The digitized document is then stored in a high-capacity storage device, usually a compact disc (CD) jukebox. This is a device containing a large number of CDs that allows rapid access to the data in each one (as opposed to tape storage systems). The jukebox format can store several terabytes of data, and it needs to because a single document stored at a high image-quality level can require up to 1/2 megabyte of storage capacity. However, it is more common to choose a lower level of document resolution when scanning into a database, which results in much lower stor-

Exhibit 1-2 *Overview of the Document Imaging Process Flow*

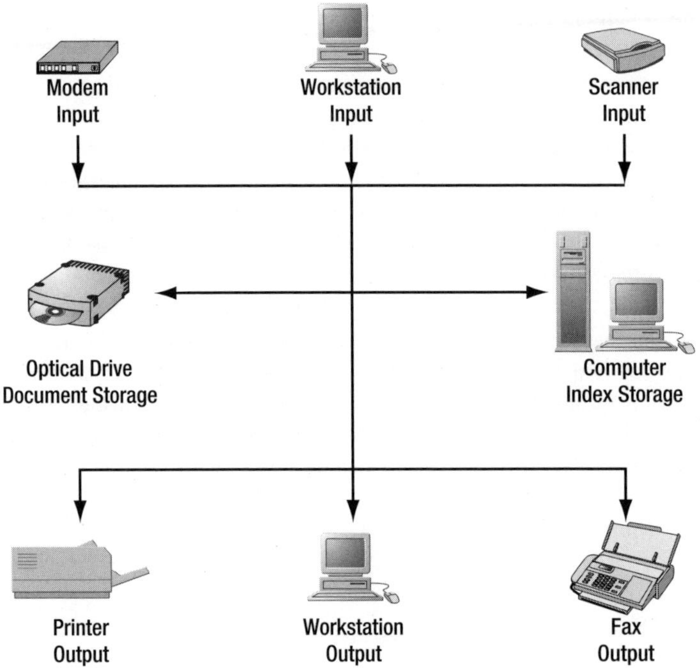

Modem
Input

Workstation
Input

Scanner
Input

Optical Drive
Document Storage

Computer
Index Storage

Printer
Output

Workstation
Output

Fax
Output

age requirements, usually in the range of 1/10 megabyte. The indexing file system is stored separately in a high-speed storage device that can rapidly sort through a large indexing file to find the correct document. This index is then used to extract a file from the CD jukebox and send it to a user on demand.

There are several ways to output the data from a document imaging system. The most common one is direct output to a user terminal, which has the dual advantages of saving paper and of allowing users to see a document on their screens side-by-side with other pertinent information. Other types of output include printing, facsimile, and modem transmission. The most common output is straight to a terminal.

The use of document imaging by an inventory accountant is primarily for drill-down analysis. It makes research efforts much easier by allowing the accountant to find all of the materials relevant to an information search without ever having to leave the terminal. For example, if he is looking for the reason for a specific purchase, he can drill down into the accounting system from the general ledger account to the purchasing journal, which shows the date and amount of the purchase as well as the purchase order number. If the system is linked to a materials management system, he may even be able to drill down to a copy of the purchase order, but he cannot reference the purchase requisition used to derive the purchase order. Now, with document imaging, he can use the requisition number noted on the purchase order to index the scanned requisition, which shows precisely what was ordered and who ordered it. There is no need to conduct research in a paper file, which makes this a much faster way to conduct inventory accounting research.

An added benefit of document imaging is that more than one person can access the same document at the same time. With a paper-based system, there is always the problem of files being missing because they are being used by someone (and the added problem of their not being returned to the appropriate location), resulting in a delay in research efforts until the files are returned. With document imaging, the file remains in the same storage location in the CD jukebox, no matter how many users are reviewing it at the same time. Thus, research is never delayed by missing documents.

The document imaging solution is a good one, but its costs must be considered. For a small organization, the cost of the computer hardware and software may be too high in relation to the cost savings anticipated from converting a small volume of documents to a digitized format. However, large-volume organizations dealing with tens or hundreds of thousands of documents find that the cost of such a system is negligible in comparison to the benefits gained. Prices are constantly dropping in this area, so it is difficult to itemize imaging system prices that will be valid for any length of time. In general, a low-end imaging system can be obtained for a price in the low five-figure range, while the cost of a high-volume transaction solution can easily exceed $1 million. When preparing a cost-benefit transaction solution for a document imaging system, one should consider the benefits not only of reducing research time but also of eliminating rent on document storage space, staff positions for filing work, and the cost of locating misfiled documents.

1-6 Electronic Data Interchange

Data collection is particularly painful when data is received from a company's trading partner and must then be reentered into the company's database. The problem is that the information sent to the company may not be the same as that required by the internal system, so someone must contact the trading partner for the missing information. In addition, there is always the risk of data entry errors, which can be caused by simple retyping mistakes or a misreading of the received document (as may be caused by a blurry fax). All of these costs are non-value-added because they contribute nothing to the underlying value of the product or service the company provides. These issues can be eliminated through the use of electronic data interchange.

For a few hundred dollars, one can purchase an elementary EDI software package that reveals an electronic form on the computer screen. One enters all of the data needed into a set of required fields for whatever standard transaction is required—more than 100 have been carefully defined by an international standard organization. Once all of the transactions have been entered, the computer sends the information to the business partner by modem or broadband connection. The recipient then accesses the data through its modem, prints it, and manually transfers the information to its computer system. Although very simple, this approach is not much better than sending the same information by fax machine, because it still requires manual entry of data at both ends of the transaction. The only improvement over the fax machine is the higher quality of the received image, which cannot be blurred by electronic transmission.

A much better approach is to have the computer system at the sending organization automatically reformat a transaction into EDI format and also send it automatically—no operator intervention required! The same process can be achieved at the receiving end, where incoming transactions are automatically received, reformatted, and inserted into the in-house computer system. With this approach, all risk of data entry error is completely eliminated. This is a particularly valuable capability at companies with large volumes of data flowing between them and their trading partners.

A final issue for EDI application is how to send a transaction between companies. It is possible to send a transmission directly to each business partner, which can have a computer permanently dedicated to the task of receiving such transactions. However, this computer may be tied up receiving a transaction from some other company and the transmission cannot go through. There may also be a problem with incompatible modem transmission and reception speeds, although this is not an issue when broadband connections are used. To avoid these problems, consider signing up with a value-added network (VAN), which is a central computing facility that receives EDI transmissions from trading partners and stores them in electronic mailboxes for recipients. The recipients automatically poll their mailboxes every few hours and extract the messages that have arrived. The VAN operator charges a fee for each transaction flowing through its computer system, but this arrangement provides a much more error-free environment in which to transact business. The complete EDI process is shown in Exhibit 1-3.

Despite its advantages, EDI is not used by many companies. One reason is that the system takes a great deal of time to set up, involving travel to business partner locations to convince them to participate and programming time to automate all linkages to and from partner computer systems. Given these difficulties, many companies only use EDI with their highest-volume trading partners.

1-7   Specialized Forms of Inventory Data Collection[3]

In warehouse situations where the staff is required to pick large numbers of inventory items, there is a significant risk of transactional error, simply because of the massive number of individual item-specific transactions involved. This is a particular problem in picking operations involving hard-to-handle items, because the staff must constantly stop picking to enter transactions, inevitably resulting in missed transactions.

---

[3]Adapted with permission from Chapter 5 of Bragg, *Inventory Best Practices,* John Wiley & Sons, 2004.

Exhibit 1-3 *Electronic Data Interchange Process Flow*

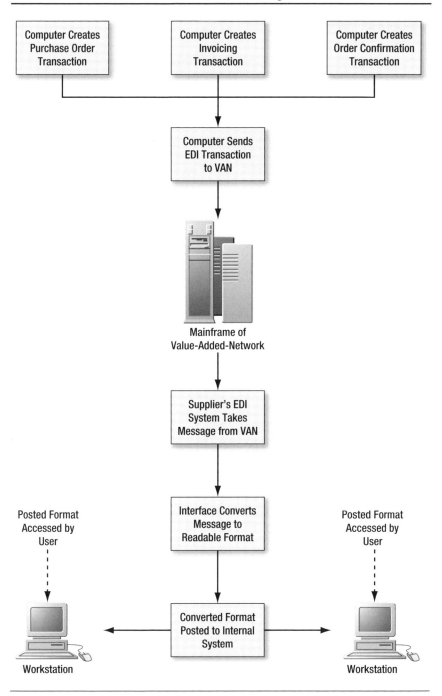

In some situations, a good way to reduce the transaction error rate is the use of *voice picking*. Under this technology, employees wear a self-contained computer on a belt. The computer communicates by radio frequency with the company computer in real time; it accepts picking information from the main computer and translates this information into English, which it communicates to the worker in English for hands-free picking with no written pick sheet. The worker also talks to the computer via a headset, telling it when items have been picked. The computer converts these spoken words into electronic messages for immediate transfer back to the main computer. This approach allows employees to record transactions in real time while they pick and to do so without having to walk to a computer terminal to enter the information. This is a particularly effective solution for people with limited writing skills.

There are a few problems with voice picking, however. First, very loud warehouse environments can interfere with communications. Second, batteries on these units can fail, so one should only acquire units with extended-life batteries, or at least keep extra units on hand to replace failed ones. Also, only acquire computers that can operate independently from the main computer if communications are interrupted for a short time. Finally, this approach works best in a low-volume picking environment.

Transaction processing is particularly difficult in situations where stock pickers must quickly pick very high volumes of small-size stock keeping units (SKUs), especially in eaches or broken case situations. Given the need to record transactions coincident to the picking, this environment tends to result in a high incidence of transactional errors. Also, using the traditional approach of picking from a printed pick list, employees must spend time locating SKUs, ensuring that they pick the correct quantity, and entering these changes into the computer system; this is an inefficient way to use warehouse staff time.

A good alternative for this type of picking is a *pick-to-light* solution. Under this approach, light sensors are mounted on the front of each bin location in the warehouse. Each sensor unit is linked to the computer system's picking module and contains a light that illuminates to indicate that picking is required for an order, a liquid crystal display (LCD) readout listing the number of required SKUs, and a button to press to indicate completion of a pick. When a stock picker enters or scans a bar-coded order number into the system, the bin sensors for those bins containing required picks will light up, and their LCD displays will show the number of units to pick. When a stock picker has completed picking from a bin, he or she presses the button, and the indicator lights shut off.

This system not only allows pickers to accurately pick without a pick list, but it also transmits successful picks back to the inventory database for real-time record updates. Also, because the system itemizes the exact quantity to pick, as well as the bin from which to pick, it is difficult to pick an incorrect quantity or bin, thereby increasing transactional accuracy. More advanced systems also include increment or decrement buttons, so cycle counters can enter inventory quantity adjustments into the inventory database on the spot. It is also possible to summarize several orders into a master order and pick just once in larger quantities for this master order, thereby reducing pick time.

Although this approach to picking is excellent, it is expensive. Besides the cost of indicator panels for each rack location, one must also invest in the integration of all related software into the existing warehouse management system. Given the cost of this approach, it is most common to see it being used only for the highest-volume SKUs. As prices fall, we may see a larger proportion of inventory being picked using this system. Another issue is changes in picker training and related procedures to mesh with the new system, which one should consider well in advance of system implementation. Any new training and procedures should be tested with a small group of pickers before rolling them out to the full picking staff.

1-8 Backflushing

The preceding discussions have all focused on the uses of technology to make data collection easier. What about using a different production tracking system to eliminate the need for data collection? In this section, we discuss how backflushing works and how it can be used to reduce the volume of data collection.

A traditional inventory tracking system traces inventory as it moves from the warehouse, through the production process, and to the shipping dock. This approach requires one to record a transaction for every physical inventory movement. Each time this occurs, another computer entry is needed to tell the production control staff where the inventory is now located, as well as to inform the accounting staff of what new manufacturing charges can be added to products as they are converted into finished goods form. This is clearly a labor-intensive approach that is also highly prone to data entry error.

A different approach is used by the backflushing system. With this method, no transaction entry is made until a product has been completed—there is no entry to show that anything has left the warehouse or traveled through the various stages of production. Instead, the computer system takes the final production figure entered, breaks it down into its constituent parts, and removes these items from the warehouse records.

This procedure can save a significant amount of data entry time, but it is useful only in certain situations. First, it should be used only when the production staff is fully capable of achieving accurate final production counts, because miscounts result in incorrect changes to warehouse records. This is a particular problem for companies with high levels of production employee turnover or low educational levels, because such conditions result in poor levels of employee knowledge of procedures, which in turn leads to inaccurate data entry. Second, there must be accurate systems in place to trace any fallout from the production process, such as for scrap or rework. These items are not eliminated from the inventory database through the standard backflushing system, and so must be accounted for separately. If this is not done, the reported inventory levels will be too high. Finally, the production process must be a short one, preferably completing products in a single day. If not, backflushing of components from stock may not occur for some time, which renders the inventory database inaccurate. It may state that inventory is on hand that is actually currently in production. This factor is also important from an inventory valuation perspective, because a rapid production process allows a company to flush out its production lines at the end of a reporting period so there is no work-in-process to be valued by the accounting staff. If these factors have not been considered by the management team, it is probable that a backflushing system will lead to incorrect data in a company's materials management database, despite the greatly reduced level of data entry it requires. Consequently, the backflushing option should be used with care.

1-9 Summary of Data Collection Techniques

Many data collection methods have been described in this section. Of the items presented, bar coding (preferably using wireless technology) is the most broadly applicable. Although it may be heavily supplemented by and even partially supplanted by radio-frequency identification, this transformation will not occur until the RFID technology becomes less expensive and more reliable. In the meantime, bar coding is the most reliable and error-free approach to inventory data collection.

Electronic data interchange is used for the exchange of information between trading partners, and so tends to be an add-on application to a corporate data collection system. Likewise, document imaging is a useful additional application that provides extra information about documents whose text cannot otherwise be incorporated into an inventory database. Nonetheless, it is a peripheral application whose importance is strictly secondary to the recording of basic inventory transactions.

Both voice picking and pick-to-light are excellent data collection techniques, but they are expensive and only apply to a small (although important) subset of all inventory transactions.

Finally, the use of backflushing can result in a massive reduction in the volume of inventory transactions but can also lead to a considerable reduction in inventory accuracy unless properly installed.

Thus, the best approach to inventory data collection is to first install bar coding to improve overall inventory transactional accuracy. Then, if it is necessary to conduct extensive communications with business partners, bolt on an EDI application. Otherwise, consider the use of pick-to-light or voice picking if there are many picking transactions. At this point, nearly all inventory transactions will contain some degree of automation, and inventory record accuracy should be relatively high. This is a good time to consider the pros and cons of implementing backflushing, but with the knowledge that it may not be applicable to a company's specific circumstances. The last step is to review the need for a document imaging system in order to layer more information onto the inventory database.

2

Inventory and Manufacturing Systems[1]

2-1 Introduction

In the preceding chapter, we discussed a variety of methods for collecting data about inventory. The next question one might ask is: What information do I need to collect, and how might this vary depending on the manufacturing system in use? This chapter covers the flow of information through a bare-bones manufacturing system using minimal transactions, one organized under a manufacturing resources planning (MRP II) system, as well as one under a just-in-time system. The differences in transactions required for the various systems, as you will see, are significant.

2-2 The Simplified Manufacturing System

An entrepreneur decides to manufacture a new product and does so out of his garage until expanded sales allow him to move into a small production facility and hire a few staff to assist in the process. In this home-grown environment, the first required inventory transaction occurs when the fledgling company receives billings from its suppliers subsequent to having ordered supplies, requiring it to record a liability to the supplier and an offsetting inventory asset for whatever was bought. When the company eventually sells products, it must record another transaction to relieve the inventory account for the amount sold, with an offsetting increase in a cost of goods sold account. The basic transactions are noted in Exhibit 2-1 at the points in the cost of goods sold cycle where they occur.

Although this approach is admirable for its spare style, it is severely lacking from both a control and costing standpoint. First, the entrepreneur has no idea if there is any scrap in the manufacturing process, because the system does not relieve

---

[1]The MRP II and JIT system descriptions in this chapter were adapted with permission from Chapters 26 and 27 of Bragg, *Cost Accounting: A Comprehensive Guide,* John Wiley & Sons, 2001.

Exhibit 2-1 Inventory Transactions in a Simplified Manufacturing System

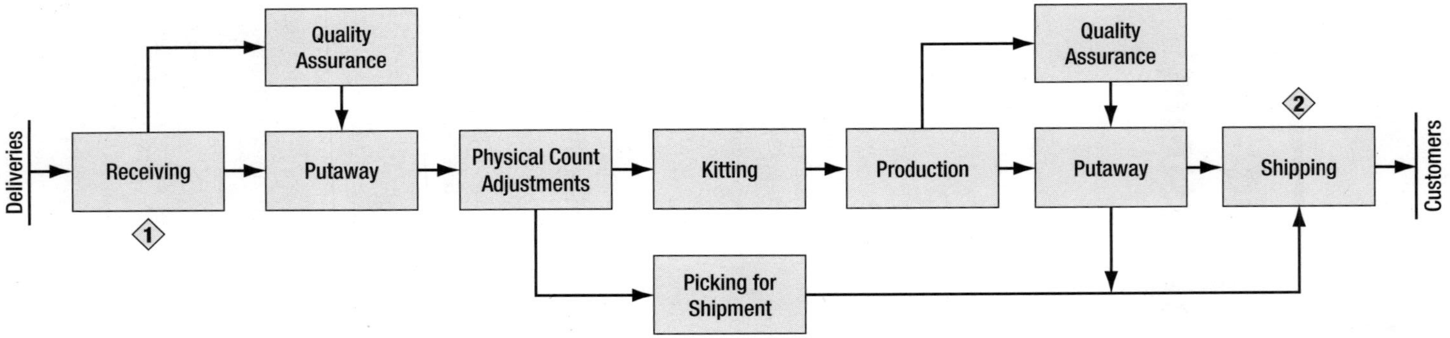

Journal Entries

⟨1⟩ Inventory receipt

	Db	Cr
Inventory	xx	
Accounts Payable		xx

⟨2⟩ Inventory sale

	Db	Cr
Cost of goods	xx	
Inventory		xx

any scrap from the system. Second, the purchasing department staff can order inventory whenever they want and in any quantities without anyone knowing if they are doing a good job, because the system has no way of determining how much inventory is actually in stock. Third, the inventory accountant cannot assign production costs to inventory, because there is no device for tracking the status of inventory through production; instead, all production costs must be charged to expense in the current period, even if the company is deliberately building its inventory stocks, resulting in probable losses in the current period and disproportionately high profits when the inventory is later sold. Consequently, the bare-bones style requires little accounting but has a severe impact on one's ability to run the business.

The problems just noted will have a considerable negative impact on the company as it grows, so the entrepreneur is usually forced to add more inventory transactions. These added transactions are noted in Exhibit 2-2.

The exhibit shows journal entries being initiated whenever inventory physically moves to a different part of the company, including raw materials inventory (shown as "R/M Inventory" in the related journal entry), work-in-process inventory (shown as "WIP Inventory"), and finished goods inventory (shown as "F/G Inventory). There is also a journal entry to record any quantity adjustments encountered during a physical count; the related journal entry indicates that either a debit or credit can be used, because adjustment may increase or decrease the on-hand balance. Note that the entrepreneur has just gone from two journal entries to eight, thereby quadrupling the required volume of transactions. At this point, one should seriously consider the use of bar coding data entry methods as described in the preceding chapter, because transaction errors are likely to increase dramatically at this stage.

Although the entrepreneur may have a much better handle on the location of and quantity of his inventory with this more advanced system, the state of his product costs has not improved much: He is now recording scrap as soon as it occurs, but he is not adding costs to inventory for direct labor or overhead costs incurred. Furthermore, he is not tracking the changing cost of raw materials over time with any sort of cost layering system. Finally, there is no consideration of reducing inventory costs for either obsolescence or the lower of cost or market rule. Without these added calculations, the inventory is not in compliance with generally accepted accounting principles for inventory costing and would fail an audit. The details of these added transactions are described in detail in Part II (Inventory Transactions) of this book, and they are illustrated here in Exhibit 2-3. This reveals the same inventory flow shown in Exhibit 2-2, but now shows only costing entries.

The costing entries shown in Exhibit 2-3 are in their most simplified form and do not include cost layering calculations at all, because they are much too complex to list in the simplified journal entry format listed in the exhibit. The intent of Exhibits 2-2 and 2-3 is to present the considerable amount of inventory unit tracking and costing entries required for even a relatively elementary materials flow. In the next section, we explore how a more advanced system, called the manufacturing resources planning (MRP II) system works, and how the flow of inventory and related transactions are impacted by it.

Exhibit 2-2 Additional Inventory Transactions to Improve Physical Controls

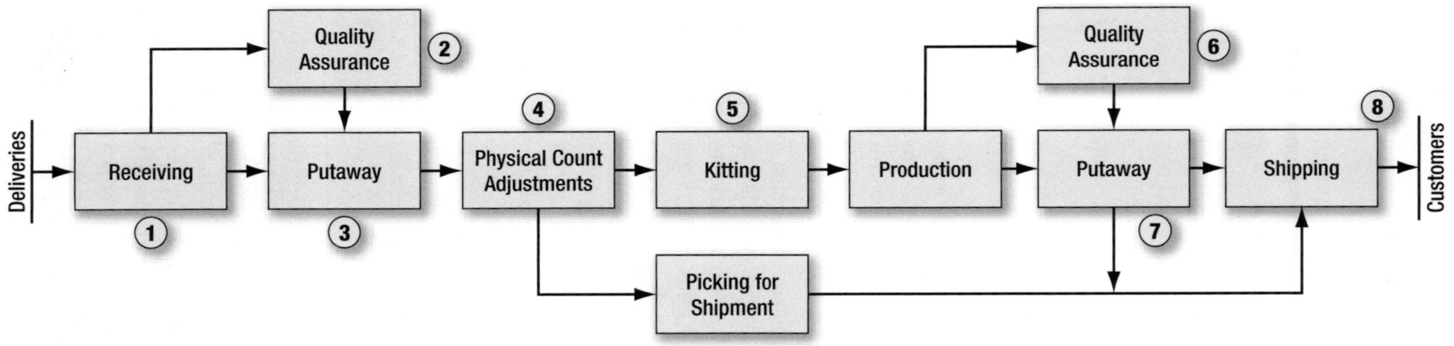

Journal Entries

(1) Inventory receipt

	Db	Cr
R/M Inventory	xx	
Accounts Payable		xx

(2) Move to QA review

	Db	Cr
QA Review	xx	
R/M Inventory		xx

(3) Move to raw materials inventory

	Db	Cr
R/M Inventory	xx	
QA Review		xx

(4) Record counting adjustments

	Db	Cr
R/M Inventory	xx	xx
Counting Adj.	xx	xx

(5) Move to work-in-progress

	Db	Cr
WIP Inventory	xx	
R/M Inventory		xx

(6) Move to QA review

	Db	Cr
QA Review	xx	
WIP Inventory		xx

(7) Move to finish goods

	Db	Cr
F/G Inventory	xx	
QA Review		xx

(8) Inventory sale

	Db	Cr
Cost of Goods	xx	
R/M Inventory		xx
F/G Inventory		xx

Exhibit 2-3 Additional Inventory Transactions to Improve Costs

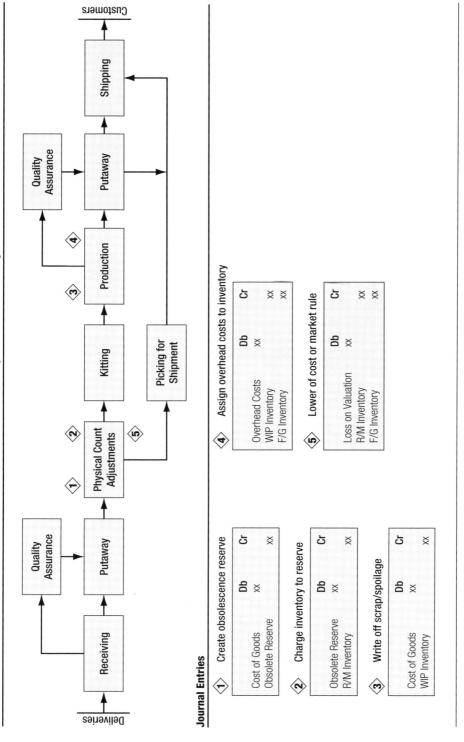

Journal Entries

① Create obsolescence reserve

	Db	Cr
Cost of Goods	xx	
Obsolete Reserve		xx

② Charge inventory to reserve

	Db	Cr
Obsolete Reserve	xx	
R/M Inventory		xx

③ Write off scrap/spoilage

	Db	Cr
Cost of Goods	xx	
WIP Inventory		xx

④ Assign overhead costs to inventory

	Db	Cr
Overhead Costs	xx	
WIP Inventory		xx
F/G Inventory		xx

⑤ Lower of cost or market rule

	Db	Cr
Loss on Valuation	xx	
R/M Inventory		xx
F/G Inventory		xx

19

2-3   A Description of the MRP II System

The MRP II system was a gradual development of computer systems that were designed to bring the advantages of computerization to the manual manufacturing systems in existence before the 1960s. It began with the creation of databases that tracked inventory. This information had historically been tracked with manually updated index cards or some similar device and was highly prone to error. By shifting to a computer system, companies could make this information available to the purchasing department, where it could be readily consulted when determining how many additional parts to purchase. In addition, the data could now be easily sorted and sifted to see which items were being used the most (and least), which yielded valuable information about what inventory should be kept in stock and what discarded.

The purchasing staff now had better information about the amount of inventory on hand, but they did not know what quantities of materials were going to be used without going through a series of painfully tedious manual calculations. To alleviate this problem, the MRP II system progressed another step by incorporating a production schedule and a bill of materials for every item listed on it. This was an immense step forward, because now the computer system could multiply the units listed on the production schedule by the component parts for each item, as listed on the bills of material, and arrive at the quantities that had to be purchased in order to meet production requirements. This total amount of purchases was then netted against the available inventory to see if anything in stock could be used, before placing orders for more materials. The lead times for the purchase of each part was also incorporated into the computer system, so that it could determine for the purchasing staff the exact dates on which orders for parts must be placed. This new level of automation was called material requirements planning (MRP), because (as the name implies) it revealed the exact quantities and types of materials needed to run a production operation.

However, the computer programmers were not done yet. As the 1960s gave way to the next decade, the MRP system evolved into the manufacturing resources planning (MRP II) system. This newer version contained all of the elements of the old MRP system, while also adding on several new features. One was the use of labor routings, which itemized the exact amounts of labor required to complete a product, as well as the identities of the machines on which this work must be done. By multiplying labor routings by the production quantities listed on the production schedule, the computer system could now report on the number of laborers required for a production facility for each day of production and even itemize the skill classifications needed. This was of great assistance in planning out headcount requirements on the production floor. Of even greater importance was the use of the same information to determine the capacity usage of each machine in the facility. If the MRP II system revealed that the scheduled production would result in a machine overload in any part of the plant, then the production schedulers could reshuffle the schedule to shift work to other machines, thereby avoiding bottlenecks that would keep the company from meeting its production targets. The main features of the MRP II system are noted in Exhibit 2-4.

Exhibit 2-4 *The Flow of Information in an MRP II System*

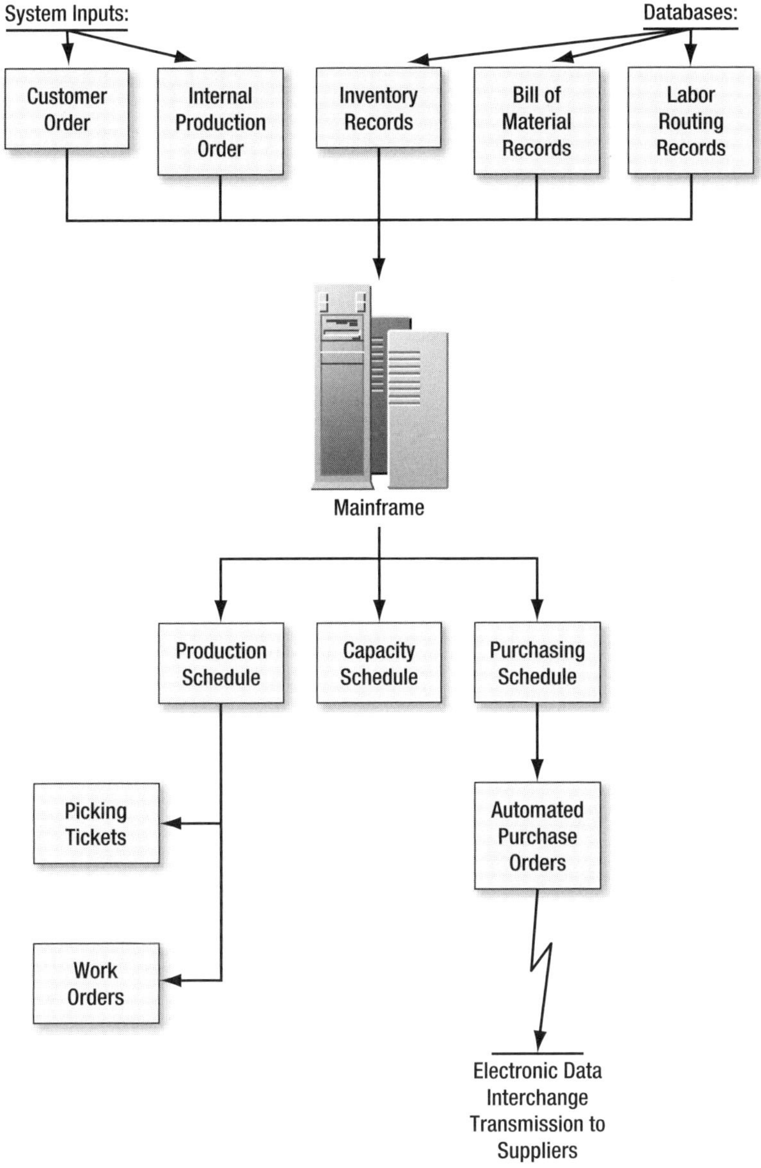

This capacity planning feature was of particular concern as the attention of companies shifted from simple material planning to ensuring that customers received their shipments on the promised dates. By verifying in advance that customer orders would be completed on time, there was no longer any last-minute scrambling to ship out orders for which there was no available machine time. Another benefit was that customers could be told at or near the time of order placement when their orders could be shipped. Also, if problems of any kind arose, the computer system would notify the production planners, who could reschedule customer orders and tell the customers as far in advance as possible of changes in their ship dates. All of these changes led to a major advance in the levels of customer service that companies could offer.

Although this is an extremely abbreviated description of MRP II, it touches on the highlights of how the system functions and what kinds of results are obtained by using it. The underlying software is exceedingly complex and requires lengthy hands-on training and course work to fully understand. However, the basic operating principles are the same, no matter what type of software is used, so expert MRP II practitioners do not have great difficulty in learning new MRP II software packages.

The MRP II system is essentially an enormous scheduling tool. It was originally designed to bring structure to the chaos of the manufacturing floor, which it certainly has done in many cases. However, the system was designed to track and plan for *existing* manufacturing practices, rather than attempt to impose a new methodology for production onto a company. As a result, the same old methods of production still underlie the system—only now everyone knows exactly how those inefficient methods work and can plan around them. The MRP II system still allows suppliers to ship in low-quality goods, requires periodic quality inspection points, allows work-in-process to build up, scrap to occur, and machines to have excessively long setup times—all factors that are directly addressed and reduced by the just-in-time (JIT) manufacturing methodology. Consequently, the MRP II system is much more of a tactical weapon for a company than a strategic one: It will not allow an organization to make great leaps in cost reduction or invested capital, but it can certainly allow it to improve inventory turnover to a significant degree and leads to a much smoother production process.

2-4 The Importance of Databases in an MRP II System

The foundation of the MRP II system is the three databases that feed it information. The most important is the bill of materials database, which consists of a separate record for each product manufactured, with each record itemizing the exact quantities of components, as well as their standard anticipated scrap rates. If there are large subassemblies, then these are usually recorded in a separate record and only referenced in the main record; this practice keeps the bills down to a tolerably short length. The bill of materials database is the driving force behind the material requirements planning portion of the MRP II system, so its accuracy is of the highest importance. An accuracy level of 98% is generally considered to be the bare minimum that will allow the MRP II system to generate accurate information. To attain such a high level, access to the database is closely guarded, and the engineering, purchasing, and production staffs are actively encouraged to warn of problems derived from it. Without a sufficient level of accuracy in this database, employees will experience problems with the information produced by the system, such as incorrect or missing purchasing quantities, that will rapidly lead to production shutdowns that are caused by missing materials.

The bill of materials database is also an outstanding tool for the inventory accountant, because it contains accurate information about product components. With that information in hand, it is usually a simple matter to reference the most current costs for each item and derive a product cost for anything in the database, which can then be used for a variety of variance and margin analyses.

Another key database is for labor routings. Each record in this database contains a detailed list of the exact times that each labor position needs to complete a product, and usually includes the required machine time, as well. Accuracy levels in this database are expected to exceed 95%. Some small inaccuracies here will not bring down a production facility, but there will be occasional work stoppages caused by inaccurate labor or capacity calculations that cause bottlenecks to arise.

The inventory accountant can use the labor information in these records to determine the standard labor cost of each product, which has applications in the reporting of variances and margins. The information in this database is best used in concert with the bill of materials database, because the two include between them all of the direct costs that are applied to a product.

The final database is for inventory. This one records the exact quantity of all items in stock. Better inventory databases also keep exact track of the usage patterns of inventory for several years. Once again, the accuracy level must be extremely high, in the 95% range, or the system will yield inaccurate reports that can lead to production shutdowns. For example, if the inventory database says that there are ten units of a gasket in stock, but there are really only five, then the MRP II system will not place an order for additional gaskets when production is scheduled that calls for ten gaskets. As a result, the production line will use all five remaining gaskets and grind to a halt because the remaining five are not in stock, which causes the purchasing staff to place a rush order for the extra gaskets, to be delivered by expensive overnight mail.

The inventory accountant will find that this database is also a gold mine of information, because one can extract from it the last dates when inventory items were used and thereby determine component or product obsolescence. It is also useful for sorting the inventory by total cost (always of concern to auditors), as well as for calculating the amount of inventory on hand (which highlights any excessive ordering practices by the purchasing department).

The key factor to consider here is the extremely high degree of accuracy that is required of these databases in order to make the MRP II system create accurate reports. If any of the databases falls short of the highest accuracy standards, then the production department will quickly fall into disarray, missing its shipment deadlines. There will also be a great deal of fingerpointing between this department and the purchasing staff, because the blame will appear to lie with the buyers, who are not bringing in the correct parts at the right time or in the correct quantities, but the real culprit is the accuracy of these databases, which are skewing the system's outputs. Consequently, the greatest possible attention must be paid to creating and maintaining an exceptional level of accuracy in these databases.

Because an MRP or MRP II system is essentially a computerized replication of the traditional manufacturing system, there is no real change in the types of inventory transactions used, so the journal entries noted earlier in Exhibits 2-2 and 2-3 are still valid. However, because the level of inventory record accuracy must be so high, there are not normally any physical count adjustments resulting from a formal count of the entire inventory; instead, companies usually adopt ongoing cycle counting in order to achieve higher levels of record accuracy, and make smaller and more frequent adjustment entries based on those counts.

2-5   A Description of Just-in-Time Systems

A JIT system is a considerable departure from the traditional manufacturing system, involving several changes that, in total, are intended to massively reduce the level of waste in a company's production systems. This also results in significant changes in the types of inventory transactions used. A JIT system has several subcomponents, which are described in this section. A complete JIT system begins with production at supplier facilities, includes deliveries to a company's production facilities, and continues through the manufacturing plant.

To begin, a company must ensure that it receives products from its suppliers on the exact date and time when they are needed. To do this, the purchasing staff must measure and evaluate every supplier, eliminating those that do not measure up to the exacting delivery standards that will now be used. In addition, deliveries will be sent straight to the production floor for immediate use in manufactured products, so there is no time to inspect incoming parts for defects. Instead, the engineering staff must visit supplier sites and examine their processes, not only to see if they can reliably ship high-quality parts, but also to provide them with engineering assistance to bring them to a higher standard of product quality.

Once suppliers have been certified for their delivery and product quality, a company must install a notification system, which may be as simplistic as a fax machine or as advanced as an electronic data interchange system or linked computer systems, that tells suppliers exactly how much of which parts to send to the company. Drivers then bring small deliveries of product to the company, possibly going to the extreme of dropping them off at the specific machines that will use them first. So far, we have achieved a process that vastly reduces the amount of raw materials inventory and improves the quality of received parts.

Next, we shorten the setup times for company machinery. In most factories, equipment is changed over to new configurations as rarely as possible, because the conversion is both lengthy and expensive. When setups take so long, company management authorizes very long production runs, which spreads the cost of the setup over far more units, thereby reducing the setup cost on a per-unit basis. However, this approach often results in too many products being made at one time, resulting in product obsolescence, inventory carrying costs, and many defective products (because problems may not be discovered until many products have already been completed). A JIT system takes a different approach to the setup issue, focusing instead on reducing the length of the equipment setups, thereby eliminating the need to create long production runs to reduce per-unit costs. To do this, a videotape is made of a typical setup, and then a team of industrial engineers and machine users peruse the tape, spotting and gradually eliminating steps that contribute to a lengthy setup. It is not unusual, after several iterations, to achieve setup times of minutes or seconds, when the previous setup times were well into the hours. By taking this step, a company reduces the amount of work-in-process, while also shrinking the number of products that can be produced before defects are identified and fixed, thereby reducing scrap costs.

It is not sufficient to reduce machine setup times, because there are still problems with machines not being coordinated properly, so that there is a smooth and stream-lined flow of parts from machine to machine. In most companies, there is such a large difference between the operating speeds of different machines that work-in-process inventory will build up in front of the slowest ones. Not only does this result in an excessive quantity of work-in-process inventory, but defective parts created by an upstream machine may not be discovered until the next downstream machine operator works his way through a pile of work-in-process to find it. By the time that happens, the upstream machine may have created quite a few more de-fective parts, all of which must now be destroyed or reworked. There are two ways to resolve both problems. The first is called the "kanban card,"[2] which is a notifi-cation card that a downstream machine sends to each machine that feeds it parts, authorizing the production of just enough parts to fulfill the production require-ments that are being authorized in turn by the next machine further downstream. This is also known as a "pull" system, because kanbans are initiated at the *end* of the production process, pulling work authorizations through the production system. By using this approach, there is no way for work-in-process inventory to build up in the production system, because it can only be created with a kanban authoriza-tion. If a kanban must be used to trigger a delivery from a supplier, this can be done with a simple fax transmission, although there is no way of knowing if it has been received by the supplier. A better approach is to add a bar code to the kanban card, which can be scanned into a production terminal, triggering an e-mail order to a sup-plier; the supplier then sends a confirming e-mail back to the company. The card is then sent to the receiving dock, where it is attached to the supplier's delivery when it eventually arrives, making the card available for a future kanban transaction when the received quantity is eventually depleted.

The second way to reduce excessive work-in-process inventory and reduce de-fective parts is to configure machines into work cells. A work cell is a small cluster of machines that can be run by a single machine operator. This person takes each

---

[2]A kanban is described in this text as a card, but it can actually be any form of notification. A common alternative is a container of a particular size. When an upstream machine re-ceives this container, it means that the machine operator is authorized to fill that container with parts—no more, no less—and then send it back to the downstream machine for im-mediate use.

part from machine to machine within the cell, so there is no way for work-in-process to build up between machines. Also, because the operator can immediately see if a part is defective, it is difficult for any but a perfect product to be created by such a machine layout. This configuration has the additional benefit of lower maintenance costs, because the smaller machines used in a machine cell are generally much simpler than the large, automated machinery that they replace. Also, because the machines are so small, it is much easier to reconfigure the production facility when it comes time to produce different products, rather than incurring a large expense to carefully reposition and align equipment.

Both kanbans and machine cells should be used together—they are not mutually exclusive. By doing so, a company can achieve extremely low product defect rates, as well as vanishingly small investments in work-in-process inventory.

Before the preceding steps are fully installed, it will become apparent that a major change must also be made in the workforce. The traditional approach is to have one worker maintain one machine, which is so monotonous that workers quickly lapse into apathy and a complete disregard for the quality of their work. Now, with full responsibility for several machines, as well as product quality, workers become much more interested in what they are doing. To enhance this favorable event, the human resources staff must prepare and implement training classes that teach employees how to operate a multitude of different machines, perform limited maintenance on the machines without having to call in the maintenance staff, spot product errors, understand how the entire system flows, and when to halt the production process to fix problems. In short, the workforce must be completely retrained and focused on a wide range of activities. This usually results in a reconfiguration of the compensation system as well, because the focus of attention now shifts away from performance based on high production volumes and in the direction of performance based on high product quality.

A major result of having an empowered workforce is that employees are now allowed to stop their machines when they see a problem and either fix it on the spot or immediately call in a repair team. In either case, the result is immediate resolution of the bulk of performance problems.

Finally, the massive changes caused by the switch to a JIT system also require several alterations to the supporting accounting systems. Because of the large number of daily supplier shipments, the accounting staff faces the prospect of wading through an enormous pile of accounts payable paperwork. To make the problem worse, there is no receiving paperwork, because the suppliers deliver parts directly to the production operation, so there is no way to determine if deliveries have been made. To avoid the first problem, the accountants can switch to a single consolidated monthly payment to each supplier. The second problem requires a more advanced solution. To prove that a supplier has delivered the part quantities it claims to have shipped, the accounting system can determine the amount of finished products created during the period and then multiply these quantities by the parts listed on the bill of materials for each product, which results in a total quantity of each part used. The accountants then pay suppliers based on this theoretical production quantity, which should also be adjusted for scrap during the production process (otherwise.

suppliers unfairly will not be paid for their parts that are scrapped during the company's production process). This approach also means that there is no need for suppliers to send invoices, because the company is relying solely on its internal production records to complete payments. The types of journal entries required in an advanced JIT system are noted in Exhibit 2-5.

The exhibit assumes no receiving function, with suppliers delivering goods straight to the production floor. This eliminates the need for an initial receiving or quality assurance review transaction, as well as movements into or out of the raw materials warehouse area. Also, because scrap is spotted by the production staff, no separate quality assurance function is needed after production is completed. There is also no transaction to move goods into the work-in-process area, because there is assumed to be too little inventory in this much leaner area to make it worth bothering with the transaction. However, scrap tracking is still necessary, as shown by the first journal entry in the JIT process. The primary JIT transaction occurs immediately after production is completed, where finished quantities are counted and used to create a purchasing liability to suppliers, while overhead is also applied to finished goods, which are shifted to a final storage area. The only other required transaction is for shipment of the goods to customers. There is no need for counting adjustments, because there are essentially no raw materials to count, and finished goods turnover is high enough to leave little inventory on hand. Please note that the process flow and transactions shown in Exhibit 2-5 represent an extremely advanced and streamlined system. In reality, a JIT system may represent a mix of some JIT components and a more traditional system, so additional transactions may be required.

2-6   Impact on Waste Costs

A key focus of the JIT system is its relentless focus on eliminating all waste from a system. This can be a waste of assets, in the case of unneeded inventory. It can also be a waste of time, in the case of assets that are unused for long periods of time (e.g., work-in-process inventory held in a production queue). It can also be the waste of materials, such as unnecessary levels of obsolete inventory, defective products, rework, and the like. When fully installed, a JIT system vastly reduces all of these types of waste. When this happens, several aspects of a product's costs decrease significantly.

For example, by reducing the amount of work-in-process, machine operators can tell immediately if an incoming part from another workstation is defective, and can notify the preceding workstation of the problem before it makes any more parts, which reduces the quantity of rework that must be done. Because a standard quantity of rework labor is often included in a product's labor routing, a reduction here will shrink the amount of labor cost charged to a product. Similarly, any material that would have been scrapped as a result of improper rework will no longer be lost, so the standard amount of scrap noted on a product's bill of materials can now be reduced. This also reduces a product's cost.

Exhibit 2-5 Inventory Transactions in a JIT Environment

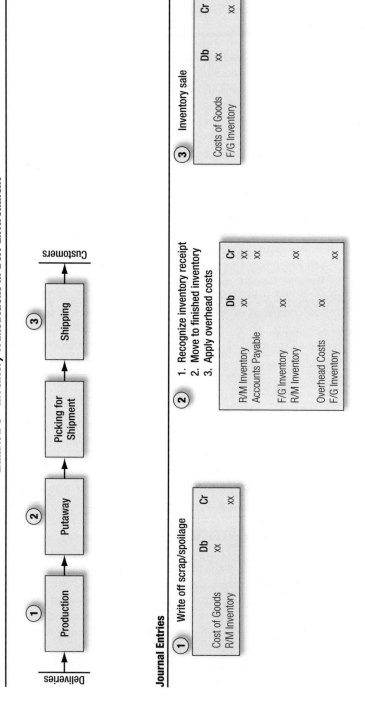

Deliveries →

| Production ① | → | Putaway ② | → | Picking for Shipment | → | Shipping ③ | → | Customers |

Journal Entries

① Write off scrap/spoilage

	Db	Cr
Cost of Goods	xx	
R/M Inventory		xx

②
1. Recognize inventory receipt
2. Move to finished inventory
3. Apply overhead costs

	Db	Cr
R/M Inventory	xx	
Accounts Payable		xx
F/G Inventory	xx	
R/M Inventory		xx
Overhead Costs	xx	
F/G Inventory		xx

③ Inventory sale

	Db	Cr
Costs of Goods	xx	
F/G Inventory		xx

28

Overhead costs that are charged to a product will also go down as other types of waste decline. For example, by clustering machines into cells, the materials handling costs that used to be incurred to shift materials among widely scattered machines can now be eliminated. This reduces the amount of materials handling costs that used to be charged to overhead. Also, machine cells tend to reduce the amount of floor space needed, because there is no longer a need for large aisles for the materials handling people to drive their forklifts through; by reducing floor space, one can also reduce facility costs, which will no longer appear in the overhead cost pool. Another form of waste is the quality inspections that used to occur for many machines. Under the JIT system, machine operators conduct their own quality checks, so there is less need for a separate group of inspectors; accordingly, the cost of their pay can be eliminated from overhead. All of these costs (and more) do not directly add value to a product, so they are wasteful costs that are subject to elimination. By eliminating them with a JIT system, fewer costs are left to charge to a product.

2-7 Impact on Overhead Costs

A key focus of any JIT system is on reducing various kinds of wasted time, so that the entire production process is focused on the time spent actually producing products. For example, all inspection time is stripped from the system by having operators conduct their own quality checks. Similarly, all move time, which involves shifting inventory and work-in-process through various parts of the plant, can be eliminated by clustering machines together in logical groupings. Third, queue time is eliminated by not allowing inventory to build up in front of machines. Finally, one can eliminate storage time by clearing out excess stocks of inventory and having suppliers deliver parts only as needed. By shrinking the amount of wasted time out of the manufacturing process, a company effectively eliminates activities that do not contribute to the value of a product, which in turn reduces the costs associated with them.

As just noted, the costs of material handling, facilities, and quality inspection will decline as a result of installing a JIT system. In addition, the reduction of all types of inventory will drastically decrease the amount of space required for the warehouse facility. Because all costs associated with the warehouse are assigned to the overhead cost pool, the amount of overhead will be reduced when the costs of staff, equipment, fixed assets, facilities, and rent associated with the warehouse are sharply cut back.

Costs will also shift from the overhead cost pool to direct costs when machine cells are introduced. The reason for this change is that a machine cell generally produces only a small range of products, which makes it easy to assign the entire cost of each machine cell to them. This means that the depreciation, maintenance, labor, and utility costs of each cell can be charged straight to a product. This is much preferable to the traditional approach of sending these costs to an overhead cost pool, from where they will be assigned to products in a much less identifiable manner. Although this change does not represent either a cost increase or reduction, it *does* increase the reliability of allocation for many more costs than was previously the case.

Despite the shift of many overhead costs to direct costs, there will still be an overhead cost pool left over that must be allocated to products. However, given the large number of changes implemented as part of the JIT system, inventory accountants may find that there are now better allocation bases available than the traditional direct labor allocation. For example, the amount of time that a product spends in each work cell may be a better measure for allocating costs, as may be the amount of space taken up by the work cells that create each product. No matter what allocation system is used, it will be somewhat different from the old system, so there will be a shift in the allocation of costs between different products.

In short, overhead costs will decline as some costs are eliminated, while other costs will shift between products as more costs are charged directly to products and the remaining overhead costs are charged out using different allocation methods.

A potentially significant one-time cost that many companies do not consider is the impact of JIT on the cost layers in their inventory costing systems. When a JIT system is installed, there is an immediate focus on eliminating inventory of all types. If a company is using some kind of layering method to track the cost of its inventory, such as last-in, first-out (LIFO) or first-in, first-out (FIFO), then it will find itself burrowing down into costing layers that may have been undisturbed for many years. If so, some unusually high or low costs may be charged off to the cost of goods sold when these inventory items are finally used up. For example, if the current market cost of a piston is $50, but a company has some very old (but serviceable) ones in stock from 20 years ago that cost $20, then only the $20 unit cost will be charged to the cost of goods sold when those units are finally used as a result of clearing out the inventory. Because of the unusually low cost of goods sold, the gross margin will be higher than usual until these early cost layers are eliminated. Because of the lower-of-cost-or-market rule (under which the cost of excessively expensive inventory must be reduced until it is no higher than the current market value), this problem tends to be less of an issue when early cost layers are *too high*, although the costs charged may still be somewhat different from those for newer layers of inventory. Once all cost layers have been used up, the only costs that management will see being charged to the cost of goods sold are those currently charged by suppliers.

2-8   Costing Allocation Differences Between a JIT and Traditional System

The chief difference between the types of cost allocations in a JIT environment and a traditional one is that most overhead costs are converted to direct costs. The primary reason for this change is the machine cell. Because a machine cell is designed to produce either a single product or a single component that goes into a similar product line, all of the costs generated by that machine cell can be charged directly to the only product it produces. When a company completely converts to the use of machine cells in all locations, then the costs related to all of those cells can now be charged directly to products, which leaves costs of any kind left to be allocated through a more traditional overhead cost pool. The result of this change is much more accurate product costs and little debate over where allocated costs should go, because there aren't enough of them left to be worth the argument.

To be specific about which costs can now be charged directly to a product, they are as follows:

- *Depreciation.* The depreciation cost of each machine in a machine cell can be charged directly to a product. It may be possible to depreciate a machine based on its actual usage, rather than charging off a specific amount per month, because this allocation variation more accurately shifts costs to a product.
- *Electricity.* The power used by the machines in a cell can be separately metered and then charged directly to the products that pass through that cell. Any excess electricity cost charged to the facility as a whole will still have to be charged to an overhead cost pool for allocation.
- *Materials handling.* Most materials handling costs in a JIT system are eliminated, because machine operators move parts around within their machine cells. Only materials handling costs between cells should be charged to an overhead cost pool for allocation.
- *Operating supplies.* Supplies are mostly used within the machine cells, so most items in this expense category can be separately tracked by individual cell and charged to products.
- *Repairs and maintenance.* Nearly all of the maintenance that a company incurs is spent on machinery, and they are all grouped into machine cells. By having the maintenance staff charge their time and materials to these cells, their costs can be charged straight to products. Only maintenance work on the facility will still be charged to an overhead cost pool.
- *Supervision.* If supervision is by machine cell, then the cost of the supervisor can be split among the cells supervised. However, the cost of general facility management, as well as of any support staff, must still be charged to an overhead cost pool.

As noted in several places in the preceding list, a few remainder costs will still be charged to an overhead cost pool for allocation. However, this constitutes a small percentage of the costs, with nearly everything now being allocable to machine cells. Only building occupancy costs, insurance, and taxes are still charged in full to an overhead cost pool. This is a vast improvement over the amount of money that the traditional system allocates to products. A typical overhead allocation pool under the traditional system may easily include 75% of all costs incurred, whereas this figure can be dropped to less than 25% of total costs by switching to a JIT system. With such a higher proportion of direct costs associated with each product, managers will then have much more relevant information about the true cost of each product manufactured.

2-9 Backflushing in a JIT System

When a JIT system is installed, management will find that it is inundated with paperwork stemming from its use of the time-honored picking system. This is a method for tracking parts as they flow through a manufacturing facility that involves making a separate inventory entry at all key steps in the production process: when an item is received, when it is stored in the warehouse, when it is picked and sent to the manufacturing floor, when it moves from machine to machine, when it returns to the warehouse for storage, and when it is sold. Because of the very large number of moves of very small quantities (and the large number of related transactions to record), a picking system is difficult to maintain in a JIT environment. Instead, companies use the backflushing system.

As described in the preceding chapter, backflushing requires no data entry of any kind until a finished product is completed. At that time, the total amount finished is entered into the computer system, which multiplies it by all of the components listed in the bill of materials for each produced item. This yields a lengthy list of components that should have been used in the production process, and which is subtracted from the beginning inventory balance to arrive at the amount of inventory that should now be left on hand. Backflushing is technically an elegant solution, because data entry only occurs once in the entire production process. Given the large transaction volumes associated with JIT, this is an ideal solution to the problem. However, some serious problems with backflushing must be corrected before it works properly. They are as follows:

- *Production reporting.* The total production figure that is entered in the system must be absolutely correct, or the wrong component types and quantities will be subtracted from stock. This is a particular problem when there is high turnover or a low level of training in the production staff that records this information, which leads to errors.

- *Scrap reporting.* All abnormal scrap must be diligently tracked and recorded, because these materials will otherwise fall outside of the backflushing system and will not be charged to inventory. Because scrap can occur anywhere in a production process, a lack of attention by any of the production staff will result in an inaccurate inventory. Once again, high production turnover or a low level of employee training will exacerbate this problem.

- *Lot tracing.* Lot tracing is impossible under the backflushing system. Lot tracing is needed when a manufacturer needs to keep records regarding which production lots were used to create a product, in case all items in a lot must be recalled. Only a picking system will adequately record this information. Some computer systems will allow a picking and backflushing system to coexist, so that pick transactions for lot tracing purposes can still be entered in the computer, so lot tracing may still be possible if the right software is available—this feature is generally only present on high-end systems.

- *Inventory accuracy.* The inventory balance will be too high at all times, because the backflushing transaction that relieves inventory usually only does so once a day, during which time other inventory has been sent to the production process; this results in a great deal of difficulty in maintaining an accurate set of inventory records in the warehouse.

Of all the issues noted here, the worst is any situation where the production staff is clearly incapable of providing sufficiently accurate scrap or production reporting for the backflushing system. If there is an easily traceable cause, such as a lower quality of staff on a particular shift, then moving a few reliable employees into those positions will provide immediate relief from the problem. It may even be possible to have an experienced shift supervisor collect this information. However, where this is not possible for whatever reason, computer system users will experience back-flushing garbage in, garbage out (GIGO). Entering inaccurate information will rapidly eliminate any degree of accuracy in the inventory records, resulting in a great many physical inventory counts to correct the problem. Consequently, the success of a backflushing system is directly related to a company's willingness to invest in a well-paid, experienced, and well educated production staff that has little turnover.

3

Inventory Control Systems

3-1   Introduction

Inventory is a difficult asset to control—it arrives and departs company premises daily, is scattered throughout the warehouse and production areas (and possibly off-site storage locations), may contain obsolete or scrap items, can involve thousands of part numbers, can include items owned by suppliers or customers, and may be valued using a variety of techniques for both direct and overhead costs. We use control systems to make it less likely that the units and costs associated with inventory are incorrect. This chapter begins with a discussion of control systems and then describes a list of 68 possible inventory controls in such areas as in-transit inventory, inventory storage, obsolete inventory, and inventory transactions. Although it is not necessary to implement all of the controls noted here, it is a representative list from which one can pick those controls that are most likely to positively affect one's inventory accuracy.

3-2   What Is an Inventory Control System?

When dealing with inventory, one should be concerned about three issues: (1) the physical quantity of goods in stock and (2) the cost at which they are valued, as well as (3) the proper billing of shipped goods. An inventory control system should be based on these issues. First, its design should minimize the risk that inventory will be lost through any number of means (e.g., pilferage, scrap losses, natural disasters). This does *not* mean that a vast array of controls should be installed that make it impossible to lose inventory, but at the price of burdening the materials management process with a multitude of non-value-added activities. On the contrary, one must customize the control system so that sufficient controls are in place to mitigate the greatest risks of inventory loss, while avoiding those controls that have comparatively little impact on inventory losses.

Second, the control system should ensure that costs are fairly and consistently applied to inventories. These controls can cover a wide array of areas, such as automation of transaction data entry to avoid entry errors, locking down access to the unit of measure field in the item master file, and controlling the contents of the overhead cost accumulation pools. Many of these controls do not require additional labor to maintain once they are set up, so there can be considerably more controls over inventory costs than may be the case over quantities.

Third, it should ensure that goods shipped are appropriately billed to customers. An inventory control system is less concerned with billing the correct amount to customers; instead, the main point is to ensure that the billing transaction is appropriately triggered by a shipment action.

All of these issues are affected by the accuracy of inventory-related transactions, which are dealt with in the final section of this chapter. The following sections describe many possible controls over various aspects of inventory quantities and controls. They are intended to be a pool of possibilities from which one can make selections, rather than a mandatory array of control requirements.

3-3   Inventory in Transit

Inventory in transit is an area that is customarily ignored by control system designers, because they tend to think only in terms of on-site inventory. However, this can be a major problem area if the terms of inbound or outbound shipment specify that the company retains ownership of the goods either before or after its arrival at or departure from the company premises. Thus, the key control issues include identification of the ownership of any in-transit inventories, mitigation of ownership risk, and inclusion of owned in-transit items in inventory valuations. The following controls address these issues:

- *Ownership: Record intercompany inventory transfers in a central inventory database.* If a company shifts inventory from one subsidiary to another, it is possible that the inventory will not be properly relieved from the shipping entity or added by the receiving entity, either of which can cause unit record error. In addition, the receiving entity may record the inventory at a different cost than the shipping entity. Both problems can be resolved by recording inventory transfers in a central inventory database that is used by both subsidiaries. However, these central databases are expensive to purchase and maintain, and also require reliable online access by multiple locations.
- *Ownership: Audit both sides of all intercompany transfer transactions.* As just noted, both sides of an intercompany inventory transfer can incorrectly record the transaction, resulting in incorrect consolidated financial results. One way to detect these issues after the fact is to regularly schedule an internal audit review of both the shipping and receiving transactions associated with a sample of intercompany transfers. These reviews should result in recommendations to alter the recording system to eliminate errors.
- *Ownership: Require a customer signature on every bill-and-hold document.* If a company builds products but does not ship them, it can still claim revenue under the assumption that customers have authorized the company to store the units on their behalf. This approach can lead to significant abuse of

revenue recognition, so a good control is to require all customers to sign a bill-and-hold transaction approval document. This document states that customers have authorized the off-site storage and accept ownership of the goods.

- *Ownership: Audit shipment terms.* Certain types of shipment terms will require that a company shipping goods must retain inventory on its books for some period after the goods have physically left the company, or that a receiving company record inventory on its books before its arrival at the receiving dock. Although in practice most companies will record inventory only when it is physically present, this is technically incorrect under certain shipment terms. Consequently, a company should perform a periodic audit of shipment terms used to see if any deliveries require different inventory treatment.

- *Ownership: Policy to prevent in-transit ownership.* The easiest form of in-transit inventory to control is when a third party owns it until it arrives at the company's receiving dock. To do so, have senior management approve a policy preventing any other type of shipping arrangement, and communicate this policy to the staff through a policy and procedures manual, as well as through periodic refresher training.

- *Mitigation: Verify existence of insurance coverage for owned in-transit goods.* If a company legally has title to in-transit goods, there is a risk that damage to those goods while in transit will result in losses to the company. Thus, the internal audit program should include an annual review of the existence and adequacy of insurance coverage for owned in-transit goods. A more passive control is to also include this requirement in a procedure listing all insurance requirements to be covered as part of the annual insurance renewal process.

- *Inclusion in valuation: Enforce rapid completion of financials.* A common problem is pressure on the accounting staff to delay the month-end cutoff date, thereby allowing the shipping department to pack a few more deliveries into the reporting period to increase revenues. This is an ongoing battle that never really goes away. An excellent control over the issue is to get management so used to receiving financial statements within one day of month-end that they tacitly approve of a stringent cutoff in order to obtain the financials as fast as possible.

- *Inclusion in valuation: Compare shipping log dates to shipper documentation.* A good way to detect an extended period-end cutoff is to compare the shipment date recorded in the corporate shipping log to any shipper documentation on which the shipper records the actual date on which it accepted the goods for delivery. If the shipping staff knows this audit will be conducted, they will be less inclined to stuff more shipments into the reporting period with an extended cutoff.

3-4 Inventory Stocking

Many of the problems associated with inventory originate with the initial decisions to set safety stock levels, add product options, and design new components into products. Although these decisions fall outside of the traditional control systems for inventory, they play a key role in the amount of a company's inventory investment, and so are included here. All controls noted relate to the addition of stock to inventory.

- *Additions: Reject all purchases that are not preapproved.* A major flaw in the purchasing systems of many companies is that all supplier deliveries are accepted at the receiving dock, irrespective of the presence of authorizing paperwork. Many of these deliveries are verbally authorized orders from employees throughout the company, many of whom are not authorized to make such purchases. This problem can be eliminated by enforcing a rule that all items received must have a corresponding purchase order on file that has been authorized by the purchasing department. By doing so, the purchasing staff can verify that there is a need for each item requisitioned and that it is bought at a reasonable price from a certified supplier.

- *Additions: Revise safety stock levels for seasonal items.* The most common approach to setting safety stock levels is to run a historical usage analysis over the past few years and use that information to decide on an average safety stock level. However, this approach ignores sudden drops in demand caused by seasonality, leaving too much inventory on hand. If demand permanently drops thereafter, safety stock levels will be too high and may represent a risk of obsolescence. A potential control is to mandate quarterly adjustments to safety stock levels of seasonal items, thereby more closely matching supply to demand.

- *Additions: Reduce the number of products and product options.* Each incremental product that a company chooses to sell requires the storage of more parts. This is a particular problem if there are many variations on the basic product, mandating storage of each product version. To control the number of these inventory additions, schedule a periodic product profitability review and cancel unprofitable products; the determination of unprofitability should certainly include an analysis of the amount of working capital tied up in inventory that is uniquely associated with a particular product.

- *Additions: Standardize parts.* When engineers design new products, they may not consider using existing components. The result is a plethora of similar but separately tracked components, each of which requires some investment in on-hand inventory. An excellent control over these unwanted inventory additions is to require a parts standardization review as an integral step in the development of any new product. To reinforce the concept, consider including the minimization of the total number of on-hand component parts in the bonus plan of the engineering manager.

- *Additions: Coordinate engineering change orders with on-hand balances.* When the engineering staff implements a change order, new parts are added to a product while the replaced items are no longer needed and remain in stock for prolonged periods. In an environment where engineering change orders are common, a nearly mandatory control is to verify the remaining on-hand balance of any components being rendered obsolete, so that the change orders can be implemented in conjunction with the maximum depletion of existing stocks.

- *Additions: Turn off reordering flags for cancelled components.* Many computer systems contain a flag in the item master file, indicating that the system should automatically create a purchase order to replenish on-hand stocks when a minimum stock level is reached. However, this contravenes a company's intent in attempting to dispose of any obsolete items, because the system will reorder what is no longer needed. Therefore, a good control is to incorporate in the obsolete inventory disposition procedure a line item stating that the reordering flag be turned off as soon as an item is declared obsolete.

- *Additions: Compare open purchase orders to current requirements.* The purchasing staff may have placed purchase orders that are no longer needed, because the production schedule was changed subsequent to placement of the purchase orders. This problem is automatically spotted by a material requirements planning system, which generates a report listing those purchase orders that should be closed. However, in the absence of an MRP system, a process should be in place to frequently compare open purchase orders to current requirements, resulting in the elimination of unneeded inventory receipts.

- *Additions: Reward managers based on a reduced working capital investment.* One of the classic frauds is to greatly increase the size of value-added on-hand inventory, so that more overhead costs are assigned to the inventory instead of flowing through the cost of goods sold and reducing reported profits. To avoid this problem, an excellent passive control is to include the reduction of a company's working capital investment in the management bonus plan. By doing so, anyone increasing inventory levels to manipulate profits would end up reducing his profit because of the increased investment in working capital.

3-5 Inventory Storage

Inventory storage tends to be the area in which the most controls are implemented. Traditionally, the key control targets have been over the loss of inventory through pilferage, as well as the record accuracy for inventory contained within the warehouse. The following list also includes a third category addressing the ownership of inventory contained within the warehouse. Additional controls related to accuracy levels are described in the "Inventory Transactions" section of this chapter. Possible controls are as follows:

- *Loss: Review for case overhang on pallets.* Inventory can be damaged if cases are incorrectly stacked on pallets. If they overhang the edge of a pallet, the weight of the stack bears down on the overhanging cardboard walls of the cases, potentially causing damage to their contents. A simple control is to include in the cycle counting review a brief visual inspection of the stacking pattern on pallets to see if any overhang is occurring. This review can also be done by audit teams as part of other investigations.

- *Loss: Restrict warehouse access to designated personnel.* Without access restrictions, the company warehouse is like a large store with no prices—just take all you want. This does not necessarily mean that employees are taking items from stock for personal use, but they may be removing excessive inventory quantities for production purposes, which leads to a cluttered production floor. Also, this leaves the purchasing staff with the almost impossible chore of trying to determine what is in stock and what needs to be bought for immediate manufacturing needs. Consequently, a mandatory control over inventory is to fence it in and closely restrict access to it.

- *Loss: Restrict access to dock doors.* As just noted, fencing in the warehouse area is an excellent approach for eliminating pilferage. However, dock doors are normally left open during business hours, allowing someone broad access to the warehouse through the doors. To avoid this situation, post "Do Not Enter" signs near the dock doors and impose a policy of immediately closing all doors that are not currently blocked by a truck.

- *Loss: Retain expensive items in the warehouse.* Although it is much more efficient to store commonly used items in storage locations near the production area, this also makes it easier for employees to steal parts from the more readily accessible bins. If there is a history of excessive parts usage from these storage locations, consider shifting the most expensive parts back into the more controlled warehouse area. This may call for the use of a formula to determine at what point a part cost is sufficiently low to make it worthwhile to retain in a floor stock location, even with a moderate amount of theft.

- *Accuracy: Review negative inventory balances.* When the inventory record database reveals a negative inventory quantity, a transaction error has caused the problem. A good control is to mandate an immediate review of the underlying transactions to determine why the negative balance occurred. This investigation requires an experienced materials management person as well as a computer system that stores a history of individual transaction records.

- *Accuracy: Pick from stock based on bills of material.* An excellent control over material costs is to require the use of bills of material for each item manufactured, and then requiring that parts be picked from the raw materials stock for the production of these items based on the quantities listed in the bills of material. By doing so, a reviewer can hone in on those warehouse issuances that were *not* authorized through a bill of material, because there is no objective reason why these issuances should have taken place.

- *Accuracy: Require approval to sign out inventory beyond amounts on the pick list.* If a standard pick list is used to take raw materials from the warehouse for production purposes, this should be the standard authorization for inventory removal. If the production staff requires any additional inventory, they should go to the warehouse gate and request it, and the resulting distribution should be logged out of the warehouse. Furthermore, any inventory that is left over after production is completed should be sent back to the warehouse and logged in. By using this approach, one can tell if there are errors in the bills of material that are used to create pick lists, because any extra inventory requisitions or warehouse returns probably represent errors in the bills.

- *Accuracy: Use standard container sizes.* Inventory counters may estimate the number of parts stored in a container rather than counting each individual item because of the extra time required to make a detailed count. To avoid the resulting record inaccuracies, consider using standard container sizes, perhaps with an egg crate design in which only a specific number of parts can be held by each container. This approach makes it much easier to determine the exact number of parts in a container. This control is particularly applicable to work-in-process, where standard part sizes are frequently moved between workstations.

- *Ownership: Segregate customer-owned inventory.* If customers supply a company with some parts that are used when constructing products for them, it becomes easy for this inventory to be mingled with the company's own inventory, resulting in a false increase in its inventory valuation. It is certainly possible to assign customer-specific inventory codes to these inventory items in order to clearly identify them, but a more easily discernible control is to physically segregate these goods in a different part of the warehouse.

- *Ownership: Segregate supplier-owned inventory.* Some suppliers retain ownership of their goods at the company site until the goods are used in the production process, at which point they bill the company for their use. A common control is to lock down access to this inventory, so that only an authorized person can both access it and log out items used. An alternative control if the supplier-owned inventory is extensive is to assign sole control over this inventory to an on-site supplier representative. Another variation is to position this inventory in an adjacent warehouse, from which deliveries can be readily made to the company while control over the inventory is more easily assured.

3-6   Off-Site Inventory Storage

When there is not sufficient on-site space available in which to store inventory, it is typically kept in storage trailers or leased off-site premises. One control issue is the loss of inventory in these locations, because access to the inventory may be less secure than in the main corporate warehouse. Another problem is the accuracy of inventory records in the off-site locations. Both control issues are dealt with through the following controls:

- *Loss: Access control.* When seasonal demand forces inventory levels higher than the storage capacity of the main warehouse area, overflow stocks must be stored elsewhere, possibly in locations having less restrictive access controls. Consider as the best alternative the use of a third-party warehouse with full access controls. If not available, at least lock down access to any additional rented space. If storage trailers are used for overflow storage, be aware that an entire trailer can easily be stolen, so fence off all storage trailers and lock the gate.

- *Accuracy: Include off-site inventory counts in the closing procedure.* A common problem is not including in the month-end inventory the inventory counts for off-site storage locations, resulting in an excessively large charge to the cost of goods sold. To avoid this, keep an updated list of all off-site locations in the month-end closing procedure, and check off the list all received inventory counts from each location, thereby highlighting missing count information. However, this control does not attest to the accuracy of the submitted counts.

- *Accuracy: Include off-site storage locations in the inventory database.* The preceding control assumed that separate records are kept for all off-site storage locations, which requires periodic consolidation in order to issue financial statements. A better approach is to use a central inventory database that is accessible from all locations, so that all additions to and deletions from all inventory locations are updated in the central database at once.

- *Accuracy: Conduct periodic audits of off-site inventory storage locations.* Although an off-site location may submit an inventory count at month-end, there is no way of knowing if the submitted information is accurate. This can be dealt with through the use of unannounced periodic audits of all major off-site locations. The intent of these reviews is to uncover record accuracy problems and possibly create suggestions for controls that will limit errors in the future.

3-7 Obsolete Inventory

Obsolete inventory can constitute a large proportion of the total inventory, so consider giving controls a high priority in this area. Controls fall into four areas: (1) prevention of obsolete inventory (described in the following "Scrap Inventory" section), (2) detection of existing obsolete inventory, (3) rapid disposal of obsolete inventory before its value drops to minimal levels, and (4) appropriate recognition of obsolescence reserves. The following controls address these issues:

- *Detection: Review inventory for obsolete items.* Despite the best prevention efforts, some inventory will not be used and will become obsolete. To detect it, periodically print a report listing which inventory items have *not* been used recently, including the extended cost of these items. A more accurate variation is to print a report itemizing all inventory items for which there are no current production requirements (only possible if an MRP system is in place). Alternately, one can use a report comparing the amount of inventory on hand to annual historical usage of each item. With this information in hand, one should then schedule regular meetings with the materials manager to determine what inventory items should be scrapped, sold off, or returned to suppliers.

- *Disposal: Create a Materials Review Board (MRB).* Obsolete inventory tends to remain in the warehouse for long periods because no one is responsible for its disposition. If it stays on-site too long, its disposal value drops and the company loses the opportunity to recover some of its obsolescence loss. To avoid this issue, a good control is for senior management to create an MRB, comprising representatives from the materials management, accounting, production, and engineering departments, who meet regularly to determine how to dispose of various items. Only through constant attention to disposition can one obtain the maximum return on obsolete inventory.

- *Reserve recognition: Include an obsolescence review in the closing procedure.* Obsolete inventory can be the great hidden secret of many warehouses, which no one wants to address. This attitude only lets the obsolescence problem build up over time until it periodically becomes a major issue. A good control is to include in the monthly closing procedure a requirement to evaluate the sufficiency of the obsolescence reserve. In order to provide sufficient time for this task, always schedule it a few days *before* the actual month-end close, so there is no excuse to ignore it on the grounds of having insufficient time or staff to allocate to the task.

3-8 Scrap Inventory

Many production processes generate a considerable amount of scrap, which requires controls over its prevention, tracking, costing, and sale. The following controls address these issues:

- *Prevention: Qualify and track supplier quality levels.* Scrap is frequently caused by parts being shipped by a supplier that do not meet company quality levels. Prevention of the problem calls for creating minimum quality standards, supplier certification, and ongoing tracking of their quality performance. The tracking control typically involves the creation of a supplier report card that includes several other factors besides quality, such as on-time deliveries and product cost.
- *Prevention: Use FIFO racking for items with a short shelf life.* If some inventory items will be rendered unusable after a specified shelf life period, consider storing them in gravity flow or pallet flow racks, so that the oldest items are always stored in front and are most accessible to stock pickers. Flow racking involves a first-in, first-out (FIFO) storage concept, where goods are put away on one side of the rack and slide downhill to the front of the rack, where they are picked.
- *Prevention: Use computer tracking for items with a short shelf life.* The preceding control to use FIFO racking is the preferred approach for tracking items with a short shelf life, because pickers automatically access the oldest items first without any need for computer tracking. An alternative is to record the receipt date of each item in the computer system and mark this information on individual units or cases, so the computer system can direct pickers to the locations where the oldest items are stored. This approach is most useful where goods cannot fit into gravity flow racks.
- *Prevention: Actively track rework status.* When a problem is detected in the production process and items are set aside for rework, they tend to languish there, because rework is not normally given a high priority. If enough time passes, items set aside for rework may be reclassified as scrap, eliminating their value.

A good control is to assign rework a high priority and track its status with a status report that is reviewed frequently.

- *Prevention: Integrate scrap results into a bonus plan.* Manufacturing executives are sometimes compensated based on the total volume of goods they can deliver to customers on time, with on-time delivery being the key bonus target. However, this system ignores scrap and rework, which in turn have a considerable impact on profits. A good control is to either include target scrap levels as a measurable objective in the bonus plan or make net profits the primary bonus criterion, thereby inherently including scrap prevention in the plan.

- *Tracking: Require transaction forms for scrap and rework transactions.* A startling amount of materials and associated direct labor can be lost through the scrapping of production or its occasional rework. This tends to be a difficult item to control, because scrap and rework can occur at many points in the production process. Nonetheless, the manufacturing staff should be well trained in the use of transaction forms that record these actions, so the inventory records will remain accurate.

- *Tracking: Track the weight of bulk scrap on a trend line.* It is often too time-consuming to require the production and materials management staffs to fill out forms documenting scrap transactions (see the preceding control). If so, and the scrap being generated is of a uniformly consistent type, consider storing it in one container and weighing it on a regularly scheduled date. If no weighing system is available, have a scrap hauler weigh it and include the weight information on a payment receipt. By tracking this information on a trend line, one can determine the general scrap level being generated by a given production volume.

- *Costing: Create a zero-cost code for all inventory designated as scrap.* It can be difficult to consistently write down the value of scrap to zero, given the large quantity of scrap items flowing through an inventory system. A simple automated approach is to have the computer system automatically assign a zero cost to any inventory that has been given a scrap code. However, this requires either an advanced or customized computer system, and so is not a generally available option for smaller companies.

- *Costing: Create a default zero-cost policy for all scrap items.* Companies may attempt to assign the scrap sale price to any inventory designated as scrap. Although this may yield a slight upward change in the total inventory valuation, it is difficult to update or justify scrap sale prices and requires extra accounting effort. A better approach to scrap costing is to enforce a default cost of zero on all scrap items. Then, by selling off the scrap regularly and recording the scrap sale as an expense reduction, there is no net change in the overall results of the financial statements.

- *Sale: Confirm scrap payments with scrap haulers.* A company's scrap is a relatively uncontrolled asset that is typically accorded a status only slightly higher than its trash—we only care about how to take it away from the company premises. However, scrap has value, and scrap haulers will pay for it. This is a particularly easy area in which to lose money, because an employee can arrange for scrap disposal through a scrap hauler who is willing to pay cash, and then pocket the funds. One can uncover this problem by confirming payments with scrap haulers, but this only works if the employee is merely skimming scrap payments, thereby leaving some transactions that show the name of the scrap hauler.

- *Sale: Track scrap receipts on a trend line.* A scrap hauler may have poor record keeping for the amounts it pays to a company for scrap. If so, create a general ledger account into which all scrap payments are recorded, and track the amount added to this account over time, especially in comparison to production levels. If there is an obvious decline in the amount of money being paid to the company, this is possible evidence that someone is skimming funds from the payments made by the scrap hauler.

- *Sale: Require check payments by scrap haulers.* The main opportunity for fraud in relation to scrap is that scrap haulers often pay in cash, which can be immediately pocketed. To avoid this temptation, require scrap haulers to only make payments with checks. Also require the haulers to mail the checks to the company's accounting department, which keeps the checks from passing through anyone else's hands and therefore further reduces the opportunity for an unauthorized person to access the funds.

3-9 Inventory Costing

There are so many components to inventory cost calculations, involving so many cost records, that there is a high risk of costing error. Principal control system targets include ensuring a proper cost roll-up, appropriately assigning fixed costs to inventory, and both consistently and appropriately assigning overhead costs to inventory. The following controls address these issues:

- *Cost roll-up: Audit inventory material costs.* Inventory costs are usually assigned either through a standard costing procedure or as part of some inventory layering concept such as LIFO or FIFO. In the case of standard costs, one should regularly compare assigned costs to the actual cost of materials purchased to see if any standard costs should be updated to bring them more in line with actual costs incurred. If it is company policy to update standard costs only at lengthy intervals, then one should verify that the variance between actual and standard costs is being written off to the cost of goods sold.

  If inventory layering is used to store inventory costs, then one should periodically audit the costs in the most recently used layers, tracing inventory costs back to specific supplier invoices.

- *Cost roll-up: Audit prices paid.* A member of the purchasing department may make an arrangement with a supplier to receive a kickback in exchange for directing business to the supplier. Because the supplier absorbs the cost of the kickback, this generally leads to higher component prices. This type of fraud is extremely difficult to detect. One possibility is to conduct a periodic audit of prices paid to see if any per-unit prices are inordinately high.

- *Cost roll-up: Rotate purchasing assignments.* As just noted, it is difficult to detect kickback schemes. One can at least make it more difficult for suppliers to enter into kickback schemes by periodically rotating supplier assignments to different members of the purchasing department. Under this approach, it is more likely that a supplier who is used to paying kickbacks will eventually run into a newly assigned staff person who has no intention of accepting payments and who may also report any supplier suggestions about kickbacks to management.

- *Cost roll-up: Assign unique part numbers to customer-owned inventory.* If a customer sends parts to a company for inclusion in a finished product and the company already owns similar or identical parts, the chances are good that the existing part numbers will be assigned to the customer-owned parts, resulting in a valuation of the parts when they should be recorded at zero cost. The best way around this problem is to assign a unique part number to the customer-owned items at the receiving dock and prominently label the items with this part number. Then assign a zero cost to the unique part number, thereby keeping any value from being assigned to it.

- *Cost roll-up: Compare unextended product costs to those for prior periods.* Product costs of all types can change for a variety of reasons. An easy way to spot these changes is to create and regularly review a report comparing the unextended cost of each product to its cost in a prior period. Any significant changes can then be traced back to the underlying costing information to see exactly what caused each change. The main problem with this control is that many less expensive accounting systems do not retain historical inventory records. If so, the information should be exported to an electronic spreadsheet or separate database once a month, where historical records can then be kept.

- *Cost roll-up: Review sorted list of extended product costs in declining dollar order.* This report is more commonly available than the historical tracking report noted in the previous list item, but contains less information. The report lists the extended cost of all inventory on hand for each inventory item, sorted in declining order of cost. By scanning the report, one can readily spot items that have unusually large or small valuations. However, finding these items requires some knowledge of what costs were in previous periods. Also, a lengthy inventory list makes it difficult to efficiently locate costing problems. Thus, this report is inferior to the unextended historical cost comparison report from a control perspective.

- *Cost roll-up: Control updates to bill of material and labor routing costs.* The key sources of costing information are the bill of materials and labor routing records for each product. One can easily modify these records in order to substantially alter inventory costs. To prevent such changes from occurring, strict security access should be placed on these records. If the accounting software has a change tracking feature that stores data about who made changes and what changes were made, then be sure to use this feature. If this feature is used, periodically print a report (if available) detailing all changes made to the records and scan it for evidence of unauthorized access.

- *Cost roll-up: Keep bill of material accuracy levels at a minimum of 98%.* The bills of material are critical for determining the value of inventory as it moves through the work-in-process stages of production and eventually arrives in the finished goods area, because they itemize every possible component that comprises each product. These records should be regularly compared to actual product components to verify that they are correct, and their accuracy should be tracked.

- *Cost roll-up: Review inventory layering calculations.* Most inventory layering systems are automatically maintained through a computer system and cannot be altered. In these cases, there is no need to verify the layering calculations. However, if the layering information is manually maintained, one should schedule periodic reviews of the underlying calculations to ensure proper cost layering. This usually involves tracing costs back to specific supplier invoices. However, one should also trace supplier invoices forward to the layering calculations, because it is quite possible that invoices have been excluded from the calculations. Also verify consistency in the allocation of freight costs to inventory items in the layering calculations.

- *Fixed-cost assignment: Audit production setup cost calculations.* If production setup costs are included in inventory unit costs, substantial costing errors could be made if the assumed number of units produced in a production run is incorrect. For example, if the cost of a production setup is $1,000 and the production run is 1,000 units, then the setup cost should be $1 per unit. However, if someone wanted to artificially increase the cost of inventory in order to create a jump in profits, the assumed production run size could be reduced. In the example, if the production run assumption were dropped to 100 units, the cost per unit would increase tenfold to $10. A reasonable control over this problem is to regularly review setup cost calculations. An early warning indicator of this problem is to run a report comparing setup costs over time for each product to see if there are any sudden changes in costs. Also, access to the computer file storing this information should be strictly limited.

- *Overhead cost assignment: Verify the calculation and allocation of overhead cost pools.* Overhead costs are usually assigned to inventory as the result of a manually derived summarization and allocation of overhead costs. This can be a lengthy calculation, which is subject to error. The best control over this process is a standard procedure that clearly defines which costs to include in the pools and precisely how these costs are to be allocated. In addition, one should regularly review the types of costs included in the calculations, verify that the correct proportions of these costs are included, and ensure that the costs are being correctly allocated to inventory. A further control is to track the total amount of overhead accumulated in each reporting period, because any sudden change in the amount may indicate an error in the overhead cost summarization.

3-10 Billing of Shipped Goods

From the perspective of a billing system, the main concern is ensuring that a delivery to a customer triggers a billing transaction, which is particularly difficult under a drop shipping arrangement where shipments are made by a third party. Thus, the key control issue is initiation of the billing transaction. The following controls address this issue:

- *Billing initiation: Automate third-party drop shipment notifications.* If a company supplier has agreed to drop-ship goods directly to a company's customers, the company is now relying on the supplier's accounting system to forward accurate shipment notifications to the company in a timely manner. If drop shipment volumes are large, the company may be relying on the supplier for a considerable proportion of its revenues, so tight controls may be needed in this area. The best approach is to arrange for automated drop shipment notifications (perhaps through electronic data interchange) directly from the supplier's computer system to that of the company. By eliminating all manual rekeying of data, there is much less chance of a billing initiation error occurring, while also creating a passive yet effective control over the process.

- *Billing initiation: Compare third-party billings to drop shipment notifications.* An excellent control over drop shipment billing initiation is to compare the quantity of units noted in a supplier's invoice to a company to the quantity listed in its drop shipment notifications. The two figures should always match. Although a supplier may have less incentive to provide accurate drop shipment notifications to the company, it will likely spend much more time ensuring that its own invoices are correct, or it will not be paid. Thus, the supplier's invoice can be considered the more accurate document against which its drop shipment notifications should be matched.

- *Billing initiation: Create an audit report matching the shipping log to billings.* The standard billing transaction begins with the receipt of a shipment notice, such as a bill of lading copy, from the shipping department. If this document never arrives in the billing department, customers are never billed. A good control over this issue is to have the computer system automatically match the shipping log file to the billing log and issue a daily report noting any variances. Of course, this requires both the warehouse and accounting departments to either use the same computer system or have an interface across which the requisite information can be exchanged.

- *Billing initiation: Manually match the shipping log to billings.* If a company-wide computer system is not available to make the preceding control usable, consider performing the same matching task manually. Even if an automated solution is available, it can be useful to conduct a periodic audit comparison, matching both the shipping records to the billing records and vice versa. Such a review may reveal that the automated system is not working as planned or that additional controls are needed for such special situations as rebillings, shipments of free samples, and warranty shipments.

3-11   Inventory Transactions

The greatest bane of maintaining a high level of record accuracy is the massive number of transactions required to process inventory from receipt through putaway, picking, production, and shipping, as well as a myriad of additional potential transactions. With such a large volume of transactions, data entry errors are bound to occur. A central control over this problem is the avoidance of the manual entry of transactions of any type. Controls in this area fall into the categories of transaction automation, avoidance, and error investigation:

- *Transaction automation: Use bar-coded data entry systems.* Although radio-frequency identification systems may eventually supplant bar-coded systems, this is by no means the case yet. The use of bar code scanning remains the single best way to keep a data entry person from keypunching transactions, thereby avoiding the inevitable risk of data entry errors. At its highest level, consider installing radio-frequency bar code scanning, so that transactions are automatically transmitted from portable scanners by radio transmissions and update the inventory database in real time.

- *Transaction avoidance: Certify suppliers for direct delivery of goods to production.* The receiving function involves transactions for receiving, putaway, and transfers to quality assurance for further review. All of these transactions introduce the possibility of record errors. By certifying suppliers in the quality and timeliness of delivery of their goods, there is no need for a receiving function, thereby allowing a company to avoid all receiving transactions and have suppliers deliver goods straight to the production process. This requires the use of backflushing (see next control).

- *Transaction avoidance: Use backflushing.* At its most detailed level, inventory transactions can be created for shifting warehoused goods to a pallet for delivery to the production area, movements between individual workstations within the production area, and a transfer back to the warehouse of finished goods—any or all of which may be keypunched incorrectly. An alternative is to enter no transactions at all until a product is finished, and then enter a single backflushing transaction to clear from raw materials stock all of the components of the completed product. This process is especially useful when suppliers are delivering goods straight to the production line, because it can also be used to determine the delivered quantities for which suppliers are to be paid. However, this approach requires extremely accurate bills of material and can result in inaccurate raw material records during the interval when goods have been removed from stock and the backflushing entry has not yet been made.

- *Transaction avoidance: Eliminate data entry backlogs.* The bane of cycle counters is to find a record inaccuracy, correct it, and then find that their correction was unnecessary because someone had not yet entered a transaction that had been physically completed several hours in the past. Thus, an important control is ensuring that transactions are entered in the computer system at once—no data entry backlog of any type is acceptable. This may call for the use of radio-frequency bar code scanners, a dedicated data entry person, or a multitude of fixed computer terminals throughout the warehouse area.

- *Transaction avoidance: Audit the receiving dock.* A significant problem from a record-keeping perspective is that the receiving staff may not have time to enter a newly received delivery into the corporate computer system, so the accounting and purchasing staffs have no idea that the items have been received. Accordingly, one should regularly compare items sitting in the receiving area to the inventory database to see if they have been recorded. One can also compare supplier billings to the inventory database to see if items billed by suppliers are not listed as having been received.

- *Transaction avoidance: Eliminate the physical count.* Although the intent of a physical inventory count is supposed to be an improvement in record accuracy, the reverse is often the case, because the count is conducted in a rush and inexperienced counters are used. Consequently, the physical count usually results in several inaccuracies that may take months to correct. A much better alternative is to use cycle counting (see next control), which is only conducted by the most experienced materials management personnel.

- *Error investigation: Implement cycle counting.* Probably the single most common and necessary inventory control is the use of cycle counting, which is the ongoing counting of small portions of the inventory and the investigation of reasons for any errors uncovered. The key element of this control is not the correction of inventory records to match physical counts, but rather the detailed investigation and correction of any problems causing the errors to occur. This is a tedious and time-consuming process that requires tenacious management support for some time before demonstrative inventory record accuracy gains are achieved.

- *Error investigation: Create and maintain a procedures manual.* An excellent way to avoid having transaction errors is to construct and regularly update a policies and procedures manual that shows employees precisely how to enter transactions into the inventory database. This control should be supplemented by a mandatory training program in the manual's use for all new hires involved with inventory, as well as periodic refresher training. If there are significant changes contemplated to these procedures, all people involved in the impacted transactions should be consulted for input, because they have the best knowledge of the ripple effect of procedural changes throughout the system.

4

Inventory Fraud[1]

4-1 Introduction

An unfortunate fact of the business world is that some companies use their inventory systems to commit fraud. Although this can involve the deliberate theft of inventory, it is even easier to artificially inflate or deflate a company's reported profits without laying a hand on the inventory. This can be done through the alteration of costing records, bills of material, the item master file, and the contents of overhead cost pools, as well as by changing the costing methodology used. In this chapter, we explore who usually commits inventory fraud, the various types of inventory-related fraud that can be perpetrated, and how it can be prevented. This chapter can be combined with the control systems noted in Chapter 3 to obtain a better picture of how fraud is caused and can be prevented.

4-2 Who Commits Inventory Fraud

Inventory-related fraud is usually instigated at the management level. The reason is that when managers are compensated based on the profitability of the company as a whole or of their individual business units, they have an incentive to stretch reported results. The problem is exacerbated when a disproportionately large part of a manager's potential income is based on "stretch" profitability goals that can only be achieved through inordinately great efforts. The reverse situation may also be true for privately held companies that are more concerned with the avoidance of taxes; these organizations may reward their managers based on their ability to improve cash flow while holding down the amount of reported profitability. In either situation, the level of fraud initially committed is relatively minor—perhaps a slight adjustment to income that results in a small change in income, but enough to reach a performance goal. However, that small step into the realm of fraudulent behavior makes it easier to make a larger adjustment in the next reporting period, and so on.

---

[1] Portions of this chapter were adapted from Chapter 40 of Bragg, *Cost Accounting*, John Wiley & Sons, 2001.

Soon, a manager is incorporating fraudulent actions into his or her daily activities and develops a range of activities that will result in skewed financial results.

The simplest detection approach is to create a trend line of all major cost categories, inventory levels, and cost allocation pools, and simply trace the levels of the items from as far back as possible, right up to the present day. Because these costs rarely change, either in total or in proportion to each other, variations will reveal the presence of a tampering manager. The level of work required to keep track of this information is minimal, so even a reduced accounting staff or one whose activities are being deliberately forced in other directions should still be able to find the time for such rudimentary analysis. The real problem is that, once detected, the very people who should be acting on the information to prevent fraud may be the ones creating it. If so, consider forwarding the information to the corporate audit committee for further action.

4-3   Change Labor Routing Assumptions

Although labor usually makes up a relatively small proportion of the total cost of a product, this cost can be artificially expanded to result in a much larger proportion, which then drives up the cost of inventory, reduces the cost of goods sold, and results in a higher level of reported profitability.

The way to increase the labor costs charged to a product is to alter the labor routings so they spread the cost of equipment setups over a smaller number of parts produced—this means that the assumed length of production runs is shortened. For example, if a metal stamping machine requires 10 hours of setup before it can stamp a particular part, then the cost of that setup can be charged to the resulting manufactured parts. If the setup cost is $1,000 and the number of parts produced during the production run is 1,000, then the cost of the operation per part will be $1. However, if the labor routing is altered so that the assumed length of the production run is much shorter, such as 100, then the cost allocated to each unit goes up to $10. Obviously, a small change in the assumption leads to a large change in cost, which makes this a worthwhile endeavor for a fraudulent manager to undertake.

The approach can be further disguised by making a series of small, incremental reductions in the assumed production run lengths in the labor routings over several years, so that auditors do not see any sudden changes in costs at one time. The author noted one situation where a shaped metal part suddenly jumped in cost from $2 to $6,000, which was so excessive that auditors spotted it at once, quickly uncovered the entire plot, and forced the company in question to restate its inventory based on prior-year labor routing information.

The best way to detect labor routing alterations is to review a selection of labor routings with the industrial engineering staff to obtain their opinions regarding the proper production run lengths. If there is some chance that the engineers are involved in the labor routing changes, then bringing in an outside consultant who can review the data and observe actual production runs may be the best alternative. Another detection technique is to turn on the tracking log option in the computer system, which notes who makes all changes to the labor routings file. The best prevention method is to restrict access to the computerized labor routings file.

4-4   Change Bill of Material Components

The bill of materials is the most sacrosanct document used by the engineering and purchasing departments, and it is considered absolutely inviolable by both of those departments. However, there is a way for a fraud-minded manager to not only alter bills of material in order to skew financial results, but to even make both departments go along with and even initiate the change.

A manager who wants to improve financial results wants to include every conceivable product component in a bill of materials, because this will create a higher per-unit cost for each item in inventory (including those already in inventory), which yields a higher inventory valuation. An easy way to do this is to put all fittings, fasteners, and shop supplies into the bills that are even remotely connected to a specific product. The engineering staff, whose job it is to do this, will think they have a micromanager on their hands and will make the changes just to humor him. Consequently, a fraudulent manager can quickly engineer a reduction in the cost of goods sold in the 1% to 2% range without raising any suspicions by anyone.

The change is small enough that most cost accountants and auditors will probably not notice it. The best way to monitor this situation is to keep tabs on the amount of monthly expense in the manufacturing supplies area; this expense should drop precipitously, because the expense is being capitalized into the inventory. Another detection technique is to turn on the tracking log option in the computer system, which notes who makes all changes to the labor routings file.

This practice is difficult to stop, because of its limited nature and theoretical justification. The best approach is to adopt a company-wide policy regarding the treatment of supplies, fittings, and fasteners, so that a fraudulent manager cannot alter the bills of material without breaking company policy. A good prevention method is to restrict access to the computerized labor routings file.

Of course, one can also make major changes to a bill of materials in order to effect immediate major changes in product costs. However, a major change will immediately flow through to excessively large picking tickets and the automated purchasing of considerable excess quantities of goods, so changes of this scope are much more easily detected.

4-5   Change Normal Scrap Assumptions

Most bills of material contain a list of each part or assembly that is used to manufacture a product, as well as the unit of measure for each part, the standard quantity used, and the standard scrap percentage that is assumed to arise in the course of production. This last item can be manipulated for short-term gains in reported levels of profitability.

If the scrap percentage is altered, then a product's cost will increase in a standard costing environment, because we multiply the cost of each inventory item by the standard scrap percentage associated with it to arrive at a total cost. As a result, both the cost of goods sold *and* the value of all work-in-process and finished goods inventory will increase, which does little to assist a fraudulent manager in the long run. However, if a company operates in a seasonal industry where there is a continuous inventory build-up for most of the year and then a short selling season, a fraudulent manager who is working toward a short-term profitability bonus can alter the scrap percentage upward, which can increase the inventory valuation by several percent, while the small proportion of sales during most months will have a minor impact on profitability. The result is a boost in the short-term reported level of profitability. However, the fraudulent manager will see these "paper profits" reversed as soon as the inventory is sold off, which should occur during the primary selling season. Consequently, this approach only works if the manager causing this activity will be rewarded for a short-term run-up in profits. It also requires a standard costing system, which relies heavily on accurate bills of material.

This is one of the most short-term approaches to fraud, but a clever manager can combine it with another method, which is a massive expansion in the level of inventory (see the "Increase Value-Added Inventory" section). By doing so, the manager can apply the extra scrap percentage to more inventory, irrespective of the level of sales. This is a particularly rewarding method if a manager is about to receive a performance bonus and then leave the company, because he or she will not care that the inventory levels and scrap percentages will have to be reduced at some point in the future, causing all "paper profits" to be reversed.

This type of fraud is most easily guarded against if the manufacturing software is designed so that a single change to a scrap percentage field in one screen will result in an automatic and cascading ripple effect that changes all of a company's bills of material. This is an easy field for a fraudulent manager to personally access and change, but it is equally easy to install password protection to it, thereby denying access to all but a few authorized employees. Given the critical nature of the information in a bill of materials, it is always a good idea to use password protection of this information, irrespective of the likelihood of fraud. At a minimum, be sure to turn on the track changes feature in the software, so an historical record is kept of all changes made.

4-6   Alter Unit Costs

A good accounting computer system will record the exact unit cost of any item purchased, so that the per-unit cost passes into a LIFO, FIFO, or some similar database that carefully tracks the costs of all parts kept in stock. When done properly, the system should represent an extremely accurate picture of all inventory costs, which can then be traced back through the accounting system to the exact supplier invoice that provides evidence of each cost. However, this system can be skewed in two ways.

One approach is to gain access to the costing data and directly alter the per-unit costs of all or selected inventory items. If the changes made are extremely small, such as tenths of a cent, the differences may appear so insignificant that an auditor will not bother to trace why there is such a tiny difference in the computer's recorded cost and the cost on the supplier's invoice. However, when there are many units of a particular item in stock, that small incremental change in the cost can result in a significant alteration in the value of the inventory, and so it is worth the effort for a fraudulent manager to undertake.

The best way to spot this problem is to use an accounting system that records and reports on all transactions in the system. Then a periodic trace of transactions relating to costing records will provide abundant evidence that someone has altered records. Another approach is to lock down all access to the costing records to all but high-level personnel. Under normal circumstances, there is no valid reason for anyone to access these records, so limiting access should not be an issue.

The other way to alter costing records is to change the assumptions under which costs are recorded from that of noting just the actual per-unit cost of each item to adding on the freight cost of each delivery from a supplier. This is perfectly acceptable under generally accepted accounting principles (GAAP), but it will result in a higher unit cost for each item in inventory, which will result in a lower cost of goods sold and a higher level of profitability. If a company is using LIFO or FIFO costing, the change will be gradual, because the new and higher costs will only gradually take over as older layers of inventory costs are used up. However, under a standard costing system where all inventory costs are replaced at once with the new cost, there will be a marked one-time jump in the inventory value that is sufficiently large to attract the attention of a fraudulent manager.

4-7   Increase Value-Added Inventory

One of the most commonly cited forms of cost accounting fraud noted in business schools is when a manager deliberately increases the amount of value-added inventory on hand, which results in a much larger allocation of overhead costs to inventory, thereby keeping the overhead from being charged to expense.

To do this, the fraudulent manager first obtains a copy of the inventory that breaks down the amount of direct labor charged to each product at either the work-in-process or finished goods stages of production (or something besides direct labor, if something else is used to allocated overhead costs to the inventory). He then sorts the list to determine which inventory items have the highest labor content, and then issues orders for exceptionally large quantities of those inventory items to be produced, usually far beyond what will actually be needed in the normal course of business. The accounting staff then allocates overhead to the inventory in its usual manner, which is probably by summarizing the direct labor content of the inventory and charging the monthly pool of overhead costs to the inventory by multiplying a standard cost of overhead to each direct labor dollar. For example, if the preset overhead allocation rate is $2.50 to be applied to each $1 of direct labor, then the overhead cost applied to inventory for $20,000 of direct labor will be $50,000. By shifting so much additional overhead cost to the inventory, there will be less left over to charge to the cost of goods sold, which results in a higher profit. The fraudulent manager then collects his performance bonus before anyone realizes just how much larger the inventories have become, and leaves the company.

This is a dangerous practice to pursue from the perspective of overall company health, because there must be a considerable additional investment in inventory before there is a noticeable increase in profits. The cash invested in this inventory may not be recovered for some time, because the inventory may have been expanded to one or more years' worth of inventory; and the larger the inventory, the greater the chance that some of it will be written off due to obsolescence or be sold at a discount.

The best way to avoid this type of fraud is to reward managers based on not only bottom-line profitability but also the amount of working capital invested in the business. Under this approach, an increase in inventory would result in an increase in working capital, so the manager would receive no bonus, and therefore would not have an incentive to perpetrate this type of fraud.

4-8   Ignore Obsolete Inventory

In even the best-run companies, some obsolete inventory will always be written off each year. The largest amount of write-offs will occur in those situations where there are poor inventory tracking systems, because employees will tend to ignore or repurchase components that are already in stock if those parts cannot be found. Obsolescence also arises when the purchasing staff buys excessive quantities of parts under the misguided notion that it is reducing per-unit costs by buying in bulk. Finally, obsolete inventories will arise when the engineering staff switches over to new parts for an existing design without first drawing down existing stocks of old parts. If all three of these issues are present in a company, then the annual write-off due to obsolescence can be remarkably high—well in excess of 10% of the total inventory balance.

Given the potential size of the write-off each year, it is no surprise that many managers will vigorously deny the existence of such large quantities of unusable inventory. Their method for eliminating this expense can cover several actions. One is to sharply reduce the obsolete inventory allowance, which is a reserve that the accounting staff accrues in each reporting period in anticipation of a future write-off of inventory. They can also pressure the warehouse and accounting staffs to stop or sharply reduce the amount of actual write-offs taken against this reserve, thereby leaving so much of the reserve in place that they successfully argue in favor of no further expense accruals to add to the reserve. They can also clean up or reshuffle the inventory, so that a casual or inexperienced observer will not notice any inventory that is covered with dust or has otherwise clearly been unused for a long period. The author is aware of one company that even hired a maid to dust off the inventory! Finally, a manager can disable the reports that itemize those inventory components or products that have not been used recently, and which are the principle and most accurate tools for identifying obsolete inventory. The combination of all of these activities can severely reduce or eliminate obsolescence write-offs.

The truly clever manager will not implement all of these changes at once, but rather will either gradually increase the usage of each technique or implement each one in a staggered fashion. By doing so, the external auditors will not see a sudden and highly suspicious drop in obsolescence write-offs, but rather a gradual decline, which the manager will have a much easier time explaining away as being caused by a gradual improvement in the company's ability to control its inventory.

This is a difficult activity to stop, especially if a manager is only reducing the obsolescence write-offs in small increments. One action is to respond promptly and in detail to any special request by the outside auditors for reports that show the age of selected inventory items, while another possibility is to ensure that the auditors have discussions with those members of the warehouse staff who can identify old inventory items; however, in this case, the severity of possible retribution by the responsible manager may keep anyone from talking. A final possibility is to suggest that the auditors run a trend line of inventory write-offs in relation to inventory turnover, because this ratio should be relatively steady from year to year. The auditors can then calculate a probable obsolescence expense based on this calculation and force the manager to accept the extra expense as part of the audit.

4-9   Change the Components of the Overhead Cost Pool

One of the areas that always seems to attract the attention of the fraudulent manager is the overhead cost pool. This pool of costs includes all overhead costs that will be allocated to inventory, rather than be directly expensed within the reporting period. If the number of expenses listed here can be increased, then the proportion of costs charged to the current period will drop, resulting in an increase in profits for the period.

The types of costs charged to the overhead cost pool are relatively standard and are as follows:

- Depreciation of factory equipment and facilities
- Factory administration expenses
- Indirect labor associated with production activities
- Indirect materials expended in support of production activities
- Factory maintenance
- Officers' salaries related to production
- Benefits of production employees
- Quality control costs
- Rent of any production equipment or facilities
- Rework labor
- Taxes related to production assets
- Utilities related to production activities

Although the specific types of costs that can be allocated are clear-cut, there are two ways to still commit fraud in this area. The first approach is to dump unrelated costs into approved accounts that will be summarized into the overhead cost pool. For example, the manager may require the accounts payable staff to code all office supply billings into the "production supplies" account, rather than a separate "office expenses" account. Another variation is to record all fixed-asset purchases into the production equipment asset account, so that the resulting depreciation and personal property taxes will all be loaded into the overhead cost pool. The second and more common approach is to increase the proportion of costs allocated between the production cost pool and period expenses. This is particularly likely when allocating the cost of officer salaries to production, because this is a highly subjective measure that cannot be precisely proven without a time-consuming study of the activities of each company officer.

A combination of the activities noted here will result in a larger overhead cost pool, which will increase profits as long as the amount of inventory (to which all of these additional costs are being directed) does not fall, which would result in the expensing of some portion of these previously capitalized costs.

Prevention is primarily in the hands of either internal or external auditors, who can run historical trend lines on the size of individual line items within each cost pool, as well as question the reasons for changes in allocated amounts.

4-10   Change the Basis for Overhead Allocation

When allocating overhead costs to products, the most common approach is to charge a predetermined amount of overhead to each dollar of direct labor that is used in each product. The direct labor component of the equation has been used for decades and is still the most common one used, despite the incursions of the much more sophisticated and accurate activity-based costing (ABC) allocation system. When a manager wants to inflate the value of inventory, thereby driving down the cost of goods sold, one possible approach is to cast around for a different allocation system that results in more overhead dollars being allocated to the inventory. It does not really matter to the manager which system is more accurate; he just wants the one that allocates the most overhead dollars to inventory.

The way in which this type of fraud begins is that a manager piously proclaims that it is time to throw out the outdated direct labor allocation system (which may be a valid claim), and so commissions a study by the accounting staff to find several allocation systems that are "more accurate." The accountants go off in a corner, chuckling to themselves that they finally have a manager who cares about cost accounting, and come back with several possible allocation systems. The manager expresses deep interest in all of the new systems, and asks that the accountants revalue the inventory based on each system, just to see what happens. When the study is completed, the manager runs through the list of inventory valuations and picks the one that yields the highest possible valuation; he does not care about the theoretical underpinnings of the system selected, he just wants a higher valuation.

Because this type of cost accounting change appears to be perfectly valid, and cannot even be considered fraud (because the new system may actually allocate costs better than the old one), there is not a great deal to be done about it. However, one should consider this a warning sign that if a manager is fiddling with the allocation system, he may have designs on other alterations to the costing system that will arise later.

4-11   Overallocate Overhead Costs

The normal approach for allocating overhead to inventory is to either compile all overhead costs for each reporting period and then allocate the actual amounts based on some allocation methodology or enter in the computer system a standard overhead cost for each item, and then adjust the total standard amount at the end of the reporting period so that it matches the total cost actually accumulated during the period. The first method is difficult for a fraudulent manager to alter, but the second one is subject to some manipulation, with the assistance of the accounting staff.

If the standard overhead system is used (the second method just noted), then the amount automatically allocated to each item in inventory will stay the same in every period, until someone goes into the computer records and manually alters them. A fraudulent manager can take advantage of this system by convincing the controller that there is no need to adjust this standard amount to match actual overhead costs in each period; making an adjustment at the end of the reporting year is sufficient. The manager can then raise the standard overhead rates charged, which has a dramatic upward impact on the value of inventory, thereby showing excellent reported profits until the end of the year. Even then, knowing that auditors are sure to review the adequacy of the overhead allocation, a manager who is working in concert with the accounting staff can shift actual costs from other accounts into the overhead cost accounts to make it appear as though actual overhead costs have risen, thereby validating the increased standard overhead costs charged to each product.

The greatest failing of this type of fraud is that it requires collusion between the fraudulent manager and the accounting staff—and the more people involved in the farce, the greater the chance that the secret will leak out. Also, a thorough auditing staff has a good chance of finding this type of fraud by carefully examining year-to-year changes in the various accounts that are used to compile overhead costs, and then closely investigating those accounts in which large year-to-year cost increases have occurred.

4-12   Shift Cost Allocations Away from Nonproduction Departments

If a company uses the traditional method of cost allocation, then all overhead costs are assigned to production activities, which means that some of the costs will be charged to inventory, and some will go into the cost of goods sold. This is the ideal situation for the fraudulent manager, because he can then concentrate on altering the system so that as much of the cost as possible is allocated to inventory, thereby driving down the cost of goods sold. However, if the cost allocation system is a more sophisticated one that also allocates costs to other departments, then those costs will probably be charged directly to expense, which leaves fewer costs to be allocated to inventory. For example, if a company has one or more service departments that provide services to other departments within the company (such as the computer services department), a reasonable allocation approach is to determine the usage of those services by all departments and allocate the costs accordingly; by doing so, some costs will be charged to general and administrative departments, whose costs are always charged directly to expense in the current reporting period.

If a fraudulent manager is looking for costs to capitalize into overhead, then such a sophisticated overhead allocation system will be a target for modification. The easiest approach is for this manager to order a reversion to the traditional allocation system that dumps all costs into production activities. If this direct conversion is not possible, then the manager will attempt to alter the allocation system so that a higher proportion of service costs are allocated to production.

The best response is to prepare a report that clearly shows the impact on reported profits that result from the manager's changes, as well as how the new allocation system is clearly skewing costs. This information should be sent up the chain of command to the controller or chief financial officer, who should use it to deal with the manager causing the changes.

4-13   Change Inventory Valuation Methods

Every inventory is valued using some underlying valuation method, such as LIFO or FIFO. These valuation methods are based on the assumed flow of inventory through a facility. For example, if you stock a shelf with inventory, the first inventory you load onto the shelf is positioned at the rear, where it will stay until all other inventory in front of it has been used. Under this assumption, the last inventory in (i.e., at the front of the shelf) is the first inventory to be used (i.e., a shopper or picker always takes the inventory at the front of the shelf first). This assumption is called the last-in, first-out (LIFO) method. The reverse assumption applies to the first-in, first-out (FIFO) method.

Whichever valuation method is used (and there are several other valid ones), there is a different impact on the inventory's valuation. For example, when there is a great deal of inflation over several years, the inventory stored at the back of the shelf will be the oldest, and so also has a lower cost than the more recent, and therefore more expensive, items near the front of the shelf. If a company currently uses the LIFO valuation methodology, and a manager wants to increase the value of the inventory, he can switch to the FIFO method; in our example, this will assign the latest, inflated, costs to inventory, while using up the oldest and least expensive inventory items first. Therefore, by altering the valuation method, one can either increase or decrease the value of the inventory, even though the inventory has never moved.

Altering the inventory valuation method is legitimate and may in fact better reflect the actual movement of costs through the inventory. However, such a change is discouraged under GAAP and requires a disclosure in the financial statements, which makes the impact of the change clear to readers of those statements. Nonetheless, if making such a change will improve the level of reported results, a manager may try it. If the accounting staff is unhappy about the switch, it can present its case to the outside auditors, who can determine if actual cost flows accurately reflect the proposed change, and who can refuse to render an opinion on the statements if they feel the change will result in misleading financial statements.

4-14   Record Sales Through Bill-and-Hold Transactions

When a manager is having difficulty selling products, a clever alternative is to enter into arrangements with customers whereby they can purchase additional quantities of product, frequently at a significant discount, but they do not have to take delivery or pay for the items until they are shipped, which may be some months in the future. Because the products do not meet the basic accounting test of having been shipped, auditors will examine these transactions in great detail and will request written confirmation from customers that these are legal and nonreversible sales.

Although this "bill and hold" transaction is not technically illegal, the end result is that a company has stuffed an excessive quantity of product into its distribution pipeline, and to such an extent that some of it has backed up into the company's facilities. At some point in the near future, there will have been so many sales recorded through bill and hold transactions that customers will no longer need to purchase additional products until they have flushed out the bulk of their bill and hold inventories. When that time arrives, sales will plunge, resulting in major losses. The fraudulent manager will try to build up bill and hold transactions to the greatest possible extent, collect his or her performance-based bonus, and leave the company just before sales suddenly dive.

This is not a difficult transaction to detect, because there must be a reasonable amount of accompanying documentation to satisfy the outside auditors. Also, it is visually apparent, because the warehouse will be overloaded with finished product that is being held for customers. The best way to stop this practice is to point out to senior management that working capital requirements have greatly expanded, because the company has now invested in inventory that is technically owned by its customers, but for which they do not have to make any payments until after they accept delivery.

4-15   Accrue Costs to Specific Jobs for Periodic Payments

When a company bills its customers on a cost-plus basis, it compiles costs under a job number and bills the customer based on the total amount of cost accumulated in that job. To increase the amount of cost in each billable job, a fraudulent manager can charge accrued costs to jobs that have not yet been incurred (and may never be incurred). If customers are not closely reviewing the contents of their job accounts to see what they are paying for, it is likely that these cost increases will be successfully billed to them. The trouble is that there may be no basis for the accrued expense; it was all a fabrication.

Once the customer has been billed, the job is closed down in the accounting system, so that no transactions can be made to or from the account. The fraudulent manager waits until the job is closed and then reverses the accrual to some other account, allegedly because the computer system will no longer allow any transactions to be made to it (which freezes the accrued expense into that account). This approach permanently leaves an unreversed accrual in the job account, so it is not at all difficult to detect the transaction. However, if the accrued amounts are kept relatively small, then their presence may escape detection by anyone who is only reviewing larger transactions on an audit basis. This approach is particularly effective for large job accounts, where a single moderate-sized accrual will be lost in a sea of other transactions.

This is a difficult situation to detect. The best method is to look for unreversed accruals in all job accounts. Also, customers who *do* review the costs in their job accounts may file a complaint about it, which is a clue to look for more widespread use of this practice.

4-16 Allocate Extra Costs to Specific Jobs

Some companies enter into time-and-materials or cost-plus projects with their customers, especially governmental entities, that allow them to pass through several costs to their customers. However, there are rules under which these contracts operate that keep companies from entering a wide array of irrelevant costs into the job records that will eventually be charged to customers. These rules typically prevent various types of overhead costs from being charged to customers. In many cases, these overhead costs cannot be charged to *any* customer, and so will be written off to expenses and absorbed by the company.

This is a fertile situation for the fraudulent manager, because the results of a deliberate skewing of the cost accounting system will be greater billings to customers and more cash when those bills are paid. The typical action taken is to deliberately change the rules regarding what expenses can be charged to specific jobs, leaving fewer expenses being allocated to unbillable overhead accounts. This fraud generally takes place in two steps, with the first one being a few small changes in cost allocations to see if the customer notices any increases in its billings. If so, and the customer sends an audit team out to investigate, then the manager can easily claim that there was an error and adjust the billings as demanded by the customer. However, if there is no response from the customer, then the next activity is a more blatant allocation of additional costs to customer-specific billings. This second step will be more targeted than the first step, because the manager may have learned to stay away from the billings of a few customers that reacted strongly to the first increase in billings, while dumping the bulk of extra costs into the billings of those customers who did not react. This approach usually results in a significant increase in billings, but runs the risk that customers will eventually determine what has happened and file a lawsuit against the company to recover their money, which results not only in damage awards but also in a public humiliation of the company.

The best prevention measure is to have the internal audit team schedule a recurring review that centers on the specific jobs to which various costs are charged, with the resulting report going straight back to the audit committee, which should include some members of the Board of Directors (who can take significant action if they discover problems).

4-17   Alter the Period-End Cutoff Date

By far the most common type of cost accounting fraud is a simple alteration in the date when a product is shipped. Many corporate managers feel intense pressure to ship as much product as possible during the last few days of a month, so that sales will be at the highest possible levels, and feel it necessary to repeatedly record shipments that actually went out in the first day or two of the next month as shipments from the previous month. This is an easily detected fraud if a company uses a third-party carrier, because all shipping documentation will clearly point toward a shipment that occurred in the next month, no matter what the internal documentation may say. This problem is so common that auditors make the cutoff review a key part of every audit.

However, the trail is somewhat more difficult to follow if a company has its own fleet of trucks, because then it can alter bills of lading and shipping records to make subsequent shipments appear as though they were actually sent in the previous month. In this case, there are still ways to detect the fraud. They are as follows:

- *Issue financial statements rapidly.* If there is a tightly enforced policy to complete financial statements as soon as possible, then the controller must complete all invoicing within the first few hours of the first day of the next month, which means that any later shipments must, by default, be recorded in the next month. This practice limits the time period when the cutoff can be extended to only a few hours past the end of the reporting period.

- *Compare driver logs to shipping documentation.* All commercial drivers must keep a detailed daily driving log. If they are caught without an up-to-date log book, their licenses can be suspended or revoked, so the logs tend to be well-kept. By comparing the driving activities noted in the logs to the shipping documentation accompanying what they are shipping, one can also detect timing differences.

- *Send an auditor to the shipping dock.* If there is an independent witness in the shipping area, there is not much chance of a cutoff problem occurring. However, this person must also examine the dates listed on all shipping documentation that then goes to the accounting department, to ensure that dates are not altered.

- *Confirm shipments with recipients.* One can also contact customers and ask them when they received shipments from the company, which is telling evidence if the customers experience a long delay in receiving shipments from the date when a company claims it sent out the shipments. However, the confirmation process is a time-consuming one and is not normally used unless there are strong suspicions that an intentional cutoff fraud exists.

The biggest problem with fraud related to the cutoff issue is that the entire management group of a company is frequently well aware of the problem and chooses to ignore it because they all stand to gain financially from the enhanced financial results that will be reported.

4-18   Delay Backflushing Adjustments

Most companies use the picking system for withdrawing goods from or entering them into the warehouse area, resulting in a specific inventory pick or receipt transaction that is easily traceable. However, backflushing does not work that way. Under this methodology, the production staff reports on the total number of products produced, which are then entered into the manufacturing computer, which in turn multiplies the total amount produced by the related bills of material for each item, resulting in a total amount of each component that should have been used, which the computer then deducts from the inventory records. This system, although technically an elegant one, is less easy to trace back through the system, because an auditor must first determine the quantity produced, then locate the bills of material for each item produced, then manually calculate the quantities of components that should have been withdrawn from inventory, and then inspect the backflushing transactions to see if those quantities were actually withdrawn. This is a tedious and highly error-prone process that only an experienced auditor can properly complete.

Knowing how difficult it is to trace this information, a fraudulent manager can simply delay the backflush processing at the end of a reporting period, so that the inventory is not reduced by it until the first day of the next reporting period. The result is an overinflated inventory for that reporting period, which may be worthwhile to a manager who needs to attain a monthly or quarterly profit figure in order to earn a bonus. Once the bonus is paid, the manager lets subsequent backflushing transactions occur at their normal times, which will result in reduced profits in the next month, because the backflushing that should have occurred in the previous month is resulting in a charge to inventory in the next month.

This is a surprisingly easy type of fraud to commit, because the fraudulent manager only has to know how to access the nightly batch processing file that schedules the backflushing transaction to run; by accessing this file and stopping that single transaction, no one will know that there is a problem. As long as the transaction is turned on again soon, it is also unlikely that anyone will notice that the resulting inventory records indicate quantities that are somewhat higher than what is actually in stock.

The best way to spot a delayed backflush is to conduct an inventory count at the end of the reporting period, during which any excessive book balances will be spotted and corrected, with the adjustments being charged to the correct reporting period. However, most companies do not count their inventories every month. Also, a clever manager can sometimes convince auditors to conduct their inventory counts slightly in advance of or after the period end, using roll-back or roll-forward calculations to verify balances; these calculations can be off by small amounts, which gives the manager sufficient room to delay a backflush and create a small change in the reported level of profitability.

4-19 Record the Cost of Customer-Owned Inventory

If customers supply a company with some parts that are used when constructing products for them, it becomes easy for this inventory to be mingled with the company's own inventory, resulting in a false increase in its inventory valuation. This is especially common when the company maintains its own inventory of the same parts, so that commingling is likely even without fraudulent intent.

A good approach for ensuring that costs are not assigned to customer-owned inventory is to rigorously enforce the rule that no items are to be received into the warehouse without a purchase order, which can be set up in advance with a zero cost by the purchasing staff. If a customer sends its inventory to the company without a purchase order authorization, it will not be accepted.

Also, once the inventory is received, the cycle counting staff may notice that there is no cost assigned to these parts and create one for them. To keep this from happening, physically segregate the goods in a different part of the warehouse, and make sure the entire warehouse staff knows what is located in that area. Also, the internal audit team can periodically run a cycle counting report for the designated storage area and see if any items within it have been assigned a cost.

In a case where someone is deliberately trying to record the cost of customer-owned inventory, these preventive techniques would require the connivance of people in the purchasing, warehouse, and internal auditing areas to complete the fraud, thereby making it more unlikely.

4-20 Steal Inventory

The most common item that people think about when they associate the words *fraud* and *inventory* is simple theft of the inventory. However, it is one of the easiest types of fraud to prevent and also tends to have a smaller impact on the financial statements than many of the other fraudulent situations already mentioned in this chapter. It is also the least likely to involve management, so there is less chance of having pressure being brought to bear on multiple people to collude in the removal of inventory. Here are several preventive measures to consider:

- *Lock up the warehouse.* Without access restrictions, the company warehouse is like a large store with no prices—just take all you want. To avoid this issue, place a fence around the warehouse, lock the main gate, and only allow authorized staff into the warehouse. Also, make sure that the warehouse is totally inaccessible after the warehouse staff goes home, so no one can enter it by climbing the fence or some other means.

- *Confirm receiving quantities at the dock door.* It is possible for shippers and the receiving staff to collude in delivering less than the full amount ordered and recording the receipt as a full receipt in the company computer system. The two parties then split the difference from the eventual sale of the stolen inventory. To prevent this problem, require that all received items be compared to purchase order quantities at the time of receipt, and have the internal audit staff verify this information during unannounced visits. Nonetheless, this is a difficult form of theft to stop.

- *Keep high-value fittings and fasteners in the warehouse.* A growing practice is to remove fittings and fasteners from the warehouse and store them in the production area, thereby reducing the picking and counting work of the warehouse staff. However, the production staff may take home some of the more expensive items. To keep this from happening, only shift low-cost items to the production area, where any theft will have an insignificant impact.

- *Investigate extra inventory requisitions.* The warehouse staff normally picks parts for the production department based on a picking list that is generated from a bill of materials. If a production person requisitions additional parts, either the bill of materials is incorrect, parts are being destroyed in the production area, or the staff are taking the parts home. Prompt investigation will determine which option is occurring. Also, require each person to sign for extra requisitioned parts, so there is a history of who took them.

5

Inventory Measurements and Internal Reports[1]

5-1 Introduction

This chapter contains 32 measurements related to inventory that can selectively be used to track changes in new product design, computer files, receiving, putaway, production, picking, shipping, and inventory storage—in that sequential order.

Don't feel compelled to use all 32 measurements. Instead, use only those measurements needed to track the most important parts of the inventory process flow. Too many measurements constitute an overflow of information and require an excessive amount of effort to calculate. For reference, the measurements are noted in their order of presentation in the following table:

5-2	Percentage of New Parts Used in New Products	5-13	Average Picking Time
		5-14	Picking Accuracy
5-3	Percentage of Existing Parts Reused in New Products		for Assembled Products
		5-15	Average Picking Cost
5-4	Bill of Material Accuracy	5-16	Order Lines Shipped per
5-5	Item Master File Accuracy		Labor Hour
5-6	On-Time Parts Delivery Percentage	5-17	Shipping Accuracy
5-7	Incoming Components Correct Quantity Percentage	5-18	Warehouse Order Cycle Time
5-8	Percentage of Receipts Authorized by Purchase Orders	5-19	Inventory Availability
		5-20	Delivery Promise Slippage
5-9	Percentage of Purchase Orders Released with Full Lead Time	5-21	Average Back Order Length
		5-22	Dock Door Utilization
5-10	Putaway Accuracy	5-23	Inventory Accuracy
5-11	Putaway Cycle Time	5-24	Inventory Turnover
5-12	Scrap Percentage	5-25	Percentage of Warehouse Stock Locations Utilized

---

[1] The measurements in this chapter are adapted with permission from Chapter 13 of Bragg, *Inventory Best Practices*, John Wiley & Sons, 2004. The forms and reports in this chapter are adapted with permission from Chapter 4 of Bragg, *GAAP Implementation Guide*, John Wiley & Sons, 2004.

In addition, this chapter contains three forms and seven reports related to the inventory function, including inventory tags, inventory sign-out and return forms, a cycle counting report, and an inventory accuracy report. One should consider integrating a selection of these offerings into one's accounting for and tracking of a corporate inventory system.

5-2 Percentage of New Parts Used in New Products

A continuing problem for a company's logistics staff is the volume of new parts that the engineering department specifies for each new product. This can result in an extraordinary number of parts to keep track of, which entails additional purchasing and materials handling costs. From the perspective of saving costs for the entire company, it makes a great deal of sense to encourage engineers to design products that share components with existing products. This approach leverages new products from the existing workload of the purchasing and materials handling staffs and has the added benefit of avoiding an investment in new parts inventory. For these reasons, the percentage of new parts used in new products is an excellent choice of performance measurement.

Divide the number of *new* parts in a bill of materials by the *total* number of parts in a bill of materials. Many companies may not include fittings and fasteners in the bill of materials, because they keep large quantities of these items on hand at all times and charge them off to current expenses. If so, the number of parts to include in the calculation will usually decline greatly, making the measurement much easier to complete. The formula is as follows:

$$\frac{\text{Number of new parts in bill of materials}}{\text{Total number of parts in bill of materials}}$$

Engineers may argue against the use of this measurement on the grounds that it provides a disincentive for them to locate more reliable and/or less expensive parts with which to replace existing components. Although this measure can act as a block to such beneficial activities, a measurement system can avoid this problem by also focusing on long-term declines in the cost of products or increases in the level of quality. A combined set of these measurements can be an effective way to focus on the most appropriate design initiatives by the engineering department.

5-3   Percentage of Existing Parts Reused in New Products

The inverse of the preceding measurement can be used to determine the proportion of existing parts that are used in new products. However, as the formula reveals, this measurement is slightly different from an inverse measurement. Companies that have compiled an approved list of parts that are to be used in new product designs, which is a subset of all existing parts, use this variation. By concentrating on the use of an *approved* parts list in new products, a company can incorporate high-quality, low-cost components into its products.

Divide the number of approved parts in a new product's bill of materials by the total number of parts in the bill. If there is no approved components list, then the only alternative is to use the set of all existing components from which to select items for the numerator, which will likely result in a higher percentage. The formula is as follows:

$$\frac{\text{Number of approved parts in bill of materials}}{\text{Total number of parts in bill of materials}}$$

Because a complex product will probably contain one or more subassemblies rather than individual components, one should verify that selected subassemblies are also on the approved parts list; otherwise, subassemblies will be rejected for the purposes of this measurement.

5-4   Bill of Material Accuracy

The engineering department is responsible for the release of a bill of materials for each product that it designs. The bill of materials should specify exactly what components are needed to build a product, plus the quantities required for each part. The logistics staff uses this information to ensure that the correct parts are available when the manufacturing process begins. At least a 98% accuracy rating is needed for this measurement in order to manufacture products with a minimum of stoppages caused by missing parts.

To calculate the measurement, divide the number of accurate parts (defined as the correct part number, unit of measure, and quantity) listed in a bill of material by the total number of parts listed in the bill. The formula is as follows:

$$\frac{\text{Number of accurate parts listed in bill of materials}}{\text{Total number of parts listed in bill of materials}}$$

Although the minimum acceptable level of accuracy is 98%, this is an area where a 100% accuracy level is required in order to ensure that the production process runs smoothly. Consequently, a great deal of attention should be focused on this measurement.

The timing of the release of the bill of materials is another problem. If an engineering staff is late in issuing a proper bill of materials, then the logistics group must scramble to bring in the correct parts in time for the start of the production process. Measuring the timing of the bill's release as well as its accuracy can avoid this problem by focusing the engineering staff's attention on it.

5-5   Item Master File Accuracy

The item master file contains all of the descriptive information about each inventory item, such as its unit of measure and cubic volume. This information must be correct or several downstream materials planning functions will issue incorrect results. Consequently, one should conduct a periodic audit of the file and report its accuracy to management.

To calculate the item master file accuracy, conduct an audit of a random sample of all item master records, verifying each field in the selected batch. Then divide the total number of records containing 100% accurate information by the total number of records sampled. The calculation is as follows:

$$\frac{\text{Total number of records reviewed having 100\% accurate information}}{\text{Total number of records sampled}}$$

An alternative approach is to divide the total number of accurate fields within the records by the total number of fields reviewed. However, this tends to result in an extremely high accuracy percentage, because there are many fields within each record, most of which are probably accurate. Because the point of using the measurement is to highlight problem areas, it is best to base the calculation on records reviewed, rather than fields, so that a lower accuracy percentage will be more likely to initiate corrective action by management.

5-6   On-Time Parts Delivery Percentage

One of the key performance measures for rating a supplier is its ability to deliver ordered parts on time, because a late delivery can shut down a production line. Furthermore, a long-standing ability to always deliver on time gives a company the ability to reduce the level of safety stock kept on hand to cover potential parts shortages, which represents a clear reduction in working capital requirements. Consequently, the on-time parts delivery percentage is crucial to the logistics function.

Subtract the requested arrival date from the actual arrival date. If one's intent is to develop a measurement that covers multiple deliveries, then one can create an average by summarizing this comparison for all of the deliveries and then dividing by the total number of deliveries. Also, if an order arrives before the requested arrival date, the resulting negative number should be converted to a zero for measurement purposes; otherwise, it will offset any late deliveries, when there is no benefit to the company of having an early delivery. Because a company must pay for these early deliveries sooner than expected, they can even be treated as positive variances by stripping away the minus sign. Any of these variations are possible, depending on a company's perception of the importance of not have early deliveries. The basic formula is as follows:

$$(\text{Actual arrival date}) - (\text{Requested arrival date})$$

This is an excellent measurement, but it does not address other key aspects of supplier performance, such as the quality of the goods delivered or their cost. These additional features can be measured alongside the on-time delivery percentage or melded into an overall rating score for each supplier.

5-7 Incoming Components Correct Quantity Percentage

If the quantity of items received in comparison to the amount ordered is too low, then the company may be faced with a parts shortage in its production operation. If the quantity is too high, then it may find itself with more inventory than it can use. Also, if an odd lot size is received, it may be difficult for the receiving staff to find a location in the warehouse in which to store it. For these reasons, the incoming components correct quantity percentage is commonly used.

Divide the number of orders to suppliers for which the correct quantity is delivered by the total quantity of orders delivered. This measurement is commonly subdivided by supplier, so the performance of each one can be measured. A variation on the formula is to only include in the numerator those orders received for which the entire order amount is shipped; this approach is used by companies that do not want to deal with multiple partial orders from their suppliers because of the increased cost of receiving and related paperwork. The formula is as follows:

$$\frac{\text{Quantity of orders with correct parts quantity delivered}}{\text{Total quantity of orders delivered}}$$

The formula can result in a low correct quantity percentage if the quantity received is only off by one unit. This may seem harsh if an order of 10,000 units is incorrect by one unit. Consequently, it is common for companies to consider an order quantity to be accurate if the quantity received is within a few percent of the ordered amount. The exact percentage used will vary based on the need for precision and the cost of the components received, although 5% is generally considered to be the maximum allowable variance.

5-8 Percentage of Receipts Authorized by Purchase Orders

One of the most difficult tasks for the receiving staff is to decide what to do with orders that are received with no accompanying purchase order. Because the orders are not authorized, the staff could simply reject them. However, they run the risk of rejecting some item that may have been bought on a priority basis and that will cause undue trouble for the logistics manager when projects in other parts of the company are held up. Accordingly, these orders are often set to one side for a few hours or days, while the receiving staff tries to find out who ordered them. This can be a significant waste of receiving time and storage space and is worth measuring on a trend line to see if the problem is worsening.

The receiving department should maintain a receiving log, on each line of which is recorded the receipt of a single product within an order. Using the line items in the receiving log that correspond to the dates within the measurement period, summarize the number of receipt line items authorized by open purchase orders by the total number of receipt line items in the log. The formula is as follows:

$$\frac{\text{Receipt line items authorized by open purchase orders}}{\text{Total receipt line items}}$$

This is an excellent measurement, because the use of purchase orders is one of the best controls over unauthorized buying, and the measurement clearly shows the extent of control problems in this area. However, it does not include other types of purchases that never run through the receiving area, such as services, subscriptions, or recurring lease payments. These other types of costs can constitute the majority of all nonpayroll costs in services industries; consequently, the measurement is of most use in businesses dealing in tangible goods.

5-9 Percentage of Purchase Orders Released with Full Lead Time

If the purchasing department is not preparing purchase orders on time, they will be forcing suppliers to deliver in less than standard lead times or incur expensive overnight air freight to bring items in on time. This may be a problem with an inefficient purchasing staff or be caused by sudden near-term changes in the production schedule. Whatever the reason may be, one should track the proportion of purchase orders released with full lead time and investigate those that are not.

To calculate the proportion of purchase orders released with full lead times, have the computer system summarize all purchase order lines in the measurement period for which there were full lead times, and divide this by the total number of purchase order lines released during the period. The calculation is as follows:

$$\frac{\text{Purchase order lines released with full lead time}}{\text{Total purchase order lines released}}$$

Given the quantity of purchase order lines involved, the summarization of data almost certainly will require a report from the computer system—manual summarization is *not* recommended! One should also use an additional report that itemizes each order line released with less than the full lead time, so that management can investigate the problem.

This measurement is not intended to apply in cases where a company orders standard parts for its manufacturing processes through the use of rolling schedules or just-in-time systems. In these instances, there should be no purchase orders at all.

5-10 Putaway Accuracy

The ability of the receiving staff to put received items away into stock locations correctly, including the proper recording of the transaction, is critical to all subsequent inventory transactions. If a putaway is done incorrectly, it is difficult to find an item, or verify that an incorrect part number or quantity has been used. An incorrect putaway also impacts the materials planning staff, which now has incorrect information about how much stock is on hand.

The basic putaway issue can be quantified with the putaway accuracy measurement. To calculate it, divide the total number of putaway transactions during the measurement period into the number of items for which an accurate putaway transaction was recorded. The formula is as follows:

$$\frac{\text{Number of accurate putaway transactions}}{\text{Total number of putaway transactions}}$$

From a practical perspective, it is usually easier to determine the number of incorrect putaways than the number of correct ones, so the numerator can be modified to be the total number of putaway transactions, less the number of putaway errors. This percentage is most easily calculated by periodically testing a sample of all inventory items.

This measurement should be clearly posted for the warehouse staff to read, thereby reinforcing the importance of a correct putaway. One should also include this measurement in the performance reviews of the warehouse staff, for the same reason.

5-11 Putaway Cycle Time

The accuracy of a putaway, as noted in the last measurement, is certainly important, but can take so long that it impacts the ability of a company to turn around items for shipment to customers or delivery to the shop floor. Consequently, one must also track the average putaway cycle time to ensure that this is being done in as short a period as possible. It is best to report the putaway cycle time and putaway accuracy measurements together in order to obtain an overall picture of the putaway function.

To measure putaway cycle time, subtract the arrival time of each receipt from its putaway time, summarize this information for all receipts during the measurement period, and divide it by the total number of receipts in the period. The calculation is as follows:

$$\frac{\text{Sum for all receiving transactions [(Putaway date/time)} - \text{(Receipt date/time)]}}{\text{Number of receipts during the measurement period}}$$

Given the large number of receiving transactions for all but the smallest warehouses, this measurement is best calculated via the materials management database. Also, because the measurement is based on the *time* of receipt and putaway (i.e., the number of minutes and seconds elapsed between these two events), the only way to obtain accurate transaction stamping is to use online, real-time data entry, which calls for the use of portable terminals linked to the materials management database. If this data collection system is not available, the measurement should not be used.

Another problem is the likely presence at the end of each measurement period of receipts that have not yet been put away. If one ignores these transactions for purposes of calculating the measurement, the average putaway cycle time will almost certainly be too low, because the items causing putaway problems are not being included. A better approach is to either delay the calculation until the unfinished transactions are completed or revise the calculation a month later when the next periodic measurement is made.

5-12 Scrap Percentage

The amount of scrap generated by a production operation is of great concern to the production manager, because it can indicate several problems: poor training of the direct labor work force, improper machine setup, materials handling problems, or even the ordering of substandard raw materials. Another reason for keeping a close watch over the scrap percentage is that inordinate amounts of scrap may require extensive revisions to the production schedule in order to produce extra goods, which in turn will require short-term changes to the purchasing schedule in order to bring in the required raw materials. For these reasons, the scrap percentage is one of the most closely watched performance measurements in the factory.

The amount of scrap that a company produces is difficult to measure, because it can be produced in many parts of a facility and in many cases is not accumulated for measurement purposes. If this is the case, the best approach is to subtract the standard cost of goods sold from the actual cost of goods sold, and divide the result by the standard cost of goods sold. By using this approach, one can compare the aggregate cost of what was produced to what should have been produced, without having to resort to a detailed count of each item scrapped. The formula is as follows:

$$\frac{(\text{Actual cost of goods sold}) - (\text{Standard cost of goods sold})}{\text{Standard cost of goods sold}}$$

A variation on this formula is to track only the scrap generated by the bottleneck production operation. This is especially important, because the scrap lost through this operation must be manufactured again, which may interfere with the production of other goods that must pass through the same operation, thereby possibly reducing the total amount of gross margin generated by the factory.

There are several problems with comparing the actual cost of goods sold to the standard amount and assuming that the difference is scrap. One problem is that there may be a standard scrap value already included in the bills of material that comprise the standard cost of goods sold, so these values must be extracted from the standard in order to determine the actual amount of scrap. Another problem is that there may be other variances contained within the actual cost of goods sold, such as a price variance on raw materials purchased. These variances must be calculated and removed from the actual cost of goods sold before the amount of scrap can be determined. Another problem is that many of the costs that make up the cost of goods sold are related to overhead, rather than the direct cost associated with scrap. To avoid this problem, one can include in the cost of goods sold only the direct labor and direct materials costs associated with production, removing all overhead costs. Finally, the inherent assumption in this formula is that standard costs are reasonably accurate; if not, the resulting scrap calculation will be incorrect.

5-13   Average Picking Time

A great many best practices in this book involve the attainment of a high level of order picking speed. Because some of the advocated changes involve a considerable capital investment or at least major changes in the scheduling or movement of the picking staff, wouldn't it be useful to see if the changes are making a difference? The measurement of average picking time is a good way to do so, although one must be aware of its shortcomings.

To measure the average picking time at the most detailed level, one can subtract the time at which an order was completed from the time when a picker received the order. Because this approach to the measurement clearly involves a massive amount of non-value-added timekeeping, one can only do it if wireless, real-time terminals are being used, so the computer system automatically tracks order duration. In the absence of such a system, the best approach is to divide the total number of orders completed during the measurement period by the total man-hours of picking time during the period. The calculation is as follows:

$$\frac{\text{Total number of orders completed}}{(\text{Total man-hours worked by picking staff}) + (\text{Total man-hours worked by contract staff})}$$

The denominator includes hours worked by both in-house and contract staff; some warehouses employ contract staff whose hours do not appear in the normal payroll system, so their hours must be added from the accounts payable system in order to obtain a full picture of the total hours being worked in the picking function.

Although this measure gives a good summary-level view of picking efficiency, it can be misinterpreted. The main issue is variations in the size of orders picked; if a larger proportion of single-line orders are processed in one month than in the next, then efficiency levels will appear to have declined, because orders are easier to fill when they only contain a single line. This problem is most common in low-volume environments when a small number of unusually large or small orders can significantly alter the measurement. However, when there are a great many orders to be picked, variations in order size tend to average out over the measurement period. If the measurement appears to be skewed by this issue, it may be possible to have the computer system summarize the total number of order lines picked during the period, and use this figure in the numerator of the measurement; this approach is usually too labor-intensive to attempt manually.

5-14 Picking Accuracy for Assembled Products

When a company ships disassembled products to customers, it is extremely important that the kits shipped out have exactly the correct number of the right parts. If the number is too high, then the company will be increasing its materials costs more than necessary. If the number is too low, then the company faces a significant customer relations problem, as well as added costs to locate and ship missing parts to customers. For these reasons, the picking accuracy of assembled products is considered important for those companies that ship kits.

To calculate this measurement, conduct an audit of a sample of completed kits, counting as an error every kit where the quantity of parts is incorrect, as well as an error for every kit where the quantity is correct, but the types of parts included are incorrect. Once a kit is considered incorrect for either reason, it cannot be counted as an error again (thereby avoiding double counting). Then divide the total number of errors by the total number of product kits sampled. Finally, subtract the resulting percentage from 100%. The formula is as follows:

$$100\% - \frac{\text{Number of quantity errors} + \text{number of part errors}}{\text{Total number of product kits sampled}}$$

If the company feels that the key issue is avoiding customer complaints, then it may be justified in not bothering to count a part overage as an error. This is especially common when counting fittings and fasteners, which are usually the least expensive parts of a product kit.

5-15 Average Picking Cost

Even if a company has achieved an extremely high level of picking efficiency and accuracy, it should not have done so at an inordinately high cost. Consequently, it is best to measure the picking cost per order line alongside efficiency and accuracy measurements in order to gain a complete picture of a company's picking capability.

To measure the average picking cost, divide the total picking cost by the number of order lines picked. The total picking cost should include the fully burdened labor cost of the picking staff, plus the depreciation on any incremental improvements in warehouse equipment or racking specifically intended to improve picking efficiency or accuracy. The calculation is as follows:

$$\frac{\text{(Fully burdened picking staff wages)} + \text{(Depreciation on picking equipment and storage)}}{\text{Total order lines picked}}$$

Obtaining the total number of order lines picked is best achieved by having the computer system summarize this information for the measurement period. Determining picking staff wages can be difficult if the warehouse staff switches among tasks, rather than having dedicated pickers; although one can use timesheets to track how much time was spent on each activity, this is a non-value-added activity, so the only alternative may be an occasional sample study of worker time. The depreciation on picking equipment and storage should be included in the numerator, because a company may invest heavily in such expensive assets as automated storage and retrieval systems or carousels in order to improve the efficiency of its picking operations. If there are such assets, use straight-line depreciation over the useful life of each asset rather than the accelerated depreciation system that may be used for accounting purposes. The straight-line method more accurately reflects the periodic expense of these assets.

5-16   Order Lines Shipped per Labor Hour

The ability to ship orders is a determinant of the efficiency of a warehouse staff. Although many other transactions are involved in warehouse activities, it must be able to reliably ship to customers on time, because this is a service issue directly experienced by customers. A warehouse manager could simply overstaff the shipping department to ensure that all possible orders are shipped on time, but this negatively impacts profits.

The best way to determine the efficiency of the shipping function is to compare the number of order line items filled to the total labor hours expended in this activity. To measure it, divide the total number of order lines shipped into the total labor hours expended to fill orders. The calculation is as follows:

$$\frac{\text{Total order lines shipped}}{\text{Total labor hours used to ship orders}}$$

The numerator cannot be the total number of orders, because some orders may contain multiple line items, thereby artificially making the shipping staff look less efficient than it really is. Also, the denominator must include all labor involved in the order fulfillment process, including all picking, packing, and shipping tasks. It is generally easiest to include in the denominator the total hours worked by all persons assigned to these tasks, so there is no chance of undercounting labor hours.

5-17   Shipping Accuracy

Although the preceding "Order Lines Shipped per Labor Hour" measurement gives
a gross measure of the efficiency of the shipping function, it yields no information
about the accuracy of the orders shipped: It does no good to ship with astonishing
efficiency if the wrong items go to the customer! Accordingly, one should report
that measure alongside a shipping accuracy percentage in order to gain a total perspective on the shipping function.

Shipping accuracy information comes from the customer, who lodges complaints about incorrect order fulfillment. This information becomes the numerator
in the shipping accuracy measurement when subtracted from the total order lines
shipped. If divided by the total order lines shipped, one can derive the measure as
a percentage. The calculation is as follows:

$$\frac{\text{(Total order lines shipped)} - \text{(Incorrect order lines reported by customers)}}{\text{Total order lines shipped}}$$

The problem with this measurement is linking the timing of the order line complaint from the customer to the order line volume for the period in which the order
was delivered. Although there may be a difference of only a few days between the
shipment and complaint dates, it is still common to mismatch a reported shipment
error to shipment volume from a different period. The best way to resolve the issue
is to record the order number over which a complaint has been lodged and have the
computer system track down the date on which that order was shipped. This approach correctly matches a shipping error to the volume of items shipped during
a specific period.

5-18   Warehouse Order Cycle Time

One of the primary customer service measures involving the warehouse is its ability to ship an order as rapidly as possible (as well as accurately—see the prior "Order
Lines Shipped per Labor Hour" measurement). Constant attention to the interval
required from receipt of a customer order to its delivery is necessary, both for bringing the order cycle time up to acceptable standards and to ensure that it does not dip
below unacceptable levels.

To calculate the warehouse order cycle time, subtract the date and time of the
order receipt into the company order entry system from the delivery date and time
of the last line item left open on the order. The calculation is as follows:

(Date and time of last line item delivery) – (Date and time of order receipt)

There are several ways to interpret this measurement. First, consider breaking down
the set of orders from which it is derived, so that the slowest 20% of all deliveries
are measured separately. One should print a detailed report of each of these slow
orders, so the management team can focus its attention not only on the gross time

interval required to ship the slowest orders, but also on the specific orders in this subset. Second, as noted in the original measurement description, be sure to measure based on delivery of the *last* order line item to be shipped—it makes no sense to measure a successful order as one for which just a few items are shipped; by doing so, management essentially chooses to ignore items placed on backlog, which is precisely where its attention should be most intensely focused. Third, if the warehouse order cycle time is initially long, don't bother to measure the time of delivery within a day; that can wait until the average cycle time has been driven down to just a day or two, after which management's measure of success will be small improvements in time intervals.

5-19 Inventory Availability

One of the primary reasons for having inventory is to satisfy customer demand in a timely manner. Maintaining a high level of inventory availability is usually cited as the primary reason why companies keep such high levels of finished goods and service parts on hand. Given this logic, one should measure a company's success in filling orders to see if high inventory retention is working as a policy.

To measure inventory availability, divide the total number of completed orders received by customers no later than their required date during the measurement period by the total number of completed orders that customers should have received during the measurement period. The calculation is as follows:

$$\frac{\text{Total number of completed orders received by customer by required date}}{\text{Total number of orders that should have been completed}}$$

The measurement emphasizes a successful order fulfillment as one *received* by the customer on time, because the customer is not being served properly if the order was merely shipped as of the required due date. Most company systems have no provision for tracking customer receipt dates. To avoid this problem, a company can train the order entry staff to subtract shipping time from a customer's required date on receipt of the order, and enter the shortened date in the order entry system.

A company can falsely assume that it has a high availability rate if it counts any sort of partial shipment as a completed order in the numerator, possibly on the grounds that it has successfully shipped nearly all of an order. This measurement approach certainly is not the view of the customer, who may well stop using the company on the basis of a "completed" order, which it sees as a failure.

5-20 Delivery Promise Slippage

An extremely common occurrence is for the customer support staff to convince a customer to take a delivery later than the originally promised date, and then enter the revised promised date into the computer system as though it were the original promised date. Then, when the order is finally delivered, the delivery is measured as being on time, because it matched the revised promised date. Management is therefore unaware of any problem with customer satisfaction resulting from continual slippage problems. The solution is to track the slippage in the delivery promised date.

There are two ways to measure delivery promise slippage. The first is to subtract the final promised date from the original promised date for all orders, and divide by the number of total orders. This approach assumes that the final promised date matches the actual shipment date, which may not be the case. The second approach, which avoids this problem, is to subtract the delivery date from the original promised date for all orders, and divide by the number of total deliveries. The calculation is as follows:

$$\frac{\text{Sum for all delivery transactions [(Delivery date/time)} - \text{(Original promised date/time)]}}{\text{Total number of deliveries}}$$

This measurement requires the presence of a field in the order entry database reserved for the original promised date, which is not available in some less-expensive software packages. Also, it is best if the original promised date field can be locked, so there is no chance of meddling with dates in order to attain a better delivery promise slippage measurement.

One problem is the likely presence at the end of each measurement period of promised orders that have not yet been delivered. If one ignores these transactions for purposes of calculating the measurement, the average delivery promise slippage will almost certainly be too low, because the items causing slippage problems are not being included. A better approach is to either delay the calculation until the unfinished transactions are completed or revise the calculation a month later when the next periodic measurement is made.

5-21 Average Back Order Length

When a company focuses solely on the inventory availability measurement just described, the status of any items placed on back order tends to fall off the map. If a customer cannot receive a shipment on time, it at least wants to receive it as soon thereafter as possible, so a company should also track the average length of its back-ordered items to ensure that customers are not excessively dissatisfied.

To measure the average back order length, compile a list of all customer orders that were not shipped on time and summarize from this list the total number of days that each order has gone past the customer receipt date without being shipped. Then divide this total number of days by the total number of back-ordered customer orders. The calculation is as follows:

$$\frac{\text{Sum of the [Number of days past the required customer receipt date for each order]}}{\text{Total number of back-ordered customer orders}}$$

Although the measurement is useful enough by itself, management will probably want to see an accompanying list of the oldest back-ordered items, so it can resolve them as soon as possible.

5-22   Dock Door Utilization

A warehouse may contain a great many dock doors, each of which must be backed by a significant amount of floor space to allow for proper materials movement and related shipping and receiving equipment. Thus, dock doors represent a considerable amount of non-value-added floor space, and so must be heavily utilized in order to release as much space as possible for other applications. One should track dock door utilization to determine if the current number of doors is optimal.

To measure dock door utilization, multiply the average dock time per trailer by the number of trailers docked during the measurement period. Then divide the result by the total number of hours in the period, multiplied by the number of dock doors. The calculation is as follows:

$$\frac{(\text{Average dock time per trailer}) \times (\text{Number of trailers docked})}{(\text{Number of hours in measurement period}) \times (\text{Number of dock doors})}$$

Proper formulation of this measurement requires tracking of all trailers docked during the measurement period, which one can back into by summarizing all shipping and receiving transactions through the computer system or by manually tracking this information. The key flaw in this measurement is the average dock time per trailer, which can seriously impact the measurement's accuracy if it is incorrectly formulated. One should schedule on the warehouse activities calendar a periodic reformulation of the average dock time, based on all trailers docked during a sample period.

5-23   Inventory Accuracy

If a company's inventory records are inaccurate, timely production of its products becomes a near impossibility. For example, if a key part is not located at the spot in the warehouse where its record indicates it should be, or its indicated quantity is incorrect, then the materials handling staff must frantically search for it and probably issue a rush order to a supplier for more of it, while the production line remains idle, waiting for the key raw materials. To avoid this problem, a company must ensure that not only the quantity and location of a raw material is correct, but also that its units of measure and part number are accurate. If any of these four items are wrong, there is a strong chance that the production process will be negatively impacted. Thus, inventory accuracy is one of the most important materials handling measurements.

Divide the number of accurate test items sampled by the total number of items sampled. The definition of an accurate test item is one whose actual quantity, unit of measure, description, and location match those indicated in the warehouse records. If any one of these items is incorrect, then the test item should be considered inaccurate. The formula is as follows:

$$\frac{\text{Number of accurate test items}}{\text{Total number of items sampled}}$$

It is extremely important to conduct this measurement using all four of the criteria noted in the formula derivation. The quantity, unit of measure, description, and location must match the inventory record. If this is not the case, then the reason for using it—ensuring that the correct amount of inventory is on hand for production needs—will be invalidated. For example, even if the inventory is available in the correct quantity, if its location code is wrong, then no one can find it in order to use it in the production process. Similarly, the quantity recorded may exactly match the amount located in the warehouse, but this will still lead to an incorrect quantity if the unit of measure in the inventory record is something different, such as dozens instead of eaches.

5-24   Inventory Turnover

Inventory is often the largest component of a company's working capital; in such situations, if inventory is not being used by operations at a reasonable pace, then a company has invested a large part of its cash in an asset that may be difficult to liquidate in short order. Accordingly, keeping close track of the rate of inventory turnover is a significant function of management. Turnover should be tracked on a trend line in order to see if there are gradual reductions in the rate of turnover, which can indicate that corrective action is required to eliminate excess inventory stocks.

The most simple turnover calculation is to divide the period-end inventory into the annualized cost of sales. One can also use an *average* inventory figure in the denominator, which avoids sudden changes in the inventory level that are likely to occur on any specific period-end date. The formula is as follows:

$$\frac{\text{Cost of goods sold}}{\text{Inventory}}$$

A variation on the preceding formula is to divide it into 365 days, which yields the number of days of inventory on hand. This may be more understandable to the layperson; for example, 43 days of inventory is more clear than 8.5 inventory turns, even though they represent the same situation. The formula is as follows:

$$365 \div \frac{\text{Cost of goods sold}}{\text{Inventory}}$$

The preceding two formulas use the entire cost of goods sold in the numerator, which includes direct labor, direct materials, and overhead. However, only direct materials costs directly relate to the level of raw materials inventory. Consequently, a clearer relationship is to compare the value of direct materials expense to raw materials inventory, yielding a raw materials turnover figure. This measurement can also be divided into 365 days in order to yield the number of days of raw materials on hand. The formula is as follows:

$$\frac{\text{Direct materials expense}}{\text{Raw materials inventory}}$$

The preceding formula does not yield as clean a relationship between direct materials expense and work-in-process or finished goods, because these two categories of inventory also include cost allocations for direct labor and overhead. However, if these added costs can be stripped out of the work-in-process and finished goods valuations, then there are reasonable grounds for comparing them to the direct materials expense as a valid ratio.

The turnover ratio can be skewed by changes in the underlying costing methods used to allocate direct labor and especially overhead cost pools to the inventory. For example, if additional categories of costs are added to the overhead cost pool, then the allocation to inventory will increase, which will reduce the reported level of inventory turnover—even though the turnover level under the original calculation method has not changed at all. The problem can also arise if the method of allocating costs is changed; for example, it may be shifted from an allocation based on labor hours worked to one based on machine hours worked, which can alter the total amount of overhead costs assigned to inventory. The problem can also arise if the inventory valuation is based on standard costs and the underlying standards are altered. In all three cases, the amount of inventory on hand has not changed, but the costing systems used have altered the reported level of inventory costs, which impacts the reported level of turnover.

A separate issue is that the basic inventory turnover figure may not be sufficient evidence of exactly where an inventory overage problem may lie. Accordingly, one can subdivide the measurement, so that there are separate calculations for raw materials, work-in-process, and finished goods (and perhaps be subdivided further by location). This approach allows for more precise management of inventory-related problems.

5-25   Percentage of Warehouse Stock Locations Utilized

One should periodically obtain a quantification of the amount of warehouse space currently being used to store stock. This measurement is useful during the annual budgeting process, because the management team needs to know if projected inventory levels for the coming year can be contained within the existing warehouse space. The information also shows the before-and-after results of having cleared out obsolete or rarely used inventory.

To measure the percentage of warehouse stock locations utilized, divide the number of stock locations containing any amount of inventory by the total number of stock locations in the warehouse. The calculation is as follows:

$$\frac{\text{Number of utilized stock locations}}{\text{Total number of stock locations in the warehouse}}$$

If inventory records are stored in a computer database, as well as cross-referenced to a file listing all possible inventory locations, it is easy to derive the proportion of registered warehouse locations currently being utilized.

If there is no inventory database, one can usually determine the total number of stock locations by walking through the warehouse and adding them up; this number does not change much, unless the warehouse is reconfigured, in which case a single walk-through will yield the new total number of locations. If one must also walk through the warehouse to count the number of utilized stock locations, it is almost always easier to count the number of stock locations in which there is *no* inventory (because warehouses rarely suffer from underutilization), and then subtract this amount from the total number of stock locations.

The main problem with this measurement is that it does not give any indication of the cubic volume of space being filled. The measure considers any stock location containing even the smallest amount of inventory to be a fully utilized location, which may grossly misrepresent the amount of unused cubic space available.

5-26   Storage Density Percentage

Although every storage rack and bin in a warehouse may be filled to the brim, indicating a 100% utilization of all stock locations, this may not indicate the true storage capacity of the warehouse. It is entirely possible that existing storage systems are not using all horizontal or vertical storage capabilities within a warehouse, because of such factors as insufficiently high racks or excessively wide aisles. Consequently, it is useful to occasionally determine a warehouse's overall storage density percentage, which measures storage capacity per square foot.

To measure the storage density percentage, divide the cubic volume of all storage locations by the total warehouse square footage and the square footage for all external staging areas. The calculation is as follows:

$$\frac{\text{Cubic volume of available storage space}}{(\text{Total warehouse square footage}) + (\text{External staging area square footage})}$$

This is an easy calculation if a company maintains a storage location file that includes the cubic volume of each location. However, this measurement can be misinterpreted, because one can create a warehouse with an excessively high storage density percentage. This can be accomplished by installing racking systems that are dangerously high or by laying out aisles that are too narrow for efficient item movement.

5-27 Inventory per Square Foot of Storage Space

It is sometimes useful to gain an understanding of overall storage space utilization, particularly in comparison to benchmarked measurements obtained elsewhere. To this end, one can relate the amount of inventory on hand to the total square feet of space it occupies. The main problem is determining the numerator in the calculation: Should it be based on the quantity, dollar value, or cubic volume of SKUs on hand? If the quantity of SKUs is used, a large number of small items can skew the measurement in favor of showing a large amount of inventory per square foot. The same logic applies to the inventory dollar value. This leaves the cubic volume of inventory on hand, which best represents space utilization.

To measure the amount of inventory per square foot of storage space, divide the cubic volume of all inventory on hand by the total warehouse square footage, plus the square footage of all external staging areas. The calculation follows:

$$\frac{\text{Cubic volume of inventory on hand}}{(\text{Total warehouse square footage}) + (\text{External staging area square footage})}$$

The cubic volume of inventory on hand can be difficult to calculate manually. The best approach is to add the cubic volume for each item to the item master file, so this information can be automatically calculated by the computer system. If this approach is used, be sure to match the cubic volume figure to the unit of measure entered in the item master file. Otherwise, an incorrect cubic volume figure will result.

A possible area of contention in this measurement is the use of total warehouse square footage in the denominator. One might be tempted to only use the square footage of actual storage racks, but doing so ignores the efficient use of other space in the warehouse. For example, one could limit the denominator to square footage occupied by existing racks to obtain an excellent result, but it would hide the existence of excessively wide aisles that could be narrowed to yield additional storage space.

5-28 Storage Cost per Item

Items can languish in the warehouse for years. During that time, one can forget their presence on the assumption that they are accumulating no costs and so can be safely ignored. Unfortunately, inventory accumulates more costs every day in the form of rack space taken, insurance coverage expenses, the opportunity cost of invested funds, and so on. One must be aware of these costs or be ignorant of a major portion of a company's cost structure.

There are several ways to measure the storage cost of an inventory item. At a summary level, one can simply divide the total number of SKUs actually on hand into all warehouse costs, which comprise the fully burdened wages of all warehouse staff, depreciation on all fixed assets, inventory insurance coverage, utilities, obsolescence, scrap costs resulting from damaged goods, and the corporate cost of capital on funds invested in inventory. At this simplified level, the calculation is as follows:

$$\frac{\text{Total warehouse expenses}}{\text{Total stock keeping units on hand}}$$

The problem with this calculation is that not all SKUs incur the same costs. For example, a high-value item should be charged a higher proportion of insurance costs, whereas perishable goods must be charged with a higher proportion of obsolescence costs. Thus, a better approach is to adopt an activity-based costing (ABC) approach to measuring the storage cost per item. Under ABC, costs are accumulated by activity (such as by putaway or picking transaction), and then costs are charged out to individual SKUs based on their use of these transactions. Although the ABC calculation can be lengthy, a typical finding is that a large proportion of all SKUs on hand are costing a company far more than they earn on the gross margin from their eventual sale.

5-29   Average Pallet Inventory per SKU

When planning storage requirements in a warehouse, it is extremely useful to determine in advance the likely pallet inventory required for each SKU, so a sufficient space can be set aside for each one.

To measure the average amount of pallet space required for each SKU, first divide the forecasted unit sales by the historical or planned turnover for each SKU, yielding the average number of units on hand at any time. Then divide this by the number of units per pallet, yielding the average number of pallets on hand. The calculation is as follows:

$$\frac{(\text{Forecasted SKU unit sales} \div \text{turnover})}{\text{Units per pallet}}$$

One can take the measurement a step further by dividing the average pallet inventory by the number of storage levels available in the pallet storage area in order to derive the storage requirement per square foot.

There are three problems with this measurement: (1) it relies heavily on an accurate forecast from the marketing department; (2) it assumes that an average inventory level is sufficient for year-round demand, when in fact there may be considerable demand spikes requiring much higher storage levels; and (3) the measurement should be used at the SKU level, which can require a prohibitive amount of calculations unless the underlying data is available on a computer for automatic calculations.

5-30   Rate of Change in Inactive, Obsolete, and Surplus Inventory

The header for this best practice refers to three types of inventory: (1) parts having no forecasted usage (inactive), (2) parts that are no longer incorporated into any current product (obsolete), and (3) parts with quantities exceeding forecasted usage (surplus). For brevity, we will refer to all three categories of inventory as IOS.

The accounting staff can have a difficult time quantifying its ongoing obsolescence reserve for IOS inventory. In a typical company, a team of reviewers periodically designates specific items in the warehouse as obsolete, at which point the accounting staff adjusts its obsolescence reserve to match the total amount of identified obsolete stock. This tends to result in sudden and large changes in the obsolescence expense that can skew reported financial results. In order to make a more gradual adjustment in the obsolescence reserve, one can use the following formula to arrive at a smaller incremental monthly adjustment in the reserve, based on the monthly growth rate in the IOS:

$$\frac{(\text{Current IOS inventory balance}) - ((\text{Beginning IOS balance}) - (\text{Actual write-off in the period}))}{\text{Number of months covered by calculation}}$$

Although this approach will result in fewer massive increases in the obsolescence reserve, such adjustments are still possible. The formula is based on historical changes in obsolescence, not any forward-looking adjustments that may include substantial write-downs related to such events as a product termination. Consequently, one can use this formula to make incremental adjustments to the obsolescence accrual, but also adjust these entries for estimated changes in the future rate of obsolescence.

5-31   Obsolete Inventory Percentage

A company needs to know the proportion of its inventory that is obsolete, for several reasons. First, external auditors will require that an obsolescence reserve be set up against these items, which drastically lowers the inventory value and creates a charge against current earnings. Second, constantly monitoring the level of obsolescence allows a company to work on eliminating the inventory through such means as returns to suppliers, taxable donations, and reduced-price sales to customers. Finally, obsolete inventory takes up valuable warehouse space that could otherwise be put to other uses; monitoring it with the obsolete inventory percentage allows management to eliminate these items in order to reduce space requirements.

Summarize the cost of all inventory items having no recent usage, and divide by the total inventory valuation. The amount used in the numerator is subject to some interpretation, because there may be occasional usage that will eventually use up the amount left in stock, even though it has not been used for some time. An alternative summarization method for the numerator that avoids this problem is to only include those inventory items that do not appear on any bill of material for a currently produced item. The formula is as follows:

$$\frac{\text{Cost of inventory items with no recent usage}}{\text{Total inventory cost}}$$

A high level of obsolete inventory does not reflect well on the logistics manager, who is responsible for maintaining a high level of inventory turnover. If this person has any influence over the calculation, it is possible that he or she will attempt to alter the amount listed in the numerator, either by defining "recent usage" as anything within a long time period or by ensuring that all inventory items are included on some sort of bill of material, which is generally considered evidence that it may eventually be used. To avoid this problem, the calculation should be given to someone outside of the logistics department.

5-32 Percentage of Inventory More Than XX Days Old

A company may not have any obsolete inventory, but it may have a sufficient amount of older inventory that it is concerned about the possibility of obsolescence at some point in the future. By determining the amount of inventory that is older than a certain fixed date, the logistics staff can determine which items should be returned to suppliers (see the next measurement) or which items should be sold off at a reduced price.

Determine a number of days after which inventory is considered to be old enough to require liquidation action. Then determine the dollar value of all items whose age exceeds this number of days. Divide that total by the total dollar value of inventory. The measurement should be accompanied by a report that lists the detailed amounts and locations of each inventory item in the numerator, so that the logistics staff can review them in detail. The formula is as follows:

$$\frac{\text{Dollars of inventory more than XX days old}}{\text{Total dollars of inventory}}$$

The measurement can give one some idea of the total amount of inventory that may require liquidation, but it gives no visibility into the raw material usage requirements of the production schedule, which may be scheduled to use these items during an upcoming production run. One can only tell if this is the case by comparing the old inventory list to the production requirements report.

If this report is used to determine the proportion of old finished goods, it yields a better idea of what products may need to be sold off. However, it also requires some knowledge of the timing of the sales season for each product on the list. For example, an article of clothing may appear to be old, but if its prime selling season is just starting, then it would make sense to leave it alone through much of the season to see if it can be sold at its full retail price before considering any type of price discounting.

5-33 Percentage of Returnable Inventory

Over time, a company will tend to accumulate either more inventory than it can use or inventory that is no longer used at all. These overaccumulations may be caused by an excessively large purchase or the scaling back of production needs below original expectations, or perhaps a change in a product design that leaves some components completely unnecessary. Whatever the reason may be, it is useful to review the inventory occasionally in order to determine what proportion of it can be returned to suppliers for cash or credit.

Summarize all inventory items for which suppliers have indicated that they will accept a return in exchange for cash or credit. For these items, one may use in the numerator either the listed book value of returnable items or the net amount of cash that can be realized by returning them (which will usually include a restocking fee charged by suppliers). The first variation is used when a company is more interested in the amount of total inventory that it can eliminate from its accounting records, while the second approach is used when one is more interested in the amount of cash that can be realized through the transaction. The denominator is the book value of the entire inventory. The formula is as follows:

$$\frac{\text{Dollars of returnable inventory}}{\text{Total dollars of inventory}}$$

Even though a large proportion of the inventory may initially appear to be returnable, one must also consider that near-term production needs may entail the repurchase of some of those items, resulting in additional freight charges to bring them back into the warehouse. Consequently, the underlying details of the measurement should be reviewed in order to ascertain not only which items can be returned but also more specifically which ones can be returned that will not be needed in the near term. This will involve the judgment of the logistics staff, perhaps aided by a reorder quantity calculation, to see if the cost is justifiable to return goods to a supplier that will eventually be needed again. A reduced version of the measurement that avoids this problem is to only include in the numerator those inventory items for which there is no production need whatsoever, irrespective of the time line involved.

5-34 Inventory Forms and Reports

This section contains three forms and seven reports related to the inventory function. Some of these forms, such as the receiving log and inventory tag, are used to track the physical existence of inventory. Others, such as the standard-to-actual cost comparison report and the standard cost changes report, are more concerned with the cost of inventory. It is useful to peruse this section and see if any of the forms and reports can be integrated into one's inventory operations. At a minimum, perhaps one's existing form or report formats can be altered to match the layouts provided here.

If a company has a fully integrated computer system into which the receiving staff can directly enter all receipts, no forms will be required for goods in transit. If not, a receiving log will be used, such as the one shown in Exhibit 5-1. The report may contain additional room for notations by the receiving staff, such as the condition of the items received.

The same information is commonly used in receiving reports, which are sorted either by date, supplier, part number, or part description.

A physical inventory count is usually taken by using a tag to be affixed to each lot. The tags are numbered serially in advance, and because a portion of the tag is left on the stock, it serves as a means of ensuring that all lots are counted. A sample inventory tag is shown in Exhibit 5-2. This is a two-part tag, with the lower section being collected for summarization. Space is provided on the reverse side for noting movements so that slow-moving items can be counted in advance of the regular count.

A cycle counting report is used by cycle counters to compare inventory records from the accounting database to physical counts in the warehouse. The sample report in Exhibit 5-3 is usually sorted by warehouse location code, so that counters can verify all items within a small area, which is the most efficient accounting method. The report has space on it to record physical inventory counts, although one can also write in any adjustments to part descriptions or units of measure as well.

Once cycle counting information has been collected, accuracy levels for each part of the inventory should be recorded on a trend line, preferably on a wall-mounted display board. By doing so, management makes a statement that this information is extremely important and that it wishes to see improvement in the accuracy statistics. An example of an inventory accuracy report is shown in Exhibit 5-4.

Most inventory to be used on the production floor is kitted by the warehouse staff based on bills of material and issued on pallets to the production floor. However, if the amounts listed on the bill of materials is too low, more inventory will be requested from the warehouse. Alternately, if the bill of materials is too high, some inventory will be returned. More inventory may also be requested if parts are

Exhibit 5-1 *Receiving Log*

Date	Supplier	Item	Quantity Shipped	Quantity Received
9/10/05	Acme Acorn Co.	Pistachio Nuts	3 barrels	3 barrels
9/10/05	Acme Acorn Co.	Pine Nuts	2 barrels	2 barrels
9/10/05	Durango Nut Co.	Pine Cones	100 pounds	98 pounds

Exhibit 5-2 *Inventory Tag*

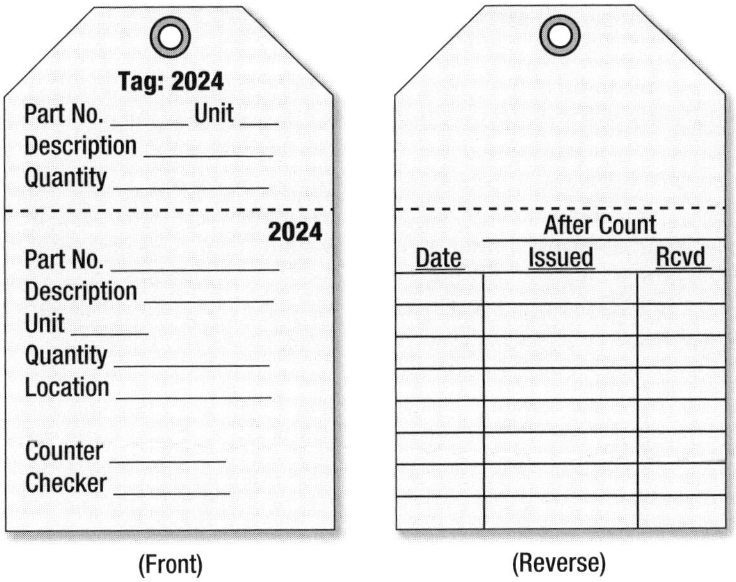

Tag: 2024

Part No. _____ Unit ____
Description _____
Quantity _____

2024
Part No. _____
Description _____
Unit _____
Quantity _____
Location _____

Counter _____
Checker _____

(Front)

Date	After Count Issued	Rcvd

(Reverse)

Exhibit 5-3 *Cycle Counting Report*

Location	Item No.	Description	U/M	Quantity
A-10-C	Q1458	Switch, 120V, 20A	EA	
A-10-C	U1010	Bolt, Zinc, $3 \times \frac{1}{4}$	EA	
A-10-C	M1458	Screw, Stainless Steel, $2 \times \frac{3}{8}$	EA	

Exhibit 5-4 *Inventory Accuracy Report*

Aisles	Responsible Person	2 Months Ago	Last Month	Week 1	Week 2	Week 3	Week 4
A-B	Fred P.	82%	86%	85%	84%	82%	87%
C-D	Alain Q.	70%	72%	74%	76%	78%	80%
E-F	Davis L.	61%	64%	67%	70%	73%	76%
G-H	Jeff R.	54%	58%	62%	66%	70%	74%
I-J	Alice R.	12%	17%	22%	27%	32%	37%
K-L	George W.	81%	80%	79%	78%	77%	76%
M-N	Robert T.	50%	60%	65%	70%	80%	90%

damaged on the production floor. When any of these issues arise, the warehouse staff should record all related transactions on an inventory sign-out and return form, such as the one shown in Exhibit 5-5. It is useful not only as a written record of transactions that must be entered into the inventory database, but also as a record of prospective adjustments to erroneous bills of material.

Production operations frequently result in either scrapped inventory or inventory that must be reworked in some manner before it can be completed. The accounting department needs to know as soon as scrap is created, so it can charge off the related cost to the cost of goods sold. Many companies give the same treatment to items requiring rework, only reassigning a cost to them once they are fixed and sent back into production. The two-part form shown in Exhibit 5-6 can be filled out by the production or materials management staff whenever scrap or rework occurs, with one copy being attached to the inventory and the other being forwarded to accounting. The form is prenumbered, in case the accounting staff wants to verify that all forms are submitted. If the "Scrapped" block is filled out, accounting charges off the inventory cost to the cost of goods sold. If the "Sent to Rework" block is filled out, accounting must also shift the related inventory to a rework inventory category in the inventory database, where it will stay until rework activities are completed. The form can later be sent to the production or engineering managers, in case they wish to review the reasons why scrap or rework occurred. When standard costs are used to create an inventory valuation, there will inevitably be some differences between standard and actual costs that will create variances that appear in the cost of goods sold. The report shown in Exhibit 5-7 itemizes these variances.

Standard costs will be altered from time to time in order to bring them more in line with actual costs. When this happens, it is useful to show the changes on a report, along with the reasons why costs were changed. If management is particularly sensitive about altering standard costs, one could also add a manager sign-off section to the report in order to record formal approval of the changes. An example of this report is shown in Exhibit 5-8.

More parts than are normally needed may be taken from stock to complete various items in production, which will unexpectedly reduce inventory levels and increase the cost of goods sold. Given its potentially large impact on inventory valuation, this issue may require a separate report, such as the one shown in Exhibit 5-9. If excess parts usage continues over time, the report can also be used as proof of a need for changes to an item's underlying bill of materials.

Exhibit 5-5   *Inventory Sign-Out and Return Form*

Description	Part No.	Quantity Issued	Quantity Returned	Job No.	Date

Exhibit 5-6   *Scrap/Rework Transaction Form*

	7403

Date: _____

Item Number: _____

Description: _____

Scrapped	*Sent to Rework*
Quantity Scrapped: _____	Quantity to Rework: _____
Reason: _____	Reason: _____
_____	_____
_____	_____
Signature: _____	Signature: _____

Exhibit 5-7   *Standard to Actual Cost Comparison Report*

Part Description	Standard Cost ($)	Actual Cost ($)	Variance ($)	Unit Volume	Extended Variance ($)
Antenna	1.20	2.00	–0.80	500	$–400.00
Speaker	0.50	0.70	–0.20	375	–75.00
Battery	2.80	3.10	–0.30	201	–60.30
Plastic case, top	0.41	0.50	–0.09	14,000	–1,260.00
Plastic case, bottom	0.23	0.41	–0.18	11,000	–1,980.00
Base unit	4.00	4.25	–0.25	820	–205.00
Cord	0.90	0.91	–0.01	571	–5.71
Circuit board	5.78	4.00	+1.78	1,804	+3,211.12
Total	—	—	—	—	$–774.89

Exhibit 5-8 *Standard Cost Changes Report*

Part Description	Beginning Standard Cost	Cost Changes	Ending Standard Costs	Remarks
Power unit	$820.00	+30.00	$850.00	Price increase
Fabric	142.60		142.60	
Paint	127.54	−22.54	105.00	Modified paint type
Instruments	93.14	−1.14	92.00	New altimeter
Exhaust stock	34.17		34.17	
Rubber grommet	19.06	−.06	19.00	New material
Aluminum forging	32.14	−2.00	30.14	Substitute forging
Cushion	14.70		14.70	
Total	**$1,283.35**	**4.26**	**$1,287.61**	

One of the easiest ways to detect obsolete inventory is to create a list of inventory items for which there has been no usage activity. The version shown in Exhibit 5-10 compares total inventory withdrawals to the amount on hand, which by itself may be sufficient information to conduct an obsolescence review. It also lists planned usage, which calls for information from an MRP system, and which informs one of any upcoming requirements that might keep one from otherwise disposing of an inventory item. An extended cost for each item is also listed, in order to give report users some idea of the write-off that might occur if an item is declared obsolete. In the exhibit, the subwoofer, speaker bracket, and wall bracket appear to be obsolete based on prior usage, but the planned use of more wall brackets would keep that item from being disposed of.

Exhibit 5-9 *Excess Material Usage Report*

Material Used	Standard Usage (Units)	Actual Usage (Units)	Excess Usage (Units)	Unit Cost	Total Excess Cost	Comments
A	3,960	4,110	150	$4.75	$712.50	(a)
B	15,840	15,960	120	2.00	240.00	(b)
C	3,960	4,000	40	21.50	860.00	(c)
D	3,960	3,970	10	65.40	654.00	(d)
E	15,840	15,920	80	3.25	260.00	(e)
Total	—	—	—	—	**$2,726.50**	

(a) Parts defective
(b) Careless workmanship
(c) Power down
(d) Wrong speed drilling
(e) Maintenance technician dropped case

Exhibit 5-10 *Inventory Obsolescence Review Report*

Description	Item No.	Location	Quantity on Hand	Last Year Usage	Planned Usage	Extended Cost
Subwoofer case	0421	A-04-C	872	520	180	$9,053
Speaker case	1098	A-06-D	148	240	120	1,020
Subwoofer	3421	D-12-A	293	14	0	24,724
Circuit board	3600	B-01-A	500	5,090	1,580	2,500
Speaker, bass	4280	C-10-C	621	2,480	578	49,200
Speaker bracket	5391	C-10-C	14	0	0	92
Wall bracket	5080	B-03-B	400	0	120	2,800
Gold connection	6233	C-04-A	3,025	8,042	5,900	9,725
Tweeter	7552	C-05-B	725	6,740	2,040	5,630

6

Budgeting for Inventory[1]

6-1 Introduction

Inventory is an extremely difficult part of the balance sheet to budget, because of the multitude of individual inventory items, as well as the impact of seasonality, purchasing volumes, product customization, and other factors. Many companies do not attempt a detailed budgeting effort in this area, instead opting to back into an inventory budget by applying the existing inventory turnover rate to the projected sales level. Although this approach may work in a general sense, a company's investment in inventory is sometimes so large that a more detailed approach is warranted. This chapter discusses how to apply a variety of budgeting techniques to the three main areas of inventory: raw materials, work-in-process, and finished goods.

6-2 Budgeting for Raw Materials Inventory

There are two methods of developing the raw materials inventory budget. First, budget each important inventory item separately based on the production plan. Second, budget materials as a whole or classes of material, based on selected production factors. Practically all companies must use both approaches to some extent, although one or the other predominates. The former method is always preferable to the extent that it is practicable, because it allows quantities to be budgeted more precisely.

The following steps should be taken in budgeting the major individual items of raw materials:

1. Determine the physical units of material required for each item of goods to be produced during the budget period.
2. Accumulate these into total physical units of each material item required for the entire production plan.

---

[1] Adapted with permission from pp. 585–594 of Bragg and Roehl-Anderson, *Controllership 7E*, John Wiley & Sons, 2004.

3. Determine for each item of material the quantity that should be on hand periodically to fulfill the production plan with a reasonable margin of safety.
4. Deduct material inventories that are expected to be on hand at the beginning of the budget period to ascertain the total quantities to be purchased.
5. Develop a purchasing plan that will ensure that the quantities will be on hand at the time they are needed. The purchasing plan must consider such factors as economically sized orders, economy of transportation, and margin of safety against delays.
6. Test the resulting budgeted inventories by standard turnover rates.
7. Translate the inventory and purchasing requirements into dollars by applying the expected prices of materials to budgeted quantities.

In practice, many difficulties arise in executing the foregoing plan. In fact, it is practicable to apply the plan only to important items of material that are used regularly and in relatively large quantities. Most manufacturing companies find that they must carry hundreds or even thousands of different items of raw materials to which this plan cannot be practically applied. Moreover, some companies cannot express their production plans in units of specific products. This is true, for example, where goods are partially or entirely made to customers' specifications. In such cases, it is necessary to look to past experience to ascertain the rate and regularity of movement of individual material items and to determine the maximum and minimum quantities between which the quantities must be held. This necessitates a program of continuous review of material records as a basis for purchasing and frequent revision of maximum and minimum limits to keep the quantities adjusted to current needs.

For those raw material items that cannot be budgeted individually, the budget must be based on general factors of expected production activity, such as total budgeted labor hours, productive hours, standard allowed hours, cost of materials consumed, or cost of goods manufactured. To illustrate, assume that the cost of materials consumed (other than basic materials, which are budgeted individually) is budgeted at $1 million and that past experience demonstrates that these materials should be held to a turnover rate of five times per year; that an average inventory of $200,000 should be budgeted. This would mean that individual items of material could be held in stock approximately 73 days (one-fifth of 365 days). This could probably be accomplished by instructing the executives in charge to keep on hand an average of 60 days' supply. Although such a plan cannot be applied rigidly to each item, it serves as a useful guide in the control of individual items and prevents the accumulation of excessive inventories.

In the application of this plan, other factors must also be considered. The relationship between the inventory and the selected factor of production activity will vary with the degree of production activity. Thus, a turnover of five times may be satisfactory when materials consumed are at the $1 million level, but it may be necessary to reduce this to four times when the level goes to $750,000. Conversely, it may be desirable to hold it to six times when the level rises to $1.25 million. Moreover, some latitude may be necessitated by the seasonal factor, because it may be necessary to increase the quantities of materials and supplies in certain months in anticipation of seasonal demands. The ratio of inventory to selected production factors at various levels of production activity and in different seasons should be plotted and studied until standard relationships can be established. The entire process can be refined somewhat by establishing different standards for different sections of the raw materials inventory.

The plan, once in operation, must be closely checked by monthly comparisons of actual and standard ratios. When the rate of inventory movement falls below the standard, study the records of activity for individual raw material items to detect the slow-moving items.

Some of the problems and methods of determining the total amount of expected purchases may be better understood by illustration. Assume, for example, that this information is made available regarding production requirements after a review of the production budget:

	Class			
	Units		Amount	
Period	**W**	**X**	**Y**	**Z**
January	400	500		
February	300	600		
March	500	400		
Subtotal	1,200	1,500		
2nd quarter	1,500	1,200		
3rd quarter	1,200	1,500		
4th quarter	1,000	1,700		
Total	**4,900**	**5,900**	**10,000**	**$20,000**

Solely for illustrative purposes, the following four groups of products have been assumed:

Class W	Material of high unit value, for which a definite quantity and time program is established in advance, such as for stock items. Also, the inventory is controlled on a Min-Max inventory basis for budget purposes.
Class X	Similar to Item W, except that, for budget purposes, Min-Max limits are not used.
Class Y	Material items for which definite quantities are established for the budget period but for which no definite time program is established, such as special orders on hand.
Class Z	Miscellaneous material items grouped together and budgeted only in terms of total dollar purchases for the budget period.

In actual practice, of course, decisions about production time must be made regarding items using Y and Z classifications. However, the bases described later in this chapter are applicable in planning the production level. Further discussion of each inventory class follows:

(i) Class W. Where the items are budgeted on a Min-Max basis, it usually is necessary to determine the range within which purchases must fall to meet production needs and stay within inventory limits. A method of making such a calculation is shown next:

	Units	
	For Minimum Inventory	**For Maximum Inventory**
January production requirements	$400	$400
Inventory limit	50	400
Total	450	800
Beginning inventory	200	200
Limit of receipts (purchases)	**$250**	**$600**

Within these limits, the quantity to be purchased will be influenced by such factors as unit transportation and handling costs, price considerations, storage space, availability of material, capital requirements, and so forth.

A similar determination would be made for each month for each such raw material, and a schedule of receipts and inventory might then be prepared, somewhat in this fashion:

	Units					
Period	**Beginning Inventory**	**Receipts**	**Usage**	**Ending Inventory**	**Unit Value**	**Purchases Budget**
January	200	$400	$400	200	$200	$80,000
February	200	400	300	300		80,000
March	300	400	500	200		80,000
Subtotal		1,200	1,200			240,000
2nd quarter	200	1,350	1,500	50		270,000
3rd quarter	50	1,200	1,200	50		240,000
4th quarter	50	1,200	1,000	250		240,000
Total		$4,950	$4,900			$990,000

(ii) Class X. It is assumed that the class X materials can be purchased as needed. Because other controls are practical on this type of item and because other procurement problems exist, purchases are determined by the production requirements. A simple extension is all that is required to determine the dollar value of expected purchases:

Period	Quantity	Unit Price	Total
January	500	$10	$5,000
February	600		6,000
March	400		4,000
Subtotal	1,500		15,000
2nd quarter	1,200		12,000
3rd quarter	1,500		15,000
4th quarter	1,700		17,000
Total	**5,900**		**$59,000**

(iii) Class Y. The breakdown of the class Y items may be assumed to be:

Item	Quantity	Unit Price	Cost
Y-1	1,000	$1.00	$1,000
Y-2	2,000	1.10	2,200
Y-3	3,000	1.20	3,600
Y-4	4,000	1.30	5,200
Total	**10,000**		**$12,000**

A determination about the time of purchase must be made, even though no definite delivery schedules and the like have been set by the customer. In this instance, the distribution of the cost and units might be made on the basis of past experience or budgeted production factors, such as budgeted machine hours. The allocation to periods could be made on past experience, as:

Period	Past Experience Regarding Similar Units Manufactured	Units				Values (Purchases)	
		Y-1	Y-2	Y-3	Y-4	Total	Budget
January	10%	100	200	300	400	1,000	$1,200
February	15	150	300	450	600	1,500	1,800
March	10	100	200	300	400	1,000	1,200
Subtotal	35	350	700	1,050	1,400	3,500	4,200
2nd quarter	30	300	600	900	1,200	3,000	3,600
3rd quarter	20	200	400	600	800	2,000	2,400
4th quarter	15	150	300	450	600	1,500	1,800
Total	**100%**	**1,000**	**2,000**	**3,000**	**4,000**	**10,000**	**$12,000**

The breakdown of units is for the benefit of the purchasing department only, inasmuch as the percentages can be applied against the total cost and need not apply to individual units. In practice, if the units are numerous regarding types and are of small value, the quantities of each might not be determined in connection with the forecast.

(iv) Class Z. Where the materials are grouped, past experience again may be the means of determining estimated expenditures by the period of time. Based on production hours, the distribution of class Z items may be assumed to be (cost of such materials assumed to be $2 per production hour):

Period	Productive Hours	Amount
January	870	$1,740
February	830	1,660
March	870	1,740
Subtotal	2,570	5,140
2nd quarter	2,600	5,200
3rd quarter	2,230	4,460
4th quarter	2,600	5,200
Total	**10,000**	**$20,000**

When all materials have been grouped and the requirements have been determined and translated to cost, the materials budget may be summarized as in Exhibit 6-1.

Exhibit 6-1 relates to raw materials. A similar approach would be taken with respect to manufacturing supplies. A few major items might be budgeted as the class W or X items just cited, but the bulk probably would be handled as Z items.

Once the requirements as measured by delivery dates have been made firm, it is necessary for the finance department to translate such data into cash disbursement needs through average lag time and so forth.

Exhibit 6-1   *Sample Purchases Budget*

The Blank Company
Purchases Budget
For the Year 20xx

			Class		
Period	W	X	Y	Z	Total
January	$80,000	$5,000	$1,200	$1,740	$87,940
February	80,000	6,000	1,800	1,660	89,460
March	80,000	4,000	1,200	1,740	86,940
Subtotal	240,000	15,000	4,200	5,140	264,340
2nd quarter	270,000	12,000	3,600	5,200	290,800
3rd quarter	240,000	15,000	2,400	4,460	261,860
4th quarter	240,000	17,000	1,800	5,200	264,000
Total	**$990,000**	**$59,000**	**$12,000**	**$20,000**	**$1,081,000**

6-3   Budgeting for Work-in-Process Inventory

The inventory of goods actually in process of production between stocking points can be best estimated by applying standard turnover rates to budgeted production. This may be expressed either in units of production or dollars and may be calculated for individual processes and departments or for the factory as a whole. The former is more accurate. To illustrate this procedure, assume the following inventory and production data for a particular process or department:

Process inventory estimated for January 1	500 units	(a)
Production budgeted for month of January	1,200 units	(b)
Standard rate of turnover (per month)	4 times	(c)
Average value per unit of goods in this process	$10	

With a standard turnover rate of four times per month, the average inventory should be 300 units (1,200 (4). To produce an average inventory of 300 units, the ending inventory should be 100 units:

$$\frac{500 + 100}{2} = 300$$

Using the symbol X to denote the quantity to be budgeted as ending inventory, the following formula can be applied:

$$X = -\frac{2b}{c} \, a = \frac{2(1200)}{4} - 500 = 100 \text{ units}$$

Value of ending inventory is $1,000 (100 × $10)

Where the formula produces a minus quantity (as it will if beginning inventory is excessive), the case should be studied as an individual problem, and a specific estimate should be made for the process or department in question.

Control over the work-in-process inventories can be exercised by a continuous check of turnover rates. Where the individual processes, departments, or plants are revealed to be excessive, they should then be subjected to individual investigation.

The control of work-in-process inventories has been sorely neglected in many concerns. The time between which material enters the factory and emerges as the finished product is often much longer than necessary for efficient production. An extensive study of the automobile tire industry revealed an amazing spread of time among five leading manufacturers, one company having an inventory float six times that of another. This study also indicated, by an analysis of the causes of the float time, that substantial reductions could be made in all five of the companies without interfering with production efficiency. Thus, budgeting for work-in-process inventory is an excellent area in which to incorporate an active program of inventory reduction activities, usually through a program of incorporating just-in-time concepts into the production process.

Although it is desirable to reduce the investment in goods actually being processed to a minimum consistent with efficient production, it is often desirable to maintain substantial inventories of parts and partially finished goods as a means of reducing finished inventories.

Parts, partial assemblies, processed stock, or any type of work-in-process that is stocked at certain points should be budgeted and controlled in the same manner as materials. That is, inventory quantities should be set for each individual item, based on the production plan; or inventory limits should be set that will conform to standard rates of turnover. In the former case, control must be exercised through the enforcement of the production plan; in the latter case, maximum and minimum quantities must be established and enforced for each individual item.

With the planned cost input to work-in-process known from the materials usage budget, the direct labor budget, and the manufacturing expense budget, and the quantities of planned completed goods furnished by manufacturing, the inventory accountant may develop the planned work-in-process time-phased (condensed) budget, as shown in Exhibit 6-2. The reasonableness of the budgeted inventory level should be tested by comparing it to historical inventory turnover levels.

6-4   Budgeting for Finished Goods Inventory

The budget of finished goods inventory (or merchandise in the case of trading concerns) must be based on the sales budget. If, for example, it is expected that 500 units of item A will be sold during the budget period, it must be ascertained what number of units must be kept in stock to support such a sales program. It is seldom possible to predetermine the exact quantity that will be demanded by customers day by day. Some margin of safety must be maintained by means of the finished goods inventory so that satisfactory deliveries can be made. With this margin established, it is possible to develop a program of production or purchases whereby the stock will be replenished as needed.

(a) Budgeting Finished Goods by Individual Items

Two general methods may be employed in budgeting the finished goods inventory. Under the first method, a budget is established for each item separately. This is done by studying the past sales record and the sales program of each item and determining the quantity that should be on hand at various dates (usually, the close of each month) throughout the budget period. The detailed production or purchasing plan can then be developed to provide such quantities over and above current sales requirements. The total budget is merely the sum of the budgets of individual items. This total budget can then be tested by the rate of turnover desired as proof that a satisfactory relationship will be maintained between inventory and sales and that it harmonizes with the general finance plan. If it fails in either respect, revision must

Exhibit 6-2   *Budget for Work-in-Process*

The Illustrative Company
Budget for Work-in-Process
For the Plan Year 20xx
(Dollars in Hundreds)

Charges to Work-in-Process

Month/Quarter	Beginning Inventory	Direct Material	Direct Labor	Manufacturing Expense	Total	Transfers to Finished Goods	Ending Inventory
January	$264,800	$110,000	$84,700	$105,900	$300,600	$307,100	$258,300
February	258,300	120,000	92,400	115,500	327,900	314,400	271,800
March	271,800	145,000	110,200	137,750	392,950	402,800	261,950
Total Quarter 1	794,900	375,000	287,300	359,150	1,021,450	1,024,300	261,950
Quarter 2	261,950	432,000	332,640	415,800	1,180,440	1,186,210	256,180
Quarter 3	256,180	353,000	271,800	338,700	963,500	969,100	250,580
Quarter 4	250,580	327,000	250,800	314,600	892,400	880,300	262,680
Grand Total	$264,800	$1,487,000	$1,142,540	$1,428,250	$4,057,790	$4,059,910	$262,680

be made in the plans of sales, production, or finance until a proper coordination is effected.

Under this plan, control over the inventory is effected by means of enforcement of the sales and production plans. If either varies to any important degree from the budget, the other must be revised to a compensating degree and the inventory budget revised accordingly.

Where the sales and production plans can be enforced with reasonable certainty, this is the preferable method. It is particularly suitable for those concerns that manufacture a comparatively small number of items in large quantities. The application is similar in principle to that illustrated in connection with raw materials controlled budget-wise by minimums and maximums.

(b) Budgeting Total Finished Quantities and Values

Where the sales of individual items fluctuate considerably and where such fluctuations must be watched for hundreds or even thousands of items, a second plan is preferable. Here basic policies are adopted relative to the relationship that must be maintained between finished goods and sales. This may be done by establishing standard rates of turnover for the inventory as a whole or for different sections of the inventory. For example, it may be decided that a unit turnover rate of three times per year should be maintained for a certain class of goods or that the dollar inventory or another class must not average more than one-fourth of the annual dollar cost of sales. The budget is then based on such relationships, and the proper executives are charged with the responsibility of controlling the quantities of individual items in such a manner that the resulting total inventories will conform to the basic standards of inventory.

With such standard turnover rates as basic guides, those in charge of inventory control must then examine each item in the inventory; collect information about its past rate of movement, irregularity of demand, expected future demand, and economical production quantity; and establish maximum and minimum quantities, and quantities to order. Once the governing quantities are established, they must be closely watched and frequently revised if the inventory is to be properly controlled.

The establishment and use of maximum, minimum, and order quantities can never be resolved into a purely clerical routine if it is to be effective as an inventory control device. A certain element of executive judgment is necessary in the application of the plan. If, for example, the quantities are based on past sales, they must be revised as the current sales trend indicates a change in sales demand. Moreover, allowance must be made for seasonal demands. This is sometimes accomplished by setting different limits for different seasons.

The most frequent cause of the failure of such inventory control plans is the assignment of unqualified personnel to the task of operating the plan and the failure to maintain a continuous review of sales experience relative to individual items. The tendency in far too many cases is to resolve the matter into a purely clerical routine and assign it to clerks who are capable only of routine execution. The danger is particularly great in companies carrying thousands of items in finished stock, with the result that many quantities are excessive, and many obsolete and slow-moving items accumulate in stock. The successful execution of an inventory control plan requires continuous study and research, meticulous records of individual items and their movement, and a considerable amount of individual judgment.

The plan, once in operation, should be continually tested by comparing the actual rates of turnover with those prescribed by the general budget program. If this test is applied to individual sections of the finished inventory, it will reveal the particular divisions that fail to meet the prescribed rates of movement. The work of correction can then be localized to these divisions.

Whenever possible, the plan of finished inventory control should be exercised in terms of units. When this is not practicable, it may be based on dollar amounts.

In the context of preparing the annual business plan in monetary terms, and based on the quantities of finished goods (furnished by the cognizant executive) deemed necessary for an adequate inventory, the inventory accountant can develop the budget for the finished goods inventory, much as is shown in condensed form in Exhibit 6-3. When the total of the inventory segments is known, the total inventory budget for the company can be summarized as in Exhibit 6-4. Such a summary can be useful in discussing inventory levels with management. Any pertinent ratios can be included. Again, in testing the reasonableness of the annual business plan, the inventory—by segments, or perhaps in total—should be tested by turnover rate or another device suggested for control (or planning) purposes.

Exhibit 6-3 *Budget for Finished Goods Inventory*

The Illustrative Company
Finished Goods Inventory Budget
For the Plan Year 20xx
(Dollars in Hundreds)

Month/Quarter	Beginning Inventory	Transfers from Work-in-Process	Purchased Parts (a)	Cost of Goods Sold	Ending Inventory
January	$329,600	$307,100	$71,000	$365,400	$342,300
February	342,300	314,400	72,000	419,100	309,600
March	309,600	402,800	80,000	472,500	319,900
Total—Quarter 1	329,600	1,024,300	223,000	1,257,000	319,900
Quarter 2	319,900	1,186,210	64,500	1,243,700	326,910
Quarter 3	326,910	969,100	41,400	1,017,500	319,910
Quarter 4	319,910	880,300	49,600	932,900	316,910
Grand total	**$329,600**	**$4,059,910**	**$378,500**	**$4,451,10**	**$316,910**

Note (a): Certain parts are acquired for sale to customers and do not enter work-in-process.

Exhibit 6-4 *Summary of Budgeted Inventories*

The Illustrative Company
Summary of Budgeted Inventories
For the Plan Year 20xx
(Dollars in Thousands)

Item	Raw Materials and Purchased Parts	Work-in-Process	Finished Goods	Total
Beginning inventory	$186,400	$264,800	$329,600	$780,800
Quarter ending inventory				
March	183,400	261,950	319,900	765,250
June	176,400	256,180	326,910	759,490
September	169,400	250,580	319,910	739,890
Year ending inventory	**$200,400**	**$262,680**	**$316,910**	**$779,990**
Total annual usage— estimated	$1,487,000	$4,059,910	$4,451,100	
Daily average (255 days)	$5,831	$15,921	$17,455	
Number of days usage on hand— year end	34.4	16.5	18.2	

7

LIFO, FIFO, and Average Costing[1]

7-1 Introduction

The type of costing method used to value inventory is the central inventory costing topic, because the method used can have a significant impact on the level of reported income. According to Statement 4 in Chapter 4 of *Accounting Research Bulletin* 43, one can derive the cost of inventory using a variety of cost flow assumptions, as long as the method chosen is the one most clearly reflecting periodic income. There are several costing methods from which to choose. In this chapter, we cover the reasons for using the first-in, first-out (FIFO), last-in, first-out (LIFO), dollar-value LIFO, link-chain, and weighted-average methods and also provide examples for how they are calculated. There is also a brief discussion of the specific identification method, which is rarely used.

7-2 First-In, First-Out (FIFO) Inventory Valuation

A computer manufacturer knows that the component parts it purchases are subject to extremely rapid rates of obsolescence, sometimes rendering a part worthless in a month or two. Accordingly, it will be sure to use up the oldest items in stock first, rather than running the risk of scrapping them a short time into the future. For this type of environment, the first-in, first-out (FIFO) method is the ideal way to deal with the flow of costs. This method assumes that the oldest parts in stock are always used first, which means that their associated old costs are used first, as well.

The concept is best illustrated with an example, which we show in Exhibit 7-1. In the first row, we create a single layer of inventory that results in 50 units of inventory, at a per-unit cost of $10. So far, the extended cost of the inventory is the same as we saw under the LIFO, but that will change as we proceed to the second row of data. In this row, we have monthly inventory usage of 350 units, which FIFO

---

[1]This chapter is adapted with permission from pp. 45–51 of Bragg, *GAAP Implementation Guide*, John Wiley & Sons, 2004.

assumes will use the entire stock of 50 inventory units that were left over at the end of the preceding month, as well as 300 units that were purchased in the current month. This wipes out the first layer of inventory, leaving us with a single new layer that is composed of 700 units at a cost of $9.58 per unit. In the third row, there is 400 units of usage, which again comes from the first inventory layer, shrinking it down to just 300 units. However, because extra stock was purchased in the same period, we now have an extra inventory layer that consists of 250 units, at a cost of $10.65 per unit. The rest of the exhibit proceeds using the same FIFO layering assumptions.

There are several factors to consider before implementing a FIFO costing system. They are as follows:

- *Fewer inventory layers.* The FIFO system generally results in fewer layers of inventory costs in the inventory database. For example, the LIFO model shown in Exhibit 7-2 contains four layers of costing data, whereas the FIFO model shown in Exhibit 7-1, which used exactly the same data, resulted in no more than two inventory layers. This conclusion generally holds true, because a LIFO system will leave some layers of costs completely untouched for long time periods, if inventory levels do not drop, whereas a FIFO system will continually clear out old layers of costs, so that multiple costing layers do not have a chance to accumulate.

- *Reduces taxes payable in periods of declining costs.* Although it is unusual to see declining inventory costs, it sometimes occurs in industries where there is either ferocious price competition among suppliers or extremely high rates of innovation that in turn lead to cost reductions. In such cases, using the earliest costs first will result in the immediate recognition of the highest possible expense, which reduces the reported profit level, and therefore reduces taxes payable.

- *Shows higher profits in periods of rising costs.* Because it charges off the earliest costs first, any recent increase in costs will be stored in inventory, rather than being immediately recognized. This will result in higher levels of reported profits, although the attendant income tax liability will also be higher.

- *Less risk of outdated costs in inventory.* Because old costs are used first in a FIFO system, there is no way for old and outdated costs to accumulate in inventory. This prevents the management group from having to worry about the adverse impact of inventory reductions on reported levels of profit, either with excessively high or low charges to the cost of goods sold. This avoids the dilemma noted earlier for LIFO, where just-in-time systems may not be implemented if the result will be a dramatically different cost of goods sold.

In short, the FIFO cost layering system tends to result in the storage of the most recently incurred costs in inventory and higher levels of reported profits. It is most useful for those companies whose main concern is reporting high profits rather than reducing income taxes.

Exhibit 7-1 FIFO Valuation Example

FIFO Costing
Part Number BK0043

Column 1 Date Purchased	Column 2 Quantity Purchased	Column 3 Cost per Unit	Column 4 Monthly Usage	Column 5 Net Inventory Remaining	Column 6 Cost of 1st Inventory Layer	Column 7 Cost of 2nd Inventory Layer	Column 8 Cost of 3rd Inventory Layer	Column 9 Extended Inventory Cost
05/03/03	500	$10.00	450	50	(50 × $10.00)	—	—	$500
06/04/03	1,000	$9.58	350	700	(700 × $9.58)	—	—	$6,706
07/11/03	250	$10.65	400	550	(300 × $9.58)	(250 × $10.65)	—	$5,537
08/01/03	475	$10.25	350	675	(200 × $10.65)	(475 × $10.25)	—	$6,999
08/30/03	375	$10.40	400	650	(275 × $10.40)	(375 × $10.40)	—	$6,760
09/09/03	850	$9.50	700	800	(800 × $9.50)	—	—	$7,600
12/12/03	700	$9.75	900	600	(600 × $9.75)	—	—	$5,850
02/08/04	650	$9.85	800	450	(450 × $9.85)	—	—	$4,433
05/07/04	200	$10.80	0	650	(450 × $9.85)	(200 × $10.80)	—	$6,593
09/23/04	600	$9.85	750	500	(500 × $9.85)	—	—	$4,925

7-3   Last-In, First-Out (LIFO) Inventory Valuation

In a supermarket, the shelves are stocked several rows deep with products. A shopper will walk by and pick products from the front row. If the stocking person is lazy, he or she will then add products to the front row locations from which products were just taken, rather than shifting the oldest products to the front row and putting new ones in the back. This concept of always taking the newest products first is called last-in, first-out (LIFO).

The following factors must be considered before implementing a LIFO system:

- *Many layers.* The LIFO cost flow approach can result in a large number of inventory layers, as shown in Exhibit 7-2. Although this is not important when a computerized accounting system that will automatically track a large number of such layers is used, it can be burdensome if the cost layers are manually tracked.

- *Alters the inventory valuation.* If there are significant changes in product costs over time, the earliest inventory layers may contain costs that are wildly different from market conditions in the current period, which could result in the recognition of unusually high or low costs if these cost layers are ever accessed. Also, LIFO costs can never be reduced to the lower of cost or market (see Chapter 8), thereby perpetuating any unusually high inventory values in the various inventory layers.

- *Interferes with the implementation of just-in-time systems.* As noted in the previous list item, clearing out the final cost layers of a LIFO system can result in unusual cost of goods sold figures. If these results will cause a significant skewing of reported profitability, company management may be put in the unusual position of opposing the implementation of advanced manufacturing concepts, such as just-in-time, that reduce or eliminate inventory levels.

- *Reduces taxes payable in periods of rising costs.* In an inflationary environment, costs that are charged off to the cost of goods sold as soon as they are incurred will result in a higher cost of goods sold and a lower level of profitability, which in turn results in a lower tax liability. This is the principle reason why LIFO is used by most companies.

- *Requires consistent usage for all reporting.* Under IRS rules (see Chapter 13), if a company uses LIFO to value its inventory for tax reporting purposes, then it must do the same for its external financial reports. The result of this rule is that a company cannot report lower earnings for tax purposes and higher earnings for all other purposes by using an alternative inventory valuation method. However, it is still possible to mention what profits would have been if some other method have been used, but only in the form of a footnote appended to the financial statements. If financial reports are only generated for internal management consumption, then any valuation method may be used.

In short, LIFO is used primarily for reducing a company's income tax liability. This single focus can cause problems, such as too many cost layers, an excessively

Exhibit 7-2 **LIFO Valuation Example**

LIFO Costing
Part Number BK0043

Column 1	Column 2	Column 3	Column 4	Column 5	Column 6	Column 7	Column 8	Column 9	Column 10
Date Purchased	Quantity Purchased	Cost per Unit	Monthly Usage	Net Inventory Remaining	Cost of 1st Inventory Layer	Cost of 2nd Inventory Layer	Cost of 3rd Inventory Layer	Cost of 4th Inventory Layer	Extended Inventory Cost
05/03/03	500	$10.00	450	50	(50 × $10.00)	—	—	—	$500
06/04/03	1,000	$9.58	350	700	(50 × $10.00)	(550 × $9.58)	—	—	$6,727
07/11/03	250	$10.65	400	550	(50 × $10.00)	(500 × $9.58)	—	—	$5,290
08/01/03	475	$10.25	350	675	(50 × $10.00)	(500 × $9.58)	(125 × $10.25)	—	$6,571
08/30/03	375	$10.40	400	650	(50 × $10.00)	(500 × $9.58)	(100 × $10.25)	—	$6,315
09/09/03	850	$9.50	700	800	(50 × $10.00)	(500 × $9.58)	(100 × $10.25)	(150 × $9.50)	$7,740
12/12/03	700	$9.75	900	600	(50 × $10.00)	(500 × $9.58)	(50 × $9.58)	—	$5,769
02/08/04	650	$9.85	800	450	(50 × $10.00)	(400 × $9.58)	—	—	$4,332
05/07/04	200	$10.80	0	650	(50 × $10.00)	(400 × $9.58)	(200 × $10.80)	—	$6,492
09/23/04	600	$9.85	750	500	(50 × $10.00)	(400 × $9.58)	(50 × $9.85)	—	$4,825

low inventory valuation, and a fear of inventory reductions because of the recognition of inventory cost layers that may contain very low per-unit costs, which will result in high levels of recognized profit and therefore a higher tax liability. Given these issues, one should carefully consider the utility of tax avoidance before implementing a LIFO cost layering system.

As an example, The Magic Pen Company has made 10 purchases, which are itemized in Exhibit 7-2. In the exhibit, the company has purchased 500 units of a product with part number BK0043 on May 3, 2003 (as noted in the first row of data), and used 450 units during that month, leaving the company with 50 units. These 50 units were all purchased at a cost of $10 each, so they are itemized in Column 6 as the first layer of inventory costs for this product. In the next row of data, an additional 1,000 units were bought on June 4, 2003, of which only 350 units were used. This leaves an additional 650 units at a purchase price of $9.58, which are placed in the second inventory layer, as noted on Column 7. In the third row, there is a net decrease in the amount of inventory, so this reduction comes out of the second (or last) inventory layer in Column 7; the earliest layer, as described in Column 6, remains untouched, because it was the first layer of costs added and will not be used until all other inventory has been eliminated. The exhibit continues through seven more transactions, at one point increasing to four layers of inventory costs.

7-4   Dollar-Value LIFO Inventory Valuation

This method computes a conversion price index for the year-end inventory in comparison to the base year cost. This index is computed separately for each company business unit. The conversion price index can be computed with the *double-extension method*. Under this approach, the total extended cost of the inventory at both base year prices and the most recent prices are calculated. Then the total inventory cost at the most recent prices is divided by the total inventory cost at base year prices, resulting in a conversion price percentage, or index. The index represents the change in overall prices between the current year and the base year. This index must be computed and retained for each year in which the LIFO method is used.

There are two problems with the double-extension method. First, it requires a massive volume of calculations if there are many items in inventory. Second, tax regulations require that any new item added to inventory, no matter how many years after the establishment of the base year, have a base year cost included in the LIFO database for purposes of calculating the index. This base year cost is supposed to be the one in existence at the time of the base year, which may require considerable research to determine or estimate. Only if it is impossible to determine a base year cost can the current cost of a new inventory item be used as the base year cost. For these reasons, the double-extension inventory valuation method is not recommended in most cases.

As an example, a company carries a single item of inventory in stock. It has retained the following year-end information about the item for the past four years:

Year	Ending Unit Quantity	Ending Current Price	Extended at Current Year-end Price
1	3,500	$32.00	$112,000
2	7,000	34.50	241,500
3	5,500	36.00	198,000
4	7,250	37.50	271,875

The first year is the base year on which the double-extension index will be based in later years. In the second year, we extend the total year-end inventory by both the base year price and the current year price, as follows:

Year-End Quantity	Base Year Cost	Extended at Base Year Cost	Ending Current Price	Extended at Ending Current Price
7,000	$32.00	$224,000	$34.50	$241,500

To arrive at the index between year two and the base year, we divide the extended ending current price of $241,500 by the extended base year cost of $224,000, yielding an index of *107.8%*.

The next step is to calculate the incremental amount of inventory added in year two, determine its cost using base year prices, and then multiply this extended amount by our index of 107.8% to arrive at the cost of the incremental year two LIFO layer. The incremental amount of inventory added is the year-end quantity of 7,000 units, less the beginning balance of 3,500 units, which is 3,500 units. When multiplied by the base year cost of $32, we arrive at an incremental increase in inventory of $112,000. Finally, we multiply the $112,000 by the price index of 107.8% to determine that the cost of the year two LIFO layer is $120,736.

Thus, at the end of year two, the total double-extension LIFO inventory valuation is the base year valuation of $112,000 plus the year two layer's valuation of $120,736, totaling $232,736.

In year three, the amount of ending inventory has declined from the previous year, so no new layering calculation is required. Instead, we assume that the entire reduction of 1,500 units during that year were taken from the year two inventory layer. To calculate the amount of this reduction, we multiply the remaining amount of the year two layer (5,500 units less the base year amount of 3,500 units, or 2,000 units) times the ending base year price of $32 and the year two index of 107.8%. This calculation results in a new year two layer of $68,992.

Thus, at the end of year three, the total double-extension LIFO inventory valuation is the base layer of $112,000 plus the reduced year two layer of $68,992, totaling $180,992.

In year four, there is an increase in inventory, so we can calculate the presence of a new layer using the following table:

Year-End Quantity	Base Year Cost	Extended at Base Year Cost	Ending Current Price	Extended at Ending Current Price
7,250	$32.00	$232,000	$37.50	$271,875

Again, we divide the extended ending current price of $271,875 by the extended base year cost of $232,000, yielding an index of *117.2%*. To complete the calculation, we then multiply the incremental increase in inventory over year three of 1,750 units, multiply it by the base year cost of $32 per unit, and then multiply the result by our new index of 117.2% to arrive at a year four LIFO layer of $65,632.

Thus, after four years of inventory layering calculations, the double-extension LIFO valuation consists of the following three layers:

Layer Type	Layer Valuation	Layer Index
Base layer	$112,000	0.0%
Year 2 layer	68,992	107.8%
Year 4 layer	65,632	117.2%
Total	$246,624	—

7-5   Link-Chain Inventory Valuation

Another way to calculate the dollar-value LIFO inventory is to use the link-chain method. This approach is designed to avoid the problem encountered during double-extension calculations, where one must determine the base year cost of each new item added to inventory. However, tax regulations require that the link-chain method only be used for tax reporting purposes if it can be clearly demonstrated that all other dollar-value LIFO calculation methods are not applicable because of high rates of churn in the types of items included in inventory.

The link-chain method creates inventory layers by comparing year-end prices to prices at the beginning of each year, thereby avoiding the problems associated with comparisons to a base year that may be many years in the past. This results in a rolling cumulative index that is linked (hence the name) to the index derived in the preceding year. Tax regulations allow one to create the index using a representative sample of the total inventory valuation that must comprise at least one-half of the total inventory valuation. In brief, a link-chain calculation is derived by extending the cost of inventory at both beginning-of-year and end-of-year prices to arrive at a pricing index within the current year; this index is then multiplied by the ongoing cumulative index from the previous year to arrive at a new cumulative index that is used to price out the new inventory layer for the most recent year.

The following example of the link-chain method assumes the same inventory information just used for the double-extension example. However, we have also noted the beginning inventory cost for each year and included the extended beginning inventory cost for each year, which facilitates calculations under the link-chain method.

Year	Ending Unit Quantity	Beginning-of-Year Cost/each	Extended at End-of-Year Cost/Each	Extended at Beginning-of-Year Price	End-of-Year Price
1	3,500	$—	$32.00	$—	$112,000
2	7,000	32.00	34.50	224,000	241,500
3	5,500	34.50	36.00	189,750	198,000
4	7,250	36.00	37.50	261,000	271,875

As was the case for the double-extension method, there is no index for year one, which is the base year. In year two, the index will be the extended year-end price of $241,500 divided by the extended beginning-of-year price of $224,000, or 107.8%. This is the same percentage calculated for year two under the double-extension method, because the beginning-of-year price is the same as the base price used under the double-extension method.

We then determine the value of the year two inventory layer by first dividing the extended year-end price of $241,500 by the cumulative index of 107.8% to arrive at an inventory valuation restated to the base year cost of $224,026. We then subtract the year one base layer of $112,000 from the $224,026 to arrive at a new layer at the base year cost of $112,026, which we then multiply by the cumulative index of 107.8% to bring it back to current year prices. This results in a year two inventory layer of $120,764. At this point, the inventory layers are as follows:

Layer Type	Base Year Valuation	LIFO Layer Valuation	Cumulative Index
Base layer	$112,000	$112,000	0.0%
Year 2 layer	112,026	120,764	107.8%
Total	$224,026	$232,764	—

In year three, the index will be the extended year-end price of $198,000 divided by the extended beginning-of-year price of $189,750, or 104.3%. Because this is the first year in which the base year was not used to compile beginning-of-year costs, we must first derive the cumulative index, which is calculated by multiplying the preceding year's cumulative index of 107.8% by the new year three index of 104.3%, resulting in a new cumulative index of 112.4%. By dividing year three's extended year-end inventory of $198,000 by this cumulative index, we arrive at inventory priced at base year costs of $176,157.

This is less than the amount recorded in year two, so there will be no inventory layer. Instead, we must reduce the inventory layer recorded for year two. To do so, we subtract the base year layer of $112,000 from the $176,157 to arrive at a reduced year two layer of $64,157 at base year costs. We then multiply the $64,157 by the cumulative index in year two of 107.8% to arrive at a inventory valuation for the year two layer of $69,161. At this point, the inventory layers and associated cumulative indexes are as follows:

Layer Type	Base Year Valuation	LIFO Layer Valuation	Cumulative Index
Base layer	$112,000	$112,000	0.0%
Year 2 layer	64,157	69,161	107.8%
Year 3 layer	—	—	112.4%
Total	$176,157	$181,161	—

In year four, the index will be the extended year-end price of $271,875 divided by the extended beginning-of-year price of $261,000, or 104.2%. We then derive the new cumulative index by multiplying the preceding year's cumulative index of 112.4% by the year four index of 104.2%, resulting in a new cumulative index of 117.1%. By dividing year four's extended year-end inventory of $271,875 by this cumulative index, we arrive at inventory priced at base year costs of $232,173. We then subtract the preexisting base year inventory valuation for all previous layers of $176,157 from this amount to arrive at the base year valuation of the year four inventory layer, which is $56,016. Finally, we multiply the $56,016 by the cumulative index in year four of 117.1% to arrive at an inventory valuation for the year four layer of $62,575. At this point, the inventory layers and associated cumulative indexes are as follows:

Layer Type	Base Year Valuation	LIFO Layer Valuation	Cumulative Index
Base layer	$112,000	$112,000	0.0%
Year 2 layer	64,157	69,161	107.8%
Year 3 layer	—	—	112.4%
Year 4 layer	56,016	62,575	117.1%
Total	$232,173	$243,736	—

Compare the results of this calculation to those from the double-extension method. The indexes are nearly identical, as are the final LIFO layer valuations. The primary differences between the two methods is the avoidance of a base year cost determination for any new items subsequently added to inventory, for which a current cost is used instead.

7-6   Weighted-Average Inventory Valuation

The weighted-average costing method is calculated exactly in accordance with its name—it is a weighted average of the costs in inventory. It has the singular advantage of not requiring a database that itemizes the many potential layers of inventory at the different costs at which they were acquired. Instead, the weighted average of all units in stock is determined, at which point *all* of the units in stock are accorded that weighted-average value. When parts are used from stock, they are all issued at the same weighted-average cost. If new units are added to stock, then the cost of the additions are added to the weighted average of all existing items in stock, which will result in a new, slightly modified weighted average for *all* of the parts in inventory (both the old and new ones).

This system has no particular advantage in relation to income taxes, because it does not skew the recognition of income based on trends in either increasing or declining costs. This makes it a good choice for those organizations that do not want to deal with tax planning. It is also useful for small inventory valuations, where there would not be any significant change in the reported level of income even if the LIFO or FIFO methods were to be used.

Exhibit 7-3 illustrates the weighted-average calculation for inventory valuations, using a series of 10 purchases of inventory. There is a maximum of one purchase per month, with usage (reductions from stock) also occurring in most months. Each of the columns in the exhibit show how the average cost is calculated after each purchase and usage transaction.

We begin the illustration with the first row of calculations, which shows that we have purchased 500 units of item BK0043 on May 3, 2003. These units cost $10 per unit. During the month in which the units were purchased, 450 units were sent to production, leaving 50 units in stock. Because there has been only one purchase thus far, we can easily calculate, as shown in column 7, that the total inventory valuation is $500, by multiplying the unit cost of $10 (in column 3) by the number of units left in stock (in column 5). So far, we have a per-unit valuation of $10.

Next we proceed to the second row of the exhibit, where we have purchased another 1,000 units of BK0043 on June 4, 2003. This purchase was less expensive, because the purchasing volume was larger, so the per-unit cost for this purchase is only $9.58. Only 350 units are sent to production during the month, so we now have 700 units in stock, of which 650 are added from the most recent purchase. To determine the new weighted-average cost of the total inventory, we first determine the extended cost of this newest addition to the inventory. As noted in column 7, we arrive at $6,227 by multiplying the value in column 3 by the value in column 6. We then add this amount to the existing total inventory valuation ($6,227 plus $500) to arrive at the new extended inventory cost of $6,727, as noted in column 8. Finally, we divide this new extended cost in column 8 by the total number of units now in stock, as shown in column 5, to arrive at our new per-unit cost of $9.61.

The third row reveals an additional inventory purchase of 250 units on July 11, 2003, but more units are sent to production during that month than were bought, so the total number of units in inventory drops to 550 (column 5). This inventory reduction requires no review of inventory layers, as was the case for the LIFO and FIFO calculations. Instead, we simply charge off the 150-unit reduction at the average per-unit cost of $9.61. As a result, the ending inventory valuation drops to $5,286, with the same per-unit cost of $9.61. Thus, reductions in inventory quanti-

Exhibit 7-3   Weighted-Average Costing Valuation Example

Average Costing
Part Number BK0043

Column 1	Column 2	Column 3	Column 4	Column 5	Column 6	Column 7	Column 8	Column 9
Date Purchased	Quantity Purchased	Cost per Unit	Monthly Usage	Net Inventory Remaining	Net Change in Inventory During Period	Extended Cost of New Inventory Layer	Extended Inventory Cost	Average Inventory Cost/Unit
05/03/03	500	$10.00	450	50	50	$500	$500	$10.00
06/04/03	1,000	$9.58	350	700	650	$6,227	$6,727	$9.61
07/11/03	250	$10.65	400	550	-150	$0	$5,286	$9.61
08/01/03	475	$10.25	350	675	125	$1,281	$6,567	$9.73
08/30/03	375	$10.40	400	650	-25	$0	$6,324	$9.73
09/09/03	850	$9.50	700	800	150	$1,425	$7,749	$9.69
12/12/03	700	$9.75	900	600	-200	$0	$5,811	$9.69
02/08/04	650	$9.85	800	450	-150	$0	$4,359	$9.69
05/07/04	200	$10.80	0	650	200	$2,160	$6,519	$10.03
09/23/04	600	$9.85	750	500	-150	$0	$5,014	$10.03

ties under the average costing method require little calculation—just charge off the requisite number of units at the current average cost.

The remaining rows of the exhibit repeat the concepts just noted, alternately adding units to and deleting them from stock. Although there are several columns noted in this exhibit that one must examine, it is really a simple concept to understand and work with. The typical computerized accounting system will perform all of these calculations automatically.

7-7   Specific Identification Method

When each individual item of inventory can be clearly identified, it is possible to create inventory costing records for each one, rather than summarizing costs by general inventory type. This approach is rarely used, because the amount of paperwork and effort associated with developing unit costs is far greater than under all other valuation techniques. It is most applicable in businesses such as home construction, where there are few units of inventory to track, and where each item is truly unique.

8

The Lower of Cost or Market Calculation

8-1   Introduction

A key aspect of generating an inventory valuation is the concept of the lower of cost or market. Under this concept, a company is required to recognize an additional expense in its cost of goods sold in the current period for any of its inventory whose replacement cost (subject to certain restrictions) has declined below its carrying cost. If the market value of the inventory subsequently rises back to or above its original carrying cost, its recorded value cannot be increased back to the original carrying amount.

The basis for this concept is contained within Statements 5 through 7 in Chapter 4 of *Accounting Research Bulletin Number* 43. Statement 5 notes that when the utility (as indicated by damage, obsolescence, and so forth) of a good falls below its recorded cost, one must recognize a loss for the full amount of the difference in the current period. Statement 6 defines "market" as the current replacement cost of an inventory item, except that the resulting market cost cannot be less than the item's net realizable value less a normal profit margin, nor can it exceed the net realizable value less any completion and disposal costs.

Statement 7 notes that the lower of cost or market rule can be applied either to individual items, groups of inventory, or the inventory as a whole; the application method chosen should be the one resulting in the most close approximation to periodic income. Statement 7 has been the cause of considerable interpretation, because its application to a large inventory group presents the possibility (allowed within Discussion Note 12 to the Statement) that a company can offset losses on reduced-utility items against gains experienced by increased-utility items within the same inventory group, resulting in no write-down of the total inventory valuation, as long as the offsetting items are in "balanced" quantities. However, in practice, the use of inventory groups for lower of cost or market calculations is unusual and so is not addressed further within this chapter. Discussion Note 14 accompanying Statement 7 also suggests that large write-downs caused by application of the lower of cost or market rule can be itemized separately from the cost of goods sold within the income statement.

The remainder of this chapter explores the practical application of the lower of cost or market rule.

8-2   Applying the Lower of Cost or Market Rule[1]

The lower of cost or market (LCM) calculation means that the cost of inventory cannot be recorded higher than its replacement cost on the open market; the replacement cost is bounded at the high end by its eventual selling price, less costs of disposal, nor can it be recorded lower than that price, less a normal profit percentage. The concept is best demonstrated with the four scenarios listed in the following example:

Item	Selling Price	Completion/ Selling Cost	Upper Price Boundary	Normal Profit	Lower Price Boundary	Existing Inventory Cost	Replacement Cost (1)	Market Value (2)	LCM
A	$15.00	$4.00	$11.0	$2.20	$8.80	$8.00	$12.50	$11.00	$8.00
B	40.15	6.00	34.15	5.75	28.40	35.00	34.50	34.15	34.15
C	20.00	6.50	13.50	3.00	10.50	17.00	12.00	12.00	12.00
D	10.50	2.35	8.15	2.25	5.90	8.00	5.25	5.90	5.90

(1) The cost at which an inventory item could be purchased on the open market.

(2) Replacement cost, bracketed by the upper and lower price boundaries.

In the example, the numbers in the first six columns are used to derive the upper and lower boundaries of the market values that will be used for the LCM calculation. By subtracting the completion and selling costs from each product's selling price, we establish the upper price boundary (in bold) of the market cost calculation. By then subtracting the normal profit from the upper cost boundary of each product, we establish the lower price boundary. Using this information, the LCM calculation for each of the listed products is as follows:

- *Product A, replacement cost higher than existing inventory cost.* The market price cannot be higher than the upper boundary of $11, which is still higher than the existing inventory cost of $8. Thus, the LCM is the same as the existing inventory cost.

- *Product B, replacement cost lower than existing inventory cost, but higher than upper price boundary.* The replacement cost of $34.50 exceeds the upper price boundary of $34.15, so the market value is designated at $34.15. This is lower than the existing inventory cost, so the LCM becomes $34.15.

---

[1]The contents of this section have been adapted with permission from p. 44 of Bragg, *GAAP Implementation Guide*, John Wiley & Sons, 2004.

- *Product C, replacement cost lower than existing inventory cost and within price boundaries.* The replacement cost of $12 is within the upper and lower price boundaries, and so is used as the market value. This is lower than the existing inventory cost of $17, so the LCM becomes $12.
- *Product D, replacement cost lower than existing inventory cost, but lower than lower price boundary.* The replacement cost of $5.25 is below the lower price boundary of $5.90, so the market value is designated as $5.90. This is lower than the existing inventory cost of $8, so the LCM becomes $5.90.

Whenever there is a calculated inventory write-down, use the following journal entry to record the valuation reduction. Although this loss can be recorded within the general cost of goods sold account, the magnitude of LCM losses tend to be lost that way, so use the "Loss on Inventory Valuation" account to more conspicuously record the information.

	Debit	Credit
Loss on inventory valuation	xxx	
Raw materials inventory		xxx
Work-in-process inventory		xxx
Finished goods inventory		xxx

Although the sample journal entry shows a credit to specific inventory accounts, it is also acceptable to credit an inventory valuation account instead.

8-3 Enforcement of the LCM Rule

Given the considerable amount of manual calculation required to determine if there is a loss under the LCM rule, few inventory accountants are interested in following its dictates regularly. One of the better approaches to enforcement is to have the Board of Directors formally approve a company policy requiring at least an annual LCM review, and to then include this policy in the job description of the inventory accountant. An example of possible policy wording follows:

> Lower of cost or market calculations shall be conducted at least annually for the entire inventory.

This policy may be modified to require more frequent reviews, based on the variability of market rates for various inventory items.

Even with a policy in place, the LCM calculation is only likely to be conducted at such infrequent intervals that the inventory accountant forgets how the calculation was made in the past. Thus, there is a considerable risk that the calculations will be conducted differently each time, yielding inconsistent results. To avoid this problem, consider including in the accounting procedures manual a clear definition of the calculation to be followed. A sample procedure is shown in Exhibit 8-1.

Exhibit 8-1   *Lower of Cost or Market Procedure*

Use this procedure to periodically adjust the inventory valuation for those items whose market value has dropped below their recorded cost.

1. Export the extended inventory valuation report to an electronic spreadsheet. Sort it by declining extended dollar cost, and delete the 80% of inventory items that do not comprise the top 20% of inventory valuation. Sort the remaining 20% of inventory items by either part number or item description. Print the report.
2. Send a copy of the report to the materials manager, with instructions to compare unit costs for each item on the list to market prices, and be sure to mutually agree upon a due date for completion of the review.
3. When the materials management staff has completed its review, meet with the materials manager to go over its results and discuss any major adjustments. Have the materials management staff write down the valuation of selected items in the inventory database whose cost exceeds their market value.
4. Have the accounting staff expense the value of the write down in the accounting records.
5. Write a memo detailing the results of the lower of cost or market calculation. Attach one copy to the journal entry used to write down the valuation, and issue another copy to the materials manager.

9

Applying Overhead
to Inventory

9-1   Introduction

The cost structure of most organizations contains a small proportion of variable costs and a great many other costs that are lumped into overhead. It is common for companies to have three or more times the amount of their variable costs invested in overhead. Because GAAP requires that some portion of overhead costs be assigned to inventory, the inventory accountant has the dual tasks of determining which costs to include in overhead and how to assign these costs to inventory. The latter task is especially difficult, because the basis of allocation has historically been direct labor, which usually constitutes only a small portion of a product's cost, and which therefore can result in significant misallocations of overhead costs to specific inventory items.

In this chapter, we review the types of costs to assign to inventory through overhead allocation, the assignment of overhead costs to raw materials, the contents of a bill of activities, and the use of activity-based costing to derive the most accurate possible overhead allocation.

9-2   Overhead Identification and Allocation to Inventory[1]

Some overhead costs can be charged off to inventory, rather than being recognized in the cost of goods sold or some other expense category within the current period. Because the proper allocation of these costs can have a large impact on the level of reported income in any given period, it is important for the inventory accountant to fully understand which costs can be shifted to a cost pool for eventual allocation and how this allocation is to be accomplished. The first question is answered by Exhibit 9-1, which itemizes precisely which costs can be shifted into a cost pool. The only cost category about which there is some uncertainty is rework labor, scrap,

---

[1]Adapted with permission from Chapter 14 of Bragg, *Accounting Reference Desktop*, John Wiley & Sons, 2002.

and spoilage. The exhibit shows that this cost can be charged in either direction. The rule in this case is that any rework, scrap, or spoilage that falls within a normally expected level can be charged to a cost pool for allocation, whereas unusual amounts must be charged off at once. This is clearly a highly subjective area, where some historical records should be maintained that will reveal the trend of these costs and that can be used as the basis for proving the charging of costs to either category.

With Exhibit 9-1 in hand, one can easily construct a cost pool into which the correct costs can be accumulated for later distribution to inventory as allocated overhead costs. The next problem is how to go about making the allocation. This problem consists of four issues, which are as follows:

- *How to smooth out sudden changes in the cost pool.* It is common to see an unusual expenditure cause a large jump or drop in the costs accumulated in the cost pool, resulting in a significant difference between periods in the amount of per-unit costs that are allocated out. This can cause large changes in overhead costs from period to period. Although perfectly acceptable from the perspective of GAAP, one may desire a more smoothed-out set of costs from period to pe-

Exhibit 9-1   *Allocation of Costs Between Cost Pool and Expense Accounts*

Description	Cost Pool	Expense
Advertising expenses		XXX
Costs related to strikes		XXX
Depreciation and cost depletion	XXX	
Factory administration expenses	XXX	
General and administrative expenses related to overall operations		XXX
Income taxes		XXX
Indirect labor and production supervisory wages	XXX	
Indirect materials and supplies	XXX	
Interest		XXX
Maintenance	XXX	
Marketing expenses		XXX
Officer's salaries related to production services	XXX	
Other distribution expenses		XXX
Pension contribution related to past service costs		XXX
Production employees' benefits	XXX	
Quality control and inspection	XXX	
Rent	XXX	
Repair expenses	XXX	
Research and experimental expenses		XXX
Rework labor, scrap, and spoilage	XXX	XXX
Salaries of officers related to overall operations		XXX
Selling expenses		XXX
Taxes other than income taxes related to production assets	XXX	
Tools and equipment not capitalized	XXX	
Utilities	XXX	

riod. If so, it is allowable to average the costs in the cost pool over several months, as long as the underlying inventory is actually in stock for a similar period. For example, if the inventory turns over four times a year, then it is acceptable to allocate overhead costs each month based on a rolling average of the costs for the preceding three months.

- *What basis to use when allocating costs.* The accounting literature has bemoaned the allocation of costs based on direct labor for many years. The reason for this judgment is that direct labor makes up such a small component of total product cost that small swings in the direct labor component can result in a large corresponding swing in the amount of allocated overhead. To avoid this issue, some other unit of activity can be used as the basis for allocation that not only comprises a larger share of total product cost, but that also relates to the incurrence of overhead costs. Another criterion that is frequently overlooked is that the accounting or manufacturing system must have a means of accumulating information about this activity measure, so that the inventory accountant does not have to spend additional time manually compiling the underlying data. An example of an activity measure that generally fulfills these three criteria is machine hours, because standard machine hours are readily available in the bill of materials or labor routing for each product, many overhead costs are related to machine usage, and the proportion of machine time used per product is commonly greater than the proportion of direct labor.

- *An even better alternative than the use of machine hours (or some similar single measure) as the basis for allocation is the use of multiple cost pools that are allocated with multiple activity measures.* This allows a company to (for example) allocate building costs based on the square footage taken up by each product, machine costs based on machine time used, labor costs based on direct labor hours used, and so on. The main issue to be aware of when using this approach is that the financial statements must still be produced in a timely manner, so one should not go overboard with the use of too many cost pools that will require an inordinate amount of time to allocate. Please review the discussion later in this chapter of activity-based costing for a more complete review of this subject area.

- *How to calculate the overhead allocation.* When allocating overhead costs, they are not simply charged off in total to the on-hand inventory at the end of the month, because the result would be an ever-increasing overhead balance stored in the on-hand inventory that would never be drawn down. On the contrary, much of the overhead is also related to the cost of goods sold. In order to make a proper allocation of costs between the inventory and cost of goods sold, the inventory accountant must determine the total amount of each basis of activity that occurred during the reporting period and divide this amount into the total amount of overhead in the cost pool, yielding an overhead cost per unit of activity. This cost per unit should then be multiplied by the total amount of the basis of activity related to the period-end inventory to determine the total amount of overhead that should be charged to inventory. This is then compared to the amount of overhead already charged to inventory in the previous reporting period to see if any additional overhead costs should be added or subtracted to arrive at the new allocated overhead figure. All other overhead costs, by default, are charged to the cost of goods sold. For example, if there is a cost pool of $100,000 to be allocated, and a total of 25,000 machine hours were used in the period, then the overhead cost per hour of machine time is $4. According to the standard labor routings for all inventory items in stock, it required 17,250 hours of machine time to create the items currently stored in inventory. Using the current cost per machine hour of $4, this means that $69,000 (17,250 hours × $4/hour) can be charged to inventory. However, the inventory overhead account already contains $52,000 of overhead that was charged to it in the preceding month, so the new entry is to debit the inventory overhead account for $17,000 ($69,000–$52,000), and to debit the cost of goods sold for the remaining amount of overhead, which is $83,000, while the cost pool is credited for $100,000.

■ *How to adjust for any unallocated or overallocated costs.* It was recommended earlier in this section that one could smooth out the cost totals in a company's overhead cost pools by averaging the costs on a rolling basis over several months. The only problem with this approach is that the amount of costs allocated each month will differ somewhat from the actual costs stored in the cost pools. How do we reconcile this difference? The annual financial statements should not include any differences between actual and allocated overhead costs, so the variance should be allocated between inventory and the cost of goods sold at that time, using the usual bases of allocation. If shareholder reporting occurs more frequently than that (such as quarterly), then the inventory accountant should consider making the same adjustment more frequently. However, if the amount in question will not have a material impact on the financial statement results, the adjustment can be completed just once, at the end of the fiscal year.

9-3 Overhead Allocation to Raw Materials

Overhead is not normally applied to raw materials, but arguments have been presented in favor of the following two issues:

■ *Inbound transportation costs.* Where the cost of getting the goods to the factory site is identifiable with particular material or lots, the cost may properly be added to the raw material. If such allocation is impractical, it may be considered part of the manufacturing overhead.

■ *Purchasing department expense.* The cost of this department generally would continue at the same level from period to period regardless of receipts, so allocating the cost to raw materials would not be a proper matching of expenses with effort expended. The cost may be more properly treated as manufacturing overhead for application to other types of inventory and the cost of goods sold.

9-4 The Shortcomings of Traditional Cost Allocation Systems[2]

Activity-based costing was developed in response to the shortcoming of traditional cost allocation systems. The chief problem with these systems is that they do not allocate overhead in a manner that truly reflects the usage of overhead. This is caused by the lumping of all overhead costs into one large overhead cost pool, as well as the use of inappropriate allocation measures to spread the cost of this pool to products. The end result is incorrect inventory costing, which can lead to incorrect decisions based on those costs.

The problem becomes particularly obvious when the overhead cost pool greatly exceeds the size of the allocation measure, which is frequently direct labor. In some industries, where there is a great deal of machinery or engineering staff involved (such as the automotive, drug, and aerospace industries), the ratio of overhead to allocation measure is frequently in the range of 300% to 400%. This means that a slight change in direct labor will result in the application of an inordinate additional amount of overhead to a product, which, in all likelihood, was never justified by changes in the usage pattern of the product to which the overhead costs are being charged.

Another problem is that the overhead cost pool is only being allocated based on one allocation measure. Many of the costs in the overhead cost pool have not the slightest relationship to the allocation measure, and so should not be allocated based on it. Here are some of the costs stored in the overhead cost pool that have no relationship whatsoever to the most common allocation measure, direct labor:

- *Building rent.* A better allocation is based on the square footage of the facility that the machinery and inventory storage areas related to a product line are using.
- *Building insurance.* The better allocation is again square footage.
- *Industrial engineering salaries.* A better allocation is the total number of units expected to be produced over the lifetime of the product line.
- *Machinery depreciation.* A better allocation is the hours of machine time used.
- *Machinery insurance.* A better allocation is the hours of machine time used.
- *Maintenance costs.* A better allocation is the hours of machine time used.
- *Production scheduling salaries.* A better allocation is the number of jobs scheduled during the accounting period.
- *Purchasing salaries.* A better allocation is the number of parts in a product or the number of suppliers for a product from whom parts must be purchased.
- *Utilities.* A better allocation is based on the hours of machine time used.
- *Warehouse salaries.* There are several better allocations, such as the number of receipts or shipments related to a product, or the number of parts in it.

---

[2]Adapted with permission from Chapter 16 of Bragg, *Cost Accounting: A Comprehensive Guide*, John Wiley & Sons, 2001.

It is evident from this list that most overhead costs have not the slightest relationship to direct labor and that a good cost allocation cannot depend on just one basis of allocation—several are needed in order to realistically portray the actual usage of each element of overhead.

Another issue is that traditional cost allocation systems tend to portray products made with high levels of automation as being deceptively low in overhead cost. The issue is best illustrated with an example. If a high-technology company decides to introduce more automation into one of its production lines, it will replace direct labor with machine hours by adding robots. This will shrink the allocation base, which is direct labor, while increasing the size of the overhead cost pool, which now includes the depreciation, utilities, and maintenance costs associated with the robots. When the overhead cost allocation is performed, a *smaller* amount of overhead will be charged to the now-automated production line, because the overhead costs are being charged based on direct labor usage, which has declined. This makes the products running through the automated line look less expensive than they really are. Furthermore, the increased overhead cost pool will be charged to those production lines with lots of direct labor, even though these other product lines have not the slightest association with the new overhead costs. The end result is a significant skewing of reported costs that makes products manufactured with automation look less expensive than they really are and those produced with manual labor look more expensive than they really are.

Another issue is that traditional cost allocation systems tend to portray low-volume products as those with the highest profits. This problem arises because the overhead costs associated with batch setups and teardowns, which can be a significant proportion of total overhead costs, are allocated indiscriminately to products that have both large and small production volumes; there is no allocation to a specific short production run of the special batch costs associated with it. This results in undercosting of products with short production runs and overcosting of products with long production runs. This is one of the most common cost accounting problems and results in incorrect management decisions to increase sales of short-run jobs and to reduce sales of long-run jobs, which results in reduced profits as company resources are concentrated on the lowest-profit products.

Based on these examples, it is clear that there are serious problems with the traditional cost allocation system. It does not apportion overhead costs correctly, resulting in management information about products that is only correct by accident, and which results in decisions that are not based on factual data. Activity-based costing was developed in order to correct these shortcomings.

9-5   An Overview of Activity-Based Costing

An activity-based costing (ABC) system begins with a determination of the scope of the project. This is a critical item, because creating an ABC system that encompasses every aspect of every department of all corporate subsidiaries will take an inordinate amount of time and resources and may never show valuable results for several years, if ever. To control this problem, we first determine the range of activities that the ABC system is to encompass, and the results desired from the system. It is not usually necessary to create an ABC system for simple processes for which the costs can be readily separated and reported on. Instead, activities that are deserving of inclusion in an ABC system are those that include many machines, involve complex processes, use automation, require many machine setups, or encompass a diverse product line. These are areas in which costs are difficult to clearly and indisputably assign to products or other cost objects. When creating a system scope to include these areas, it may be best to first include just a few of them on a pilot project basis, so that the installation team and the affected employees can get used to the new system. The scope can later be expanded to include other areas of sufficient complexity to warrant the use of this system.

Scope considerations should also expand to include the level of detailed information that the system should produce. For example, an ABC system that is only designed to produce information for strategic analysis will be considered satisfactory if it issues high-level information. This system requires a much lower level of detailed information handling and calculation than one that is used for the tactical-level costing of products, activities, or customers. Accordingly, the level of detailed information analysis built into the project's scope will depend entirely on the uses to which the resulting information is to be put.

Another scope issue is the extent to which the ABC system is to be integrated into the existing accounting system. If the project is to be handled on a periodic recalculation basis, rather than one that is automatically updated whenever new information is introduced into the accounting system, then all linkages can be no more than manual retyping of existing information into a separate ABC. However, a fully integrated ABC system will require the extensive coding of software interfaces between the two systems, which is both time-consuming and expensive. These changes may include some alteration of the corporate chart of accounts, the cost center structure, and the cost and revenue distributions used by the accounts payable and billing functions. These are major changes, so the level of system integration should be a large proportion of the scope discussions.

A final scope issue is a determination of how many costs from nonproduction areas should be included in the system. For those companies that have proportionately large production departments, this may not be an issue; but for service companies or those with large development departments, these other costs can be a sizable proportion of total costs, and so should be included in the ABC system. These costs can come from areas as diverse as the research and development, product design, marketing, distribution, computer services, janitorial, and administration functions. Adding each new functional area will increase the administrative cost of the ABC system, so a key issue in scope determination is whether the cost of each functional area is large enough to affect the activity costs calculated by the ABC system. Ones with a negligible impact should be excluded.

Once we have determined the scope, we must next separate all direct materials and labor costs and set them to one side. These costs are adequately identified by most existing accounting systems already, so it is usually a simple matter to identify and segregate the general ledger accounts in which these costs are stored. The remaining costs in the general ledger should be ones that can be allocated.

Next, using our statement of the scope of the project, we can identify those costs in the general ledger that are to be allocated through the ABC system. For example, if the primary concern of the new system is to determine the cost of the sales effort on each product sale, then finding the sales and marketing costs will be the primary concern. Alternately, if the purpose of the ABC system is to find the distribution cost per unit, then only those costs associated with warehousing, shipping, and freight must be located.

With the designated overhead costs in hand, we then proceed to store costs into secondary, or resource, cost pools. A secondary cost pool is one that provides services to other company functions, without directly providing services to any activities that create products or services. Examples of resource costs are administrative salaries, building maintenance, and computer services. The costs stored in these cost pools will later be charged to other cost pools with various activity measures, so the costs should be stored in separate pools that can be allocated with similar allocation measures. For example, computer services costs may be allocated to other cost pools based on the number of personal computers used, so any costs that can reasonably and logically be allocated based on the number of personal computers used should be stored in the same resource cost pool.

In a similar manner, we then store all remaining overhead costs in a set of primary cost pools. There can be a very large number of cost pools for the storage of similar costs, but one should consider that the cost of administering the ABC system (unless it is a rare case of full automation) will increase with each cost pool added. Accordingly, it is best to keep the number of cost pools to less than 10. The following standard cost pool descriptions are used in most companies:

- *Batch-related cost pools.* Many costs, such as purchasing, receiving, production control, shop floor control, tooling, setup labor, supervision, training, material handling, and quality control are related to the length of production batches.
- *Product line–related cost pools.* A group of products may have incurred the same research and development, advertising, purchasing, and distribution costs. It may be necessary to split this category into separate cost pools if there are several different distribution channels, if the cost of the channels differ dramatically from each other.
- *Facility-related cost pools.* Some costs cannot be directly allocated to specific products, because they relate more closely to the entire facility. These costs include building insurance, building maintenance, and facility depreciation.

Other cost pools can be added to these three basic cost pools, if the results will yield a significantly improved level of accuracy, or if the extra cost pools will lead to the attainment of the goals and scope that were set at the beginning of the project. In particular, the batch-related cost pool can be subdivided into several smaller cost pools depending on the number of different operations within a facility. For example, a candy-making plant will have a line of cookers, the cost of which can be included in one cost pool, while the cost of its candy extruder machines can be segregated into a separate cost pool and its cellophane wrapper machines into yet another cost pool. Costs may be allocated differently, depending on the type of machine used, so separating this category into several smaller cost pools may make sense. The various sources of product costs are noted in Exhibit 9-2.

Costs cannot always be directly mapped from general ledger accounts into cost pools. Instead, there may be valid reasons for splitting general ledger costs into different cost pools. If so, an allocation method must be found that logically splits these costs. This method is termed a *resource driver*. Examples of resource drivers are the number of products produced, direct labor hours, and the number of production orders used. Whatever the type of resource driver selected, it should provide a logical and defendable means for redirecting costs from a general ledger account into a cost pool. There should be a minimal number of resource drivers, because time and effort is required to accumulate each one. In reality, most companies will use management judgment to arrive at a set percentage of each account that is allocated to cost pools, rather than using any formal resource driver at all. For example,

Exhibit 9-2   *The Sources of Product Costs*

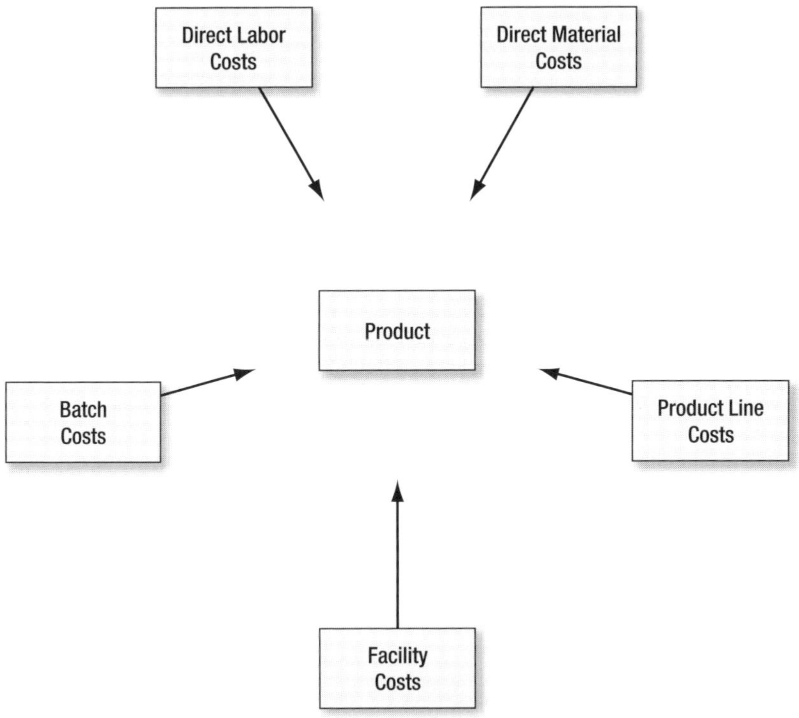

the cost of computer depreciation may be allocated 50% to a secondary cost pool, 40% to a batch-related primary cost pool, and 10% to a facility-related primary cost pool, because these percentages roughly reflect the number of personal computers located at various parts of the facility, which in turn is considered a reasonable means for spreading these costs among different cost pools.

There are varying levels of detailed analysis that one can use to assign costs to cost pools. The level of analysis will be largely driven by the need for increasingly detailed levels of information; if there is less need for accuracy, then a less expensive method can be used. For example, if there are three cost pools into which the salaries of the purchasing department can be stored, depending on the actual activities conducted, then the easiest and least accurate approach is to make a management decision to send a certain percentage of the total cost into each one. A higher level of accuracy would require that the employees be split up into job categories, with varying percentages being allocated from each category. Finally, the highest level of accuracy would require time tracking by employee, with a fresh recalculation after every set of time sheets is collected. The level of accuracy needed, the size of the costs being allocated, and the cost of the related data collection, will drive the decision to collect information at progressively higher levels of accuracy.

The next step is to allocate all of the costs stored in the secondary cost pools into the primary cost pools. This is done with activity drivers, which we will explain shortly. By allocating these cost pools to primary cost pools, we cause a redistribution of costs to occur that can then be further allocated from the primary cost pools, with considerable accuracy, to cost objects. This subsidiary step of allocating costs from resource cost centers to primary cost centers can be avoided by sending all costs straight from the general ledger to the primary cost pools, but several studies have shown that this more direct approach does not do as good a job of accurately allocating costs. The use of resource cost centers more precisely reflects how costs flow through an organization—from resource activities such as the computer services department to other departments, which in turn are focused on activities that are used to create cost objects.

Now that all costs have been allocated into primary cost pools, we must find a way to accurately charge these costs to cost objects, which are the users of the costs. Examples of cost objects are products and customers. We perform this allocation with an *activity driver*. This is a variable that explains the consumption of costs from a cost pool. There should be a clearly defined cause-and-effect relationship between the cost pool and the activity, so that there is a solid and defensible reason for using a specific activity driver. This is a key area, because the use of specific activity drivers will change the amount of costs charged to cost objects, which can raise the ire of the managers who are responsible for those cost objects. Exhibit 9-3 itemizes several activity drivers that relate to specific types of costs.

The list of activities presented in Exhibit 9-3 is by no means comprehensive. Each company has unique processes and costs that may result in the selection of different activity drivers from the ones noted here. The following key issues should be considered when selecting an activity driver:

- *Minimize data collection.* Very few activity drivers are already tracked through the existing accounting system, because few of them involve costs. Instead, they are more related to actions, such as the number of supplier reviews or the number of customer orders processed. These are numbers that may not be tracked anywhere in the existing system, and so they will require extra effort to compile. Consequently, if there are few differences between several potential activity drivers, pick the one that is already being measured, thereby saving the maintenance work for the ABC system.

- *Pick low-cost measurements.* If it is apparent that the only reasonable activity measures are ones that must be collected from scratch, then—all other items being equal—pick the one with the lowest data collection cost. This is a particularly important consideration if the ABC project is operating on a tight budget or if there is concern by employees that the new system is taking up too many resources.

- *Verify a cause-and-effect relationship.* The activity driver must have a direct bearing on the incurrence of the costs in the cost pool. To test this, perform a regression analysis; if the regression reveals that changes in the activity driver have a direct and considerable impact on the size of the cost pool, then it is a good driver to use. It is also useful if the potential activity driver can be used as an element of improvement change. For example, if management can focus the attention of the organization on reducing the quantity of the activity driver, then this will result in a smaller cost pool.

Once an activity driver has been selected for each cost pool, we then divide the total volume of each activity for the accounting period into the total amount of costs

Exhibit 9-3   *Activity Drivers for Specific Types of Costs*

Cost Type	Related Activity Driver
Facility costs	Amount of space utilization
Manufacturing costs	Number of direct labor hours
Manufacturing costs	Number of field support visits
Manufacturing costs	Number of jobs scheduled
Manufacturing costs	Number of machine hours
Manufacturing costs	Number of machine setups
Manufacturing costs	Number of maintenance work orders
Manufacturing costs	Number of parts in product
Manufacturing costs	Number of parts in stock
Manufacturing costs	Number of price negotiations
Manufacturing costs	Number of purchase orders
Manufacturing costs	Number of scheduling changes
Manufacturing costs	Number of shipments
Quality control costs	Number of inspections
Quality control costs	Number of supplier reviews
Storage time (e.g., depreciation, taxes)	Inventory turnover
Storage transactions (e.g., receiving)	Number of times handled

accumulated into each cost pool to derive a cost per unit of activity. For example, if the activity measure is the number of insurance claims processed, and there are 350 in the period, then if they were to be divided into a human resources benefits cost pool of $192,000, the resulting cost per claim processed would be $549.

Our next step is to determine the quantity of each activity that is used by the cost object. To do so, we need a measurement system that accumulates the quantity of activity driver used for each cost object. This measurement system may not be in existence yet, and so must be specially constructed for the ABC system. If the cost of this added data collection is substantial, then there will be considerable pressure to reduce the number of activity drivers, which represents a trade-off between accuracy and system cost.

Finally, we have reached our goal, which is to accurately assign overhead costs to cost objects. To do so, we multiply the cost per unit of activity by the number of units of each activity used by the cost objects. This should flush out all of the costs located in the cost pools and assign them to cost objects in their entirety. By doing so, we have found a defensible way to assign overhead costs in a manner that is not only understandable, but more important, is a way that managers can use to reduce those costs. For example, if the activity measure for the overhead costs associated with the purchasing function's cost is the number of different parts ordered for each product, then managers can focus on reducing the activity measure, which entails a reduction in the number of different parts included in each product. By doing so, the amount of purchasing overhead will be reduced, because it is directly associated with and influenced by this activity driver. Thus, the ABC system is an excellent way to focus attention on costs that can be eliminated.

The explanation of ABC has been a lengthy one, so let us briefly recap it. After setting the scope of the ABC system, we allocate costs from the general ledger to secondary and primary cost pools, using resource drivers. We then allocate the costs of the secondary cost pools to the primary ones. Next, we create activity drivers that are closely associated with the costs in each of the cost pools, and derive a cost per unit of activity. We then accumulate the number of units of each activity that are used by each cost object (such as a product or customer) and multiply the number of these units by the cost per activity driver. This procedure completely allocates all overhead costs to the cost objects in a reasonable and logical manner. An overview of the process is shown in Exhibit 9-4.

9-6   The Bill of Activities

A key outcome of an ABC system that deserves separate discussion is the bill of activities (BOA). This is similar to a bill of materials (BOM), in that it itemizes all of the components of a product, but it lists only the overhead components as defined through an ABC system, rather than the direct material and labor costs that are most commonly found in a BOM.

When combined with the costs listed in a BOM, the BOA yields a high level of detail on all costs associated with a product. These two documents then become the

Exhibit 9-4 *ABC Allocation Process*

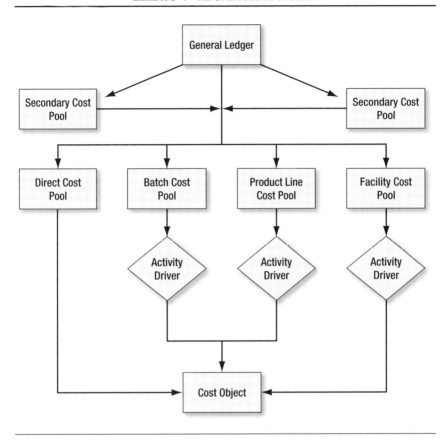

core of almost any cost-based analysis that involves products. For example, one can use the BOA to determine the exact overhead costs to apply to a product in a full costing situation, while also being able to assign costs based on only certain cost pools, depending on the analysis issue being reviewed. If there is a question regarding the development cost per unit of production, the BOA has that information. If managers are curious about the overhead cost per batch, the BOA contains that information, too.

An example of a BOA is shown in Exhibit 9-5. Note that there are different line items for each cost pool, so that one can clearly differentiate the overhead costs that are based on batch-level, product line-level, and facility-level activities. Also, note that the cost pool quantities are divided by the activity volumes associated with those pools (e.g., the product engineering cost pool is divided by the total number of units expected to be produced over the life of the product, because this quantity bears a valid relationship to the research and development costs required to create the product).

Exhibit 9-5   *The Bill of Activities*

Overhead Cost Pool	Total Pool Cost	Activity Measure	Relevant Volume	Cost per Unit
Product engineering	$300,000	Units produced	50,000/life cycle	$6.00
Process planning	175,000	Units produced	50,000/life cycle	3.50
Batch specific	90,000	Batch size	12,000/batch	7.50
Marketing and distribution	120,000	Annual volume	10,000/annually	12.00
Total Costs	—	—	—	**$29.00**

10

Joint and By-Product Costing[1]

10-1   Introduction

There are many instances where a company will operate a single production process that results in more than one product, none of which can be clearly identified through the early stages of production. Examples of such merged production are in the wood products industry, where a tree can be cut into a wide variety of end products, or meat packing, where an animal can be cut into many different finished goods. Up to the point where individual products become clearly identifiable in the production process, there is no clear-cut way to assign costs to products. This issue is of considerable importance to the inventory accountant, who must have a consistent method for assigning costs to these items. We will discuss several cost allocation methods in this chapter that deal with this problem and also note the usefulness (or lack thereof) of these allocation methods.

The key point emphasized by this chapter is that the allocation of costs through any method discussed in this chapter is essentially arbitrary in nature—it results in some sort of cost being assigned to a joint product or by-product, but these costs are only useful for financial or tax reporting purposes, not for management decisions.

10-2   The Nature of Joint Costs

To understand joint products and by-products, one must have a firm understanding of the *split-off point*. This is the last point in a production process where it is impossible to determine the nature of the final products. All costs that have been incurred by the production process up until that point—both direct and overhead—must somehow be allocated to the products that result from the split-off point. Any costs incurred thereafter can be charged to specific products in the normal manner. Thus, a product that comes out of such a process will be composed of allocated costs from

---

[1]Adapted with permission from Chapter 15 of Bragg, *Cost Accounting: A Comprehensive Guide*, John Wiley & Sons, 2001.

before the split-off point and costs that can be directly traced to it, which occur after the split-off point.

A related term is the *by-product*, which is one or more additional products that arise from a production process, but whose potential sales value is much smaller than that of the principal joint products that arise from the same process. As we will see, the accounting for by-products can be somewhat different.

A complication to the joint cost concept is that there can be more than one split-off point. As noted in Exhibit 10-1, we see the processing in a slaughterhouse, where the viscera are removed early in the process, creating a by-product. This is the first split-off point. Then the ribs are split away from the carcass, which is a second split-off point. The ribs may in turn be packaged and sold off at once, or processed further to produce additional products, such as prepackaged barbequed ribs. In this instance, some costs incurred through the first split-off point may be assigned to the by-product viscera (more on that later), while costs incurred between the first and second split-off points will no longer be assigned to the viscera, but must in turn be assigned to the remaining products that can be extracted from the carcass. Finally, costs that must be incurred to convert ribs into final products will be assigned directly to those products. This is the basic cost flow for joint products and by-products.

10-3 The Reasoning Behind Joint and By-product Costing

As we will see in the next section, the allocation of costs to products at the split-off point is essentially arbitrary in nature. Although two standard methods are used, neither one leads to information that is useful for management decision making. Why, then, must the inventory accountant be concerned with the proper cost allocation methodology for joint products and by-products?

Exhibit 10-1   *Multiple Split-Off Points for Joint Products and By-products*

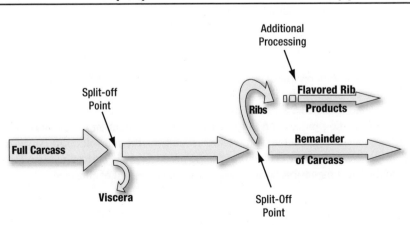

Because there are accounting and legal reasons for doing so. Generally accepted accounting principles (GAAP) require that costs be assigned to products for inventory valuation purposes. Although the costs incurred by a production process up to the split-off point cannot be clearly assigned to a single product, it is still necessary to find some reasonable allocation method for doing so, in order to obey the accounting rules. Otherwise, all costs incurred up to the split-off point could reasonably be charged off directly to the cost of goods sold as an overhead cost, which would result in enormous overhead costs and few direct costs (only those incurred after the split-off point).

The logic used for allocating costs to joint products and by-products has less to do with some scientifically derived allocation method and more with finding a quick and easy way to allocate costs that is reasonably defensible (as we will see in the next section). The reason for using simple methodologies is that the promulgators of GAAP realize there is no real management use for allocated joint costs—they cannot be used for determining break-even points, setting optimal prices, or figuring out the exact profitability of individual products. Instead, they are used for any of the following purposes, which are more administrative in nature:

- *Inventory valuation.* It is possible to manipulate inventory levels (and therefore the reported level of income) by shifting joint cost allocations toward those products that are stored in inventory. This practice is obviously discouraged, because it results in changes to income that have no relationship to operating conditions. Nonetheless, one should be on the lookout for the deliberate use of allocation methods that will alter the valuation of inventory.

- *Income reporting.* Many organizations split their income statements into sublevels that report on profits by product line or even individual product. If so, joint costs may make up such a large proportion of total production costs that these income statements will not include the majority of production costs, unless they are allocated to specific products or product lines.

- *Transfer pricing.* A company can alter the prices at which it sells products among its various divisions, so that high prices are charged to those divisions located in high-tax areas, resulting in lower reported levels of income tax against which those high tax rates can be applied. A canny inventory accounting staff will choose the joint cost allocation technique that results in the highest joint costs being assigned to products being sent to such locations (and the reverse for low-tax regions).

- *Bonus calculations.* Manager bonuses may depend on the level of reported profits for specific products, which in turn are partly based on the level of joint costs allocated to them. Thus, managers have a keen interest in the calculations used to assign costs, especially if some of the joint costs can be dumped onto products that are the responsibility of a different manager.

- *Cost-plus contract calculations.* Many government contracts are based on the reimbursement of a company's costs, plus some predetermined margin. In this situation, it is in a company's best interests to ensure that the largest possible proportion of joint costs are assigned to any jobs that will be reimbursed by the customer, while the customer will be equally interested, but because of a desire to *reduce* the allocation of joint costs.

- *Insurance reimbursement.* If a company suffers damage to its production or inventory areas, some finished goods or work-in-process inventory may have been damaged or destroyed. If so, it is in the interests of the company to fully allocate as many joint costs as possible to the damaged or destroyed stock, so that it can receive the largest possible reimbursement from its insurance provider.

Next, we will look at the two most commonly used methods for allocating joint costs to products, which are based on product revenues for one method and gross margins for the other.

10-4 Cost Allocation Methodologies

Although several cost allocation methodologies have been proposed in the accounting literature, only two methods have gained widespread acceptance. The first is based on the sales value of all joint products at the split-off point. To calculate it, the inventory accountant compiles all costs accumulated in the production process up to the split-off point, determines the eventual sales value of all products created at the split-off point, and then assigns these costs to the products based on their relative values. If there are by-products associated with the joint production process, they are considered to be too insignificant to be worthy of any cost assignment, although revenues gained from their sale can be charged against the cost of goods sold for the joint products. This is the simplest joint cost allocation method, and it is particularly attractive, because the inventory accountant needs no knowledge of any production processing steps that occur after the split-off point.

This different treatment of the costs and revenues associated with by-products can lead to profitability anomalies at the product level. The trouble is that the determination of whether a product is a by-product or not can be subjective; in one company, if a joint product's revenues are less than 10% of the total revenues earned, then it is a by-product, whereas another company might use a 1% cutoff figure instead. Because of this vagueness in accounting terminology, one company may assign all of its costs to just those joint products with an inordinate share of total revenues, and record the value of all other products as zero. If a large quantity of these by-products were to be held in stock at a value of zero, the total inventory valuation would be lower than another company would calculate, simply because of their definition of what constitutes a by-product.

A second problem with the treatment of by-products under this cost allocation scenario is that by-products may only be sold off in batches, which may only occur once every few months. This can cause sudden drops in the cost of joint products in the months when sales occur, because these revenues will be subtracted from their cost. Alternately, joint product costs will appear to be too high in those periods when there are no by-product sales. Thus, one can alter product costs through the timing of by-product sales.

A third problem related to by-products is that the revenues realized from their sale can vary considerably, based on market demand. If so, these altered revenues will cause abrupt changes in the cost of those joint products against which these revenues are netted. It certainly may require some explaining by the inventory accountant to show why changes in the price of an unrelated product caused a change in the cost of a joint product! This can be a difficult concept for a nonaccountant to understand.

The best way to avoid the three issues just noted is to avoid the designation of *any* product as a by-product. Instead, every joint product should be assigned some proportion of total costs incurred up to the split-off point, based on their total potential revenues (however small they may be), and no resulting revenues should be used to offset other product costs. By avoiding the segregation of joint products into different product categories, we can avoid a variety of costing anomalies.

The second allocation method is based on the estimated final gross margin of each joint product produced. The calculation of gross margin is based on the revenue that each product will earn at the end of the entire production process, less the cost of all processing costs incurred from the split-off point to the point of sale. This is a more complicated approach, because it requires the inventory accountant to accumulate additional costs through the end of the production process, which in turn requires a reasonable knowledge of how the production process works and where costs are incurred. Although it is a more difficult method to calculate, its use may be mandatory in those instances where the final sale price of one or more joint products cannot be determined at the split-off point (as is required for the first allocation method), thereby rendering the other allocation method useless.

The main problem with allocating joint costs based on the estimated final gross margin is that it can be difficult to calculate if there is a great deal of *customized* work left between the split-off point and the point of sale. If so, it is impossible to determine in advance the exact costs that will be incurred during the remaining production process. In such a case, the only alternative is to make estimates of expected costs that will be incurred, base the gross margin calculations on this information, and accept the fact that the resulting joint cost allocations may not be provable, based on the actual costs incurred.

The two allocation methods described here are easier to understand with an example, which is shown in Exhibit 10-2. In the exhibit, we see that $250 in joint costs have been incurred up to the split-off point. The first allocation method, based on the eventual sale price of the resulting joint products, is shown beneath the split-off point. In it, the sale price of the by-product is ignored, leaving a revenue split of 59% and 49% between products A and B, respectively. The joint costs of the process are allocated between the two products based on this percentage.

The second allocation method, based on the eventual gross margins earned by each of the products, is shown to the right of the split-off point. This calculation includes the gross margin on sale of product C, which was categorized as a by-product, and therefore ignored, in the preceding calculation. This calculation results in a substantially different sharing of joint costs between the various products than we saw for the first allocation method, with the split now being 39%,

Exhibit 10-2 Example of Joint Cost Allocation Methodologies

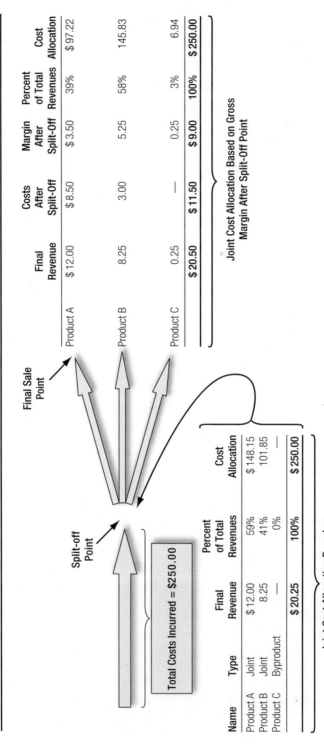

	Final Revenue	Costs After Split-Off	Margin After Split-Off	Percent of Total Revenues	Cost Allocation
Product A	$12.00	$8.50	$3.50	39%	$97.22
Product B	8.25	3.00	5.25	58%	145.83
Product C	0.25	—	0.25	3%	6.94
	$20.50	$11.50	$9.00	100%	$250.00

Joint Cost Allocation Based on Gross
Margin After Split-Off Point

Total Costs Incurred = $250.00

Name	Type	Final Revenue	Percent of Total Revenues	Cost Allocation
Product A	Joint	$12.00	59%	$148.15
Product B	Joint	8.25	41%	101.85
Product C	Byproduct	—	0%	—
		$20.25	100%	$250.00

Joint Cost Allocation Based on
Estimated Sales Value at
the Split-off Point

58%, and 3% between products A, B, and C, respectively. The wide swing in allocated amounts between the two methods can be attributed to the different bases of allocation: the first is based on revenue, whereas the second is based on gross margins.

10-5   Pricing of Joint Products and By-products

The key operational issue for which joint cost allocations should be devoutly ignored is in the pricing of joint products and by-products. The issue here is that the allocation used to assign a cost to a particular product does not really have any bearing on the actual cost incurred to create the product—either method for splitting costs between multiple products, as noted in the last section, cannot really be proven to allocate the correct cost to any product. Instead, we must realize that all costs incurred up to the split-off point are sunk costs that will be incurred, no matter what combination of products are created and sold from the split-off point forward.

Because everything before the split-off point is considered to be a sunk cost, pricing decisions are only concerned with those costs incurred *after* the split-off point, because these costs can be directly traced to individual products. In other words, incremental changes in prices should be based on the incremental increases in costs that accrue to a product after the split-off point. This can result in costs being assigned to products that are inordinately low, because there may be so few costs incurred after the split-off point. This can be in response to competitive pressures or because it only seems necessary to add a modest markup percentage to the incremental costs incurred after the split-off point. If these prices are too low, then the revenues resulting from the entire production process may not be sufficiently high for the company to earn a profit.

The best way to ensure that pricing is sufficient for a company to earn a profit is to create a pricing model for each product line. This model, as shown in Exhibit 10-3, itemizes the types of products and their likely selling points, as well as the variable costs that can be assigned to them subsequent to the split-off point. Thus far, the exhibit results in a total gross margin that is earned from all joint and by-product sales. Then we add up the grand total of all sunk costs that were incurred before the split-off point and subtract this amount from the total gross margin. If the resulting profit is too small, then the person setting prices will realize that individual product prices must be altered in order to improve the profitability of the entire cluster of products. Also, by bringing together all of the sales volumes and price points related to a single production process, one can easily see where pricing must be adjusted in order to obtain the desired level of profits. In the example, we must somehow increase the total profit by $3.68 in order to avoid a loss. A quick perusal of the exhibit shows us that two of the products—the viscera and pituitary gland—do not generate a sufficient amount of throughput to cover this loss. Accordingly, the sales staff should concentrate the bulk of its attention on the repricing of the other three listed products, in order to eliminate the operating loss.

This format can be easily adapted for use for entire reporting periods or production runs, rather than for a single unit of production (as was the case in the last

Exhibit 10-3 *Pricing Model for Joint and By-product Pricing*

Product Name	Price/ Unit	Incremental Cost/ Unit	Throughput/ Unit	No. of Sales Units	Total Throughput
Viscera	$.40	$.10	$.30	1	$.30
Barbequed ribs	3.00	1.80	1.20	4	4.80
Flank steak	5.50	1.05	4.35	2	8.70
Quarter steak	4.25	1.25	3.00	4	12.00
Pituitary gland	1.00	.48	.52	1	.52
				Total throughput	$26.32
				Total sunk costs	$30.00
				Net profit/ loss	−$3.68

exhibit). To do so, we simply multiply the number of units of joint products or by-products per unit by the total number of units to be manufactured during the period, and enter the totals in the far right column of the same format just used in Exhibit 10-3. The advantage of using this more comprehensive approach is that a production scheduler can determine which products should be included in a production run (assuming that more than one product is available) in order to generate the largest possible throughput.

11

Obsolete Inventory

11-1 Introduction

Obsolete inventory is any inventory for which there is no longer any use, either through inclusion in viable manufactured goods or by direct sale to customers. Generally accepted accounting principles (GAAP) state that obsolete inventory must be written off as soon as it is identified. Given the substantial level of interpretation that can be put on the "obsolete inventory" designation, it is evident that this subject area can have a large adverse impact on profitability. In this chapter, we review how to find obsolete inventory, how to dispose of it in the most profitable manner, how much expense to recognize, and how to prevent it from occurring.

11-2 Locating Obsolete Inventory

There are several techniques for locating obsolete inventory, as discussed in this section. However, be sure to gain the commitment of upper management to this search first; otherwise, the scope of the resulting expense (which can be substantial) may lead to multiple rounds of questions regarding how the company could have found itself saddled with so much obsolete inventory, all of which must be written off as soon as it is discovered. Conducting a search for obsolete inventory may meet with a particular level of resistance if the management team is being awarded significant profit-based bonuses. If so, consider addressing the prevention of incoming obsolete inventory instead, which may reduce inventory levels over the long term, although it will not address the existing obsolete inventory.

It is certainly encouraging to see a manager eliminate obsolete inventory, but a common problem is to see some items disposed of that were actually needed, possibly for short-term production requirements, but also for long-term service parts or substitutes for other items. In these cases, the person eliminating inventory will likely be castigated for causing problems that the logistics staff must fix. A good solution is to form a Materials Review Board (MRB). The MRB is composed of representatives from every department having any interaction with inventory issues—

149

accounting, engineering, logistics, and production. For example, the engineering staff may need to retain some items that they are planning to incorporate into a new design, while the logistics staff may know that it is impossible to obtain a rare part, and so prefer to hold onto the few items left in stock for service parts use.

It can be difficult to bring this disparate group together for obsolete inventory reviews, so one normally has to put a senior member of management in charge to force meetings to occur, while also scheduling a series of regular inventory review meetings well in advance. Meeting minutes should be written and disseminated to all group members, identifying which inventory items have been mutually declared obsolete. If this approach still results in accusations that items have been improperly disposed of, then the group can also resort to a sign-off form that must be completed by each MRB member before any disposition can occur. However, obtaining a series of sign-offs can easily cause lengthy delays or the loss of the sign-off form, and is therefore not recommended. A simpler approach is to use a negative approval process whereby items will be dispositioned as of a certain date unless an MRB member objects. The MRB is not recommended for low-inventory situations, as can arise in a just-in-time (JIT) environment, because an MRB tends to act too slowly for employees who are used to a fast-moving JIT system.

The simplest long-term way to find obsolete inventory without the assistance of a computer system is to leave the physical inventory count tags on all inventory items following completion of the annual physical count. The tags taped to any items used during the subsequent year will be thrown away at the time of use, leaving only the oldest unused items still tagged by the end of the year. One can then tour the warehouse and discuss with the MRB each of these items to see if an obsolescence reserve should be created for them. However, tags can fall off or be ripped off inventory items, especially if there is a high level of traffic in nearby bins. Extra taping will reduce this issue, but it is likely that some tag loss will occur over time.

Even a rudimentary computerized inventory tracking system is likely to record the last date on which a specific part number was removed from the warehouse for production or sale. If so, it is an easy matter to use a report writer to extract and sort this information, resulting in a report listing all inventory, starting with those products with the oldest "last used" date. By sorting the report with the oldest last-usage date listed first, one can readily arrive at a sort list of items requiring further investigation for potential obsolescence. However, this approach does not yield sufficient proof that an item will never be used again, because it may be an essential component of an item that has not been scheduled for production in some time, or a service part for which demand is low.

A more advanced version of the last used report is shown in Exhibit 11-1. It compares total inventory withdrawals to the amount on hand, which by itself may be sufficient information to conduct an obsolescence review. It also lists planned usage, which calls for information from a material requirements planning system and which informs one of any upcoming requirements that might keep the MRB from otherwise disposing of an inventory item. An extended cost for each item is also listed, in order to give report users some idea of the write-off that might occur if an item is declared obsolete. In the exhibit, the subwoofer, speaker bracket, and

Exhibit 11-1 *Inventory Obsolescence Review Report*

Description	Item No.	Location	Quantity on Hand	Last Year Usage	Planned Usage	Extended Cost
Subwoofer case	0421	A-04-C	872	520	180	$9,053
Speaker case	1098	A-06-D	148	240	120	1,020
Subwoofer	3421	D-12-A	293	14	0	24,724
Circuit board	3600	B-01-A	500	5,090	1,580	2,500
Speaker, bass	4280	C-10-C	621	2,480	578	49,200
Speaker bracket	5391	C-10-C	14	0	0	92
Wall bracket	5080	B-03-B	400	0	120	2,800
Gold connection	6233	C-04-A	3,025	8,042	5,900	9,725
Tweeter	7552	C-05-B	725	6,740	2,040	5,630

wall bracket appear to be obsolete based on prior usage, but the planned use of more wall brackets would keep that item from being disposed of.

If a computer system includes a bill of materials, there is a strong likelihood that it also generates a "where used" report, listing all of the bills of material for which an inventory item is used. If there is no "where used" listed on the report for an item, it is likely that a part is no longer needed. This report is most effective if bills of material are removed from the computer system or deactivated as soon as products are withdrawn from the market; this approach more clearly reveals those inventory items that are no longer needed.

An additional approach for determining whether a part is obsolete is reviewing engineering change orders. These documents show those parts being replaced by different ones, as well as when the changeover is scheduled to take place. One can then search the inventory database to see how many of the parts being replaced are still in stock, which can then be totaled, yielding another variation on the amount of obsolete inventory on hand.

A final source of information is the preceding period's obsolete inventory report. Even the best MRB will sometimes fail to dispose of acknowledged obsolete items. The accounting staff should keep track of these items and continue to notify management of those items for which there is no disposition activity.

In order to make any of these review systems work, it is necessary to create policies and procedures as well as ongoing scheduled review dates. By doing so, there is a strong likelihood that obsolescence reviews will become a regular part of a company's activities. In particular, consider a Board-mandated policy to conduct at least quarterly obsolescence reviews, which gives management an opportunity to locate items before they become too old to be disposed of at a reasonable price. Another Board policy should state that management will actively seek out and dispose of work-in-process or finished goods with an unacceptable quality level. By doing so, goods are kept from being stored in the warehouse in the first place, so the MRB never has to deal with it at a later date.

11-3 Disposing of Obsolete Inventory

As soon as obsolete inventory is identified, GAAP mandates that it be written off at once. However, this only applies to the unrecoverable portion of the inventory, so one should make a strong effort to earn some compensation from an inventory disposition. This section outlines several disposition possibilities, beginning with full-price sales and moving down through options having progressively lower returns.

In some situations, one can recover nearly the entire cost of excess items by asking the service department to sell them to existing customers as replacement parts. This approach is especially useful when the excess items are for specialized parts that customers are unlikely to obtain elsewhere, because these sales can be presented to customers as valuable replacements that may not be available for much longer. Conversely, this approach is least useful for commodity items or those subject to rapid obsolescence or having a short shelf life.

It is possible that some parts should be kept on hand for a few years, to be sold or given away as warranty replacements. This will reduce the amount of obsolescence expense and also keeps the company from having to procure or remanufacture parts at a later date in order to meet service/repair obligations. The amount of inventory to be held in this service/repair category can be roughly calculated based on the company's experience with similar products, or with the current product if it has been sold for a sufficiently long period. Any additional inventory on hand exceeding the total amount of anticipated service/repair parts can then be disposed of. Of particular interest is the time period over which management anticipates storing parts in the service/repair category. There should be some period over which the company has historically found that parts are required, such as five or ten years. Once this predetermined period has ended, a flag in the product master file should trigger a message indicating that the remaining parts can be eliminated. Before doing so, management should review recent transactional experience to see if the service/repair period should be extended or if it is now safe to eliminate the remaining stock.

Another possibility is to return the goods to the original supplier. Doing so will likely result in a restocking fee of 15% to 20%, which is still a bargain for otherwise useless goods. Rather than buying back parts for cash, many suppliers will only issue a credit against future purchases. This option becomes less likely if the company has owned the goods for a long time, because the supplier may no longer have a need for them stock them at all. Of course, this approach fails if the supplier will only issue a credit and the company has no need for other parts sold by the supplier.

It may be possible to sell goods online through an auction service. The best-known site is eBay, although there are other sites designed exclusively for the disposition of excess goods, such as www.salvagesale.com. These sites are more proactive in maintaining contact with potential buyers within specific commodity categories, and so can sometimes generate higher resale prices.

A poor way to sell off excess inventory to salvage contractors is to allow them to pick over the items for sale, only selecting those items they are certain to make a profit on. By doing so, the bulk of the excess inventory will still be parked in the warehouse when the contractors are gone. Instead, divide the inventory into batches, each one containing some items of value, which a salvage contractor must purchase in total in order to obtain that subset of items desired. Then have the contractors bid on each batch. Although the total amount of funds realized may not be much higher than would have been the case if the contractors had cherry-picked the inventory, they will take on the burden of removing the inventory from the warehouse, thereby allowing the company to avoid disposal expenses.

There are some instances where a company can donate excess inventory to a charity. By doing so, it can claim a tax deduction for the book value of the donated items. This will not generate any cash flow if the company has no reportable income, but the deduction can contribute to a net operating loss carry-forward that can be carried into a different tax reporting year. If this approach looks viable, request a copy of nonprofit status from the receiving entity, proving that it has been granted nonprofit status under section 501(c)(3) of the Internal Revenue Service tax code.

Finally, even if there is no hope of obtaining any form of compensation for obsolete goods, strongly consider throwing them in the dumpster. By doing so, there will be more storage space in the warehouse, the space to be allocated to other uses. Furthermore, the amount of inventory insurance coverage will be less, resulting in a smaller annual insurance premium. Depending on the local tax jurisdiction, one can also avoid paying a property tax on the inventory that has been disposed of. In addition, the number of inventory items to track in the warehouse database can be reduced, which can lead to a reduction in the number of cycle counting hours required per day to review the entire inventory on a recurring basis.

11-4   Expense Recognition for Obsolete Inventory

In brief, the proper expense recognition procedure for obsolete inventory is to determine the most likely disposition value for the targeted items, subtract this value from the book value of the obsolete inventory, and set aside the difference as a reserve. As the obsolete inventory is actually disposed of or estimates in the disposition values change, adjust the reserve account to reflect these alterations.

For example, a review of the Presto Computer Company's inventory reveals that it has $100,000 of laptop computer hard drives that it cannot sell. However, it believes there is a market for the drives through a reseller in Africa, but only at a sale price of $20,000. Accordingly, the Presto controller recognizes a reserve of $80,000 with the following journal entry:

	Debit	Credit
Cost of goods sold	$80,000	
Reserve for obsolete inventory		$80,000

After finalizing arrangements with the African reseller, the actual sale price is only $19,000, so the controller completes the transaction with the following entry, recognizing an additional $1,000 of expense:

	Debit	Credit
Reserve for obsolete inventory	$80,000	
Cost of goods sold	$1,000	
Inventory		$81,000

Sounds like a simple, mechanical process, doesn't it? It is not. The first problem is that one can improperly alter a company's reported financial results just by altering the timing of actual dispositions. For example, if a manager knows he can receive a higher-than-estimated price when selling old inventory, he can accelerate or delay the sale in order to drop some gains into a reporting period where the extra results are needed. This is unlikely to be a significant problem if the reserve is small, but it is a substantial risk if the reverse is the case. For example, the Presto Computer Company has set aside an obsolescence reserve of $25,000 for laptop computer fans. However, in January, the purchasing manager knows that the resale price for fans has plummeted, so the real reserve should be closer to $35,000, which would call for the immediate recognition of an additional $10,000 of expense. However, because this would result in an overall loss in Presto's financial results in January, he waits until April, when Presto has a profitable month, and completes the sale at that time, thereby delaying the additional obsolescence loss until the point of sale.

A second problem is the reluctance of management to suddenly drop a large expense reserve into the financial statements, which may disturb outside investors and creditors. Managers have a tendency instead to recognize small incremental amounts, thereby making it look as though obsolescence is a minor problem. There is no ready solution to this problem, because GAAP clearly mandates that all obsolete inventory be written off at once. It is a rare accountant who does not enter into a battle with management over this issue at some point during his or her career.

A third problem is the shear size of an expense recognition if there has been a long time period between obsolescence reviews. A review usually occurs at the end of the fiscal year, when this type of inventory is supposed to be investigated and written off, usually in conjunction with the auditor's review or the physical inventory count (or both). If this write-off has not occurred in previous years, the cumulative amount can be startling, which can result in the departure of the materials manager and/or the controller on the grounds that they should have known about the problem. There are three ways to keep a large write-off from occurring. First, conduct frequent obsolescence reviews to keep large write-offs from building up. Second, create an obsolescence expense reserve as part of the annual budget, and encourage the MRB to use it all. Under this approach, one can usually count on the warehouse manager to throw out the maximum possible amount of stock on the first day when the new budget takes effect. Third, implement some of the approaches described in the next section to prevent inventory from becoming obsolete.

A final expense recognition issue is that senior management simply may not believe the MRB when they arrive at an extremely high obsolescence reserve, and management may reject the recommended expense recognition. Their presumed knowledge of the business will not allow them to consider that a large part of the inventory is no longer usable. If this is the case, consider bringing in consultants to conduct an independent evaluation of the inventory. Senior managers may need this second opinion before they will authorize a large obsolescence reserve.

11-5 Preventing Obsolete Inventory

Thus far, we have only reviewed a variety of ways to locate, dispose of, and account for obsolete inventory. The real trick is to avoid all of those topics by ensuring that there is no obsolete inventory to begin with. This section addresses several ways to achieve this goal.

A major source of obsolete inventory is excessive purchasing volumes. The purchasing department may be purchasing in large quantities in order to save itself the trouble of issuing a multitude of purchase orders for smaller quantities, or because it can obtain lower prices by purchasing in large volumes. This problem can be avoided through the use of just-in-time purchasing practices, purchasing only those items authorized by a material requirements planning system, or by setting high inventory turnover goals for the materials management department.

A well run purchasing department will use bills of material to determine the parts needed to build a product and then order them in the quantities specified in the bills. However, if a bill of material is incorrect, then the items purchased will either be the wrong ones or the correct ones but in the wrong quantities. To avoid this problem, the bill of materials should be audited regularly for accuracy. An additional way to repair bills of material is to investigate why some kitted items are returned unused to the warehouse or additional items are requested by the production staff. These added transactions usually indicate incorrect bills of material.

It is easy for a part to become obsolete if no one knows where it is. If it is buried in an odd corner of the warehouse, there is not much chance that it will be used up. To avoid this problem, there should be location codes in the inventory database for every part, along with continual cycle counting to ensure that locations are correct. A periodic audit of location codes will give management a clear view of the accuracy of this information.

When the marketing department investigates the possibility of withdrawing a product from sale, it often does so without determining how much inventory of both the finished product and its component parts remain on hand. At most, the marketing staff only concerns itself with clearing out excess finished goods, because this can be readily identified. Those unique parts that are only used in the manufacture of a withdrawn product will then be left to gather dust in the warehouse and will eventually be sold off as scrap only after a substantial amount of time has passed.

To avoid this situation, the engineering, marketing, production, and accounting managers should review all proposed product cancellations to determine how much inventory will be left "hanging" on the proposed cancellation date. The result may be a revised termination date designed to first clear out all remaining stocks.

A related problem is poor engineering change control. If the engineering department does not verify that old parts are completely used up before installing a new part in a product, then the remaining quantities of the old part will be rendered obsolete. To avoid this scenario, have the accounting, production, and engineering managers determine the best time to effect the change that will minimize the old stock. Furthermore, if there is an automatic ordering flag in the computer system, shut it off for any items being withdrawn from use through an engineering change order. Otherwise, the system will reorder parts that have been deliberately drawn down below their reorder points.

Some products have limited shelf lives and must be thrown out if they are not used by a certain date. This certainly applies to all food products and can even be an issue with such other items as gaskets and seals, which will dry out over time. In a large warehouse with thousands of inventory items and only a small number of these limited-life products, it can be difficult to specially track them and ensure that they will be used before their expiration dates.

A mix of changes must be implemented to ensure proper shelf life control. First, the computer system must have a record of the ending shelf life date for each item in the warehouse. This calls for a special field in the inventory record that is not present in many standard inventory systems, so one must either obtain standard software containing this feature or have the existing database altered to make this feature available. The receiving staff must be warned by the computer system upon the arrival of a limited-shelf-life item, so a flag must also be available in the item master file for this purpose. With both of these software changes in hand, one can use the computer system to warn of impending product obsolescence for specific items. A simpler variation is to still have a flag in the item master file warn of the arrival of limited-shelf-life items, but to then have the warehouse staff manually track the obsolescence problem from that point on. This means clearly tagging each item with its shelf life date, so anyone picking inventory can clearly see which items must be picked first. Although this solution is much less expensive, it relies on both the receiving staff and stock pickers to ensure that the oldest items are used first.

A third variation is to use a gravity flow rack. This is a racking system set at a slight downward angle to the picker and containing rollers. Cartons of arriving items are loaded into the back of the rack, where they queue up behind cartons containing older items. Pickers then take the oldest items from the front of the rack. Because of this load-in-back, pick-in-front configuration, inventory is always used in a first-in, first-out manner, ensuring that the oldest items are always used first. This is an excellent way to control item shelf life, because there is no conscious need to pick one item over another in order to use the oldest one first. Similar racking systems are available for pallet-sized loads. However, this system does not absolutely ensure that items will be used before their shelf life dates; if there are many items in front of an item in a gravity flow rack, or if demand is minimal, then the older item still will not be used in time.

   If one can identify any of these problems as being the cause of obsolescence, quantify the cost of each problem and aggressively push for any changes that will eliminate it.

12

Inventory Transactions

12-1 Introduction

This chapter describes the most common inventory-related journal entries. The first section contains entries for goods in transit, beginning with the receipt of raw material and progressing through the various types of inventory to their eventual sale to customers. The second section contains entries listing common adjustments to inventory, including obsolescence, physical count adjustments, and abnormal scrap. The final block of entries shows how to shift indirect costs of various kinds into the overhead cost pool, and then how to allocate these costs back out to either the cost of goods sold or inventory. For each journal entry, there is a sample description, as well as the most likely debit and credit for each account used within the entry.

12-2 Goods in Transit

Record received goods. To increase inventory levels as a result of a supplier delivery.

	Debit	Credit
Raw materials inventory	xxx	
Accounts payable		xxx

Move inventory to work-in-process. To shift the cost of inventory to the work-in-process category once production work begins on converting it from raw materials to finished goods.

	Debit	Credit
Work-in-process inventory	xxx	
Raw materials inventory		xxx

Move inventory to finished goods. To shift the cost of completed inventory from work-in-process inventory to finished goods inventory.

	Debit	Credit
Finished goods inventory	xxx	
Work-in-process inventory		xxx

Sell inventory. To record the elimination of the inventory asset as a result of a product sale, shifting the asset to an expense and also recording the creation of an accounts receivable asset to reflect an unpaid balance from the customer on sale of the product.

	Debit	Credit
Cost of goods sold	xxx	
Finished goods inventory		xxx
Accounts receivable	xxx	
Revenue		xxx

12-3 Inventory Adjustments

Adjust inventory for obsolete items: To charge an ongoing expense to the cost of goods sold that increases the balance in a reserve against which obsolete inventory can be charged (*first entry*). The *second entry* charges off specific inventory items against the reserve.

	Debit	Credit
Cost of goods sold	xxx	
Obsolescence reserve		xxx
Obsolescence reserve	xxx	
Raw materials inventory		xxx
Work-in-process inventory		xxx
Finished goods inventory		xxx

Adjust inventory to lower of cost or market. To reduce the value of inventory to a market price that is lower than the cost at which it is recorded in the company records. The second journal entry shows an alternative approach where the credit is made to an inventory valuation account instead, from which specific write-offs can be completed at a later date.

	Debit	**Credit**
Loss on inventory valuation	xxx	
Raw materials inventory		xxx
Work-in-process inventory		xxx
Finished goods inventory		xxx
Loss on inventory valuation	xxx	
Reserve for reduction in inventory value		xxx

Adjust inventory to physical count. To adjust inventory balances, either up or down, as a result of changes in the inventory quantities that are noted during a physical count. The following entries assume that there are increases in inventory balances. If there are decreases in the inventory balances, then the debits and credits are reversed.

	Debit	**Credit**
Raw materials inventory	xxx	
Work-in-process inventory	xxx	
Finished goods inventory	xxx	
Cost of goods sold		xxx

Write off abnormal scrap/spoilage. To shift unexpected, one-time scrap or spoilage costs directly to the cost of goods sold, effectively writing off this amount in the current period.

	Debit	**Credit**
Cost of goods sold	xxx	
Work-in-process inventory		xxx

12-4 Valuation of Inventories

Record normal scrap/spoilage. To shift the normal, expected amount of scrap or spoilage cost to the overhead cost pool, from where it is allocated as a part of overhead to inventory.

	Debit	**Credit**
Overhead cost pool	xxx	
Work-in-process inventory		xxx

Transfer costs to overhead cost pools. To transfer manufacturing expenses into one or more overhead cost pools for later allocation to inventory and the cost of goods sold.

	Debit	Credit
Overhead cost pool	xxx	
Maintenance expenses		xxx
Manufacturing supplies		xxx
Rent, manufacturing related		xxx
Repairs, manufacturing related		xxx
Salaries, maintenance department		xxx
Salaries, materials handling department		xxx
Salaries, production control department		xxx
Salaries, purchasing department		xxx
Salaries, quality control department		xxx
Salaries, supervisory		xxx
Scrap, normal		xxx
Utilities		xxx
Depreciation—various accounts		xxx

Allocate overhead costs to inventory. To shift the amount of costs built up in the overhead cost pool to the work-in-process and finished goods inventory categories, as well as to the cost of goods sold for any inventory sold during the period.

	Debit	Credit
Cost of goods sold	xxx	
Work-in-process inventory	xxx	
Finished goods inventory	xxx	
Overhead cost pool		xxx

Assign manufacturing costs to joint products. Based on the cost assignment method used, to assign manufacturing cost pools to completed joint products.

	Debit	Credit
Finished goods inventory	xxx	
Overhead cost pool		xxx

13

IRS Inventory Rules

13-1 Introduction

The inventory accountant is primarily concerned with preparing accounting records that fall under the guidelines of Generally Accepted Accounting Principles (GAAP). However, the Internal Revenue Service (IRS) has its own set of rules related to inventory, which do not always match GAAP. This chapter contains the text of the IRS's inventory rules, along with commentary from the author (shown next to the "Commentary" headers). The text of the IRS rules has been truncated by the author near the end of some sections where the content does not relate to inventory. In order to locate the original IRS text, please refer to the following headings within the Internal Revenue Code:

Title 26—Internal Revenue Code
  Subtitle A—Income Taxes
    Chapter 1—Normal Taxes and Surtaxes
      Subchapter E—Accounting Periods and Methods of Accounting
        Part II—Methods of Accounting
          Subpart D—Inventories
            Section 471—General Rule for Inventories
            Section 472—Last-in, First-Out Inventories
            Section 473—Qualified Liquidations of LIFO Inventories
            Section 474—Simplified Dollar-Value LIFO Method for Certain Small Businesses

13-2 Section 471—General Rule for Inventories

Commentary: This section is an authorization for the IRS to develop its own inventory rules in order to determine a taxpayer's taxable income.

Whenever in the opinion of the Secretary the use of inventories is necessary in order clearly to determine the income of any taxpayer,

inventories shall be taken by such taxpayer on such basis as the Secretary may prescribe as conforming as nearly as may be to the best accounting practice in the trade or business and as most clearly reflecting
the income.

13-3   Section 472—Last-In, First-Out Inventories

Commentary: Section 472 (a) is a general statement that anyone using the LIFO
method shall follow IRS rules in doing so.

IRS Text:

(a) Authorization

A taxpayer may use the method provided in subsection (b) in inventorying
goods specified in an application, to use such method filed at such time and
in such manner as the Secretary may prescribe. The change to, and the use of,
such method shall be in accordance with such regulations as the Secretary may
prescribe as necessary in order that the use of such method may clearly reflect
income.

Commentary: Section 472 (b) describes a modified form of LIFO inventory,
whereby one layer includes inventory existing before the taxable year and one
subsequent layer includes inventory acquired during the taxable year.

(b) Method applicable

In inventorying goods specified in the application described in subsection (a),
the taxpayer shall:

(1) Treat those remaining on hand at the close of the taxable year as being:
First, those included in the opening inventory of the taxable year (in the
order of acquisition) to the extent thereof; and second, those acquired in
the taxable year;

(2) Inventory them at cost; and

(3) Treat those included in the opening inventory of the taxable year in
which such method is first used as having been acquired at the same time
and determine their cost by the average cost method.

Commentary: Section 472 (c) states that taxpayers can only use LIFO for tax
reporting purposes if the company already uses LIFO for its regular financial
reporting.

(c) Condition

Subsection (a) shall apply only if the taxpayer establishes to the satisfaction
of the Secretary that the taxpayer has used no procedure other than that specified in paragraphs (1) and (3) of subsection (b) in inventorying such goods to
ascertain the income, profit, or loss of the first taxable year for which the
method described in subsection (b) is to be used, for the purpose of a report or
statement covering such taxable year –

(1) to shareholders, partners, or other proprietors, or to beneficiaries, or

(2) for credit purposes.

Commentary: Section 472 (d) describes the costing method to be used for LIFO layering.

(d) 3-year averaging for increases in inventory value

The beginning inventory for the first taxable year for which the method described in subsection (b) is used shall be valued at cost. Any change in the inventory amount resulting from the application of the preceding sentence shall be taken into account ratably in each of the 3 taxable years beginning with the first taxable year for which the method described in subsection (b) is first used.

Commentary: Section 472 (e) states that a company cannot switch from LIFO to some other method once it has begun reporting taxable income with a LIFO inventory valuation, without permission from the IRS.

(e) Subsequent inventories

If a taxpayer, having complied with subsection (a), uses the method described in subsection (b) for any taxable year, then such method shall be used in all subsequent taxable years unless –

(1) with the approval of the Secretary a change to a different method is authorized; or,

(2) the Secretary determines that the taxpayer has used for any such subsequent taxable year some procedure other than that specified in paragraph (1) of subsection (b) in inventorying the goods specified in the application to ascertain the income, profit, or loss of such subsequent taxable year for the purpose of a report or statement covering such taxable year (A) to shareholders, partners, or other proprietors, or beneficiaries, or (B) for credit purposes; and requires a change to a method different from that prescribed in subsection (b) beginning with such subsequent taxable year or any taxable year thereafter. If paragraph (1) or (2) of this subsection applies, the change to, and the use of, the different method shall be in accordance with such regulations as the Secretary may prescribe as necessary in order that the use of such method may clearly reflect income.

Commentary: Section 472 (f) states that government price indexes can be used to value LIFO inventory layers.

(f) Use of government price indexes in pricing inventory

The Secretary shall prescribe regulations permitting the use of suitable published governmental indexes in such manner and circumstances as determined by the Secretary for purposes of the method described in subsection (b).

Commentary: Section 472 (g) states that if a company is to use the LIFO method for tax reporting purposes, all of the companies with which it combines its financial results must also use the LIFO method. The complete text of the IRS rule for the "section 1504" referred to in this section is listed later in Section 13-6 of this chapter.

(g) Conformity rules applied on controlled group basis

(1) In general

Except as otherwise provided in the regulations, all members of the same group of financially related corporations shall be treated as one taxpayer for purposes of subsections (c) and (e)(2).

(2) Group of financially related corporations

For purposes of paragraph (1), the term ''group of financially related corporations'' means –

(A) any affiliated group as defined in section 1504 determined by substituting ''50 percent'' for ''80 percent'' each place it appears in section 1504(a) and without regard to section 1504(b), and

(B) any other group of corporations which consolidate or combine for purposes of financial statements

13-4 Section 473–Qualified Liquidations of LIFO Inventories

Commentary: Section 473 (a) states that liquidated LIFO layers cannot be replaced with newly acquired goods.

(a) General rule

If, for any liquidation year –

(1) there is a qualified liquidation of goods which the taxpayer inventories under the LIFO method, and

(2) the taxpayer elects to have the provisions of this section apply with respect to such liquidation, then the gross income of the taxpayer for such taxable year shall be adjusted as provided in subsection (b).

Commentary: Section 473 (b) states again that liquidated LIFO layers cannot be replaced with newly acquired goods; the cost of the liquidated layers must be reflected in current taxable income.

(b) Adjustment for replacements

If the liquidated goods are replaced (in whole or in part) during any replacement year and such replacement is reflected in the closing inventory for such year, then the gross income for the liquidation year shall be –

(1) decreased by an amount equal to the excess of –

(A) the aggregate replacement cost of the liquidated goods so replaced during such year, over

(B) the aggregate cost of such goods reflected in the opening inventory of the liquidation year, or

(2) increased by an amount equal to the excess of –

(A) the aggregate cost reflected in such opening inventory of the liquidated goods so replaced during such year, over

(B) such aggregate replacement cost.

Commentary: Section 473 (c) states that a LIFO inventory layer can be liquidated and then reinstated if it is caused by a Department of Energy request or is the result of a specific type of foreign trade interruption. This section is referenced again in section 473(e)(2).

(c) Qualified liquidation defined

For purposes of this section –

(1) In general

The term ''qualified liquidation'' means –

(A) a decrease in the closing inventory of the liquidation year from the opening inventory of such year, but only if

(B) the taxpayer establishes to the satisfaction of the Secretary that such decrease is directly and primarily attributable to a qualified inventory interruption.

(2) Qualified inventory interruption defined

(A) In general the term ''qualified inventory interruption'' means a regulation, request, or interruption described in subparagraph (B) but only to the extent provided in the notice published pursuant to subparagraph (B).

(B) Determination by Secretary

Whenever the Secretary, after consultation with the appropriate Federal officers, determines –

(i) that –

(I) any Department of Energy regulation or request with respect to energy supplies, or

(II) any embargo, international boycott, or other major foreign trade interruption, has made difficult or impossible the replacement during the liquidation year of any class of goods for any class of taxpayers, and

(ii) that the application of this section to that class of goods and taxpayers is necessary to carry out the purposes of this section, he shall publish a notice of such determinations in the Federal Register, together with the period to be affected by such notice.

Commentary: Section 473 (d) defines the terms "liquidation year," "replacement year," "replacement period," "LIFO method," and "election."

(d) Other definitions and special rules

For purposes of this section –

(1) Liquidation year

The term ''liquidation year'' means the taxable year in which occurs the qualified liquidation to which this section applies.

(2) Replacement year

The term "replacement year" means any taxable year in the replacement period; except that such term shall not include any taxable year after the taxable year in which replacement of the liquidated goods is completed.

(3) Replacement period

The term "replacement period" means the shorter of –

(A) the period of the 3 taxable years following the liquidation year, or

(B) the period specified by the Secretary in a notice published in the Federal Register with respect to that qualified inventory interruption. Any period specified by the Secretary under subparagraph (B) may be modified by the Secretary in a subsequent notice published in the Federal Register.

(4) LIFO method

The term "LIFO method" means the method of inventorying goods described in section 472.

(5) Election

(A) In general

An election under subsection (a) shall be made subject to such conditions, and in such manner and form and at such time, as the Secretary may prescribe by regulation.

(B) Irrevocable election

An election under this section shall be irrevocable and shall be binding for the liquidation year and for all determinations for prior and subsequent taxable years insofar as such determinations are affected by the adjustments under this section.

Commentary: Section 473 (e) defines inventory acquired to replace earlier inventory layers.

(e) Replacement; inventory basis

For purposes of this chapter –

(1) Replacements

If the closing inventory of the taxpayer for any replacement year reflects an increase over the opening inventory of such goods for such year, the goods reflecting such increase shall be considered, in the order of their acquisition, as having been acquired in replacement of the goods most recently liquidated (whether or not in a qualified liquidation) and not previously replaced.

(2) Amount at which replacement goods taken into account

In the case of any qualified liquidation, any goods considered under paragraph (1) as having been acquired in replacement of the goods liquidated in such liquidation shall be taken into purchases and included in the closing inventory of the taxpayer for the replacement year at the inventory cost basis of the goods replaced.

Commentary: Section 473 (f) describes the periods within which tax credits or liabilities and related interest charges can be assessed as a result of adjustments to inventory layers.

(f) Special rules for application of adjustments

    (1) Period of limitations

        If –

        (A) an adjustment is required under this section for any taxable year by reason of the replacement of liquidated goods during any replacement year, and

        (B) the assessment of a deficiency, or the allowance of a credit or refund of an overpayment of tax attributable to such adjustment, for any taxable year, is otherwise prevented by the operation of any law or rule of law (other than section 7122, relating to compromises), then such deficiency may be assessed, or credit or refund allowed, within the period prescribed for assessing a deficiency or allowing a credit or refund for the replacement year if a notice for deficiency is mailed, or claim for refund is filed, within such period.

    (2) Interest

        Solely for purposes of determining interest on any overpayment or underpayment attributable to an adjustment made under this section, such overpayment or underpayment shall be treated as an overpayment or underpayment (as the case may be) for the replacement year.

13-5 Section 474–Simplified Dollar-Value LIFO Method for Certain Small Businesses

Commentary: Section 474 (a) allows a simplified LIFO valuation for small businesses.

(a) General rule

    An eligible small business may elect to use the simplified dollar-value method of pricing inventories for purposes of the LIFO method.

    Commentary: Section 474 (b) describes the simplified dollar-value method, including the use of inventory pools and cost adjustments based on the Producer Price Index or Consumer Price Index.

(b) Simplified dollar-value method of pricing inventories

    For purposes of this section –

    (1) In general

        The simplified dollar-value method of pricing inventories is a dollar-value method of pricing inventories under which –

        (A) the taxpayer maintains a separate inventory pool for items in each major category in the applicable Government price index, and

(B) the adjustment for each such separate pool is based on the change from the preceding taxable year in the component of such index for the major category.

(2) Applicable Government price index

The term "applicable Government price index" means –

(A) except as provided in subparagraph (B), the Producer Price Index published by the Bureau of Labor Statistics, or

(B) in the case of a retailer using the retail method, the Consumer Price Index published by the Bureau of Labor Statistics.

(3) Major category

The term "major category" means –

(A) in the case of the Producer Price Index, any of the 2-digit standard industrial classifications in the Producer Prices Data Report, or

(B) in the case of the Consumer Price Index, any of the general expenditure categories in the Consumer Price Index Detailed Report.

Commentary: Section 474 (c) defines what types of businesses are eligible to use the simplified dollar-value LIFO method. The reference to section 448(c)(3) covers the following points:

- If the business has not yet been in operation for three years, then the regulation shall be applied for the period of its existence.

- If any of the three preceding taxable years include a short year, that year shall be annualized.

- Gross receipts shall be reduced by any returns and allowances.

(c) Eligible small business

For purposes of this section, a taxpayer is an eligible small business for any taxable year if the average annual gross receipts of the taxpayer for the 3 preceding taxable years do not exceed $5,000,000. For purposes of the preceding sentence, rules similar to the rules of section 448(c)(3) shall apply.

Commentary: Section 474 (d) covers several special rules related to LIFO, such as the applicability of controlled groups, the ability to use LIFO, and how to transition to its use.

(d) Special rules

For purposes of this section –

(1) Controlled groups

(A) In general

In the case of a taxpayer which is a member of a controlled group, all persons which are component members of such group shall be treated as one taxpayer for purposes of determining the gross receipts of the taxpayer.

(B) Controlled group defined

For purposes of subparagraph (A), persons shall be treated as being component members of a controlled group if such persons would be treated as a single employer under section 52.

(2) Election

(A) In general

The election under this section may be made without the consent of the Secretary.

(B) Period to which election applies

The election under this section shall apply –

(i) to the taxable year for which it is made, and

(ii) to all subsequent taxable years for which the taxpayer is an eligible small business, unless the taxpayer secures the consent of the Secretary to the revocation of such election.

(3) LIFO method

The term ''LIFO method'' means the method provided by section 472(b).

(4) Transitional rules

(A) In general

In the case of a year of change under this section –

(i) the inventory pools shall –

(I) in the case of the 1st taxable year to which such an election applies, be established in accordance with the major categories in the applicable Government price index, or

(II) in the case of the 1st taxable year after such election ceases to apply, be established in the manner provided by regulations under section 472;

(ii) the aggregate dollar amount of the taxpayer's inventory as of the beginning of the year of change shall be the same as the aggregate dollar value as of the close of the taxable year preceding the year of change, and

(iii) the year of change shall be treated as a new base year in accordance with procedures provided by regulations under section 472.

(B) Year of change

For purposes of this paragraph, the year of change under this section is –

(i) the 1st taxable year to which an election under this section applies, or

(ii) in the case of a cessation of such an election, the 1st taxable year after such election ceases to apply.

13-6   Section 1504 (a)–Affiliated Group Definition

Commentary: This section contains the complete IRS text referring to an affiliated group, as referenced earlier in Section 472 (g). For the purposes of Section 472 (g), replace all references to 80% in the voting and value tests noted in Section 1504 (a)(2) with 50%.

(a)   Affiliated group defined

For purposes of this subtitle –

(1)   In general

The term ''affiliated group'' means –

(A)   1 or more chains of includible corporations connected through stock ownership with a common parent corporation which is an includible corporation, but only if –

(B)

(i)   the common parent owns directly stock meeting the requirements of paragraph (2) in at least one of the other includible corporations, and

(ii)   stock meeting the requirements of paragraph (2) in each of the includible corporations (except the common parent) is owned directly by one or more of the other includible corporations.

(2)   80-percent voting and value test

The ownership of stock of any corporation meets the requirements of this paragraph if it –

(A)   possesses at least 80 percent of the total voting power of the stock of such corporation, and

(B)   has a value equal to at least 80 percent of the total value of the stock of such corporation.

(3)   5 years must elapse before reconsolidation

(A)   In general

If –

(i)   a corporation is included (or required to be included) in a consolidated return filed by an affiliated group for a taxable year which includes any period after December 31, 1984, and

(ii)   such corporation ceases to be a member of such group in a taxable year beginning after December 31, 1984, with respect to periods after such cessation, such corporation (and any successor of such corporation) may not be included in any consolidated return filed by the affiliated group (or by another affiliated group with the same common parent or a successor of such common parent) before the 61st month beginning after its first taxable year in which it ceased to be a member of such affiliated group.

(B) Secretary may waive application of subparagraph (A)

The Secretary may waive the application of subparagraph (A) to any corporation for any period subject to such conditions as the Secretary may prescribe.

(4) Stock not to include certain preferred stock

For purposes of this subsection, the term "stock" does not include any stock which –

(A) is not entitled to vote,

(B) is limited and preferred as to dividends and does not participate in corporate growth to any significant extent,

(C) has redemption and liquidation rights which do not exceed the issue price of such stock (except for a reasonable redemption or liquidation premium), and

(D) is not convertible into another class of stock.

(5) Regulations

The Secretary shall prescribe such regulations as may be necessary or appropriate to carry out the purposes of this subsection, including (but not limited to) regulations –

(A) which treat warrants, obligations convertible into stock, and other similar interests as stock, and stock as not stock,

(B) which treat options to acquire or sell stock as having been exercised,

(C) which provide that the requirements of paragraph (2)(B) shall be treated as met if the affiliated group, in reliance on a good faith determination of value, treated such requirements as met,

(D) which disregard an inadvertent ceasing to meet the requirements of paragraph (2)(B) by reason of changes in relative values of different classes of stock,

(E) which provide that transfers of stock within the group shall not be taken into account in determining whether a corporation ceases to be a member of an affiliated group, and

(F) which disregard changes in voting power to the extent such changes are disproportionate to related changes in value.

14

Counting Inventory

14-1 Introduction

An accountant can have the finest costing system in the world and still waste time recording inventory transactions if the record accuracy level of those transactions is poor. Because the accounting department is often held responsible if recorded inventory costs are wrong, one should have a clear idea of how to set up an inventory tracking system, conduct physical inventory counts, and cycle count inventory on an ongoing basis in order to have greater confidence in the inventory record accuracy. Although the accountant may not have control over these systems, it is helpful to know how they should be run. It is also increasingly common for controllers to be given management-level control over the warehouse solely because they will then have central and undisputed responsibility for inventory record accuracy.

This chapter notes several counting policies that management should approve and support, as well as procedures for setting up inventory tracking systems, conducting physical inventory counts, ensuring a proper inventory cutoff, reconciling inventory variances, running successful cycle counting programs, and reducing the need for inventory tracking.

14-2 Inventory Counting Policies

Creating and running inventory tracking systems can require a considerable upfront investment of time and funds to which company management may be unwilling to commit. It also takes time away from other materials management chores, and so may not be followed with the consistency needed to ensure success. A good way to avoid these problems is to obtain senior management support through their approval of the following policies:

- *A complete physical inventory count shall be conducted at the end of each reporting period.* This policy ensures that an accurate record of the inventory is used as the basis for a cost of goods sold calculation.
- *The materials manager is responsible for inventory accuracy.* This policy centralizes control over inventory accuracy, thereby increasing the odds of it being kept at a high level.

■ *Cycle counters shall continually review inventory accuracy and identify related problems.* This policy is intended for perpetual inventory systems and results in a much higher level of inventory accuracy and attention to the underlying problems that cause inventory errors.

14-3 Setting up an Inventory Tracking System[1]

A physical inventory count can be eliminated if accurate perpetual inventory records are available. Many steps are required to implement such a system, requiring considerable effort. The accountant should evaluate a company's resources before embarking on this process to ensure that they are sufficient to set up and maintain this system. This section contains a sequential listing of the steps that must be completed before an accurate system is achieved. This is a difficult implementation to shortcut, because missing any of the following steps will affect the accuracy of the completed system. If a company skips a few steps, it will likely not achieve the requisite high levels of accuracy that it wants and end up having to backtrack and complete those steps at a later date. Consequently, a company should sequentially complete all of the following steps to implement a successful inventory tracking system:

1. *Select and install inventory tracking software.* The primary requirements for this software are as follows:
   - ■ *Track transactions.* The software should list the frequency of product usage, which allows the materials manager to determine what inventory quantities should be changed and which items are obsolete.
   - ■ *Update records immediately.* The inventory data must always be up-to-date, because production planners must know what is in stock, while cycle counters require access to accurate data. Batch updating of the system is not acceptable.
   - ■ *Report inventory records by location.* Cycle counters need inventory records that are sorted by location in order to more efficiently locate and count the inventory.
2. *Test inventory tracking software.* Create a set of typical records in the new software, and perform a series of transactions to ensure that the software functions properly. In addition, create a large number of records and perform the transactions again, to see if the response time of the system drops significantly. If the software appears to function properly, continue to the next step. Otherwise, fix the problems with the software supplier's assistance or acquire a different software package.
3. *Revise the rack layout.* It is much easier to move racks before installing a perpetual inventory system, because no inventory locations must be changed in the computer system. Create aisles that are wide enough for forklift operation

---

[1]Adapted with permission from pp. 159–161 of Bragg, *Accounting Reference Desktop*, John Wiley & Sons, 2002.

if this is needed for larger storage items, and cluster small parts racks together for easier parts picking. The services of a consultant are useful for arriving at the optimum warehouse configuration.

4. *Create rack locations.* A typical rack location is, for example, A-01-B-01. This means that this location code is found in Aisle A, Rack 1. Within Rack 1, it is located on Level B (numbered from the bottom to the top). Within Level B, it is located in Partition 1. Many companies skip the use of partitions, on the grounds that an aisle-rack-level numbering system will get a stock picker to within a few feet of an inventory item.

   As one progresses down an aisle, the rack numbers should progress in ascending sequence, with the odd rack numbers on the left and the even numbers on the right. Thus, the first rack on the left side of aisle D is D-01, the first rack on the right is D-02, the second rack on the left is D-03, and so on. This layout allows a stock picker to move down the center of the aisle, efficiently pulling items from stock based on sequential location codes.

5. *Lock the warehouse.* One of the main causes of record inaccuracy is removal of items from the warehouse by outside staff. To stop this removal, all entrances to the warehouse must be locked. Only warehouse personnel should be allowed access to it. All other personnel entering the warehouse should be accompanied by a member of the warehouse staff to prevent the removal of inventory.

6. *Consolidate parts.* To reduce the labor of counting the same item in multiple locations, group common parts into one place. This is not a one-shot process, because it is difficult to combine parts when there are thousands of them scattered throughout the warehouse. Expect to repeat this step at intervals, especially when entering location codes in the computer, when it tells you that the part has already been entered for a different location!

7. *Assign part numbers.* Have several experienced personnel verify all part numbers. A mislabeled part is as useless as a missing part, because the computer database will not show that it exists. Mislabeled parts also affect the inventory cost; for example, a mislabeled engine is more expensive than the item represented by its incorrect part number, which may identify it as, for example, a spark plug.

8. *Verify units of measure.* Have several experienced people verify all units of measure. Unless the software allows multiple units of measure to be used, the entire organization must adhere to one unit of measure for each item. For example, the warehouse may desire tape to be counted in rolls, but the engineering department would rather create bills of material with tape measured in inches instead of fractions of rolls. If someone goes into the inventory database to change the unit of measure to suit his or her needs, this will also alter the extended cost of the inventory; for example, when 10 rolls of tape with an extended cost of $10 is altered so that it becomes 10 inches of tape, the cost will drop to a few pennies, even though there are still 10 rolls on the shelf. Consequently, not only must the units of measure be accurate, but the file that stores this information must also be kept off limits.

9. *Pack the parts.* Pack parts into containers, seal the containers, and label them with the part number, unit of measure, and total quantity stored inside. Leave a few parts free for ready use. Only open containers when additional stock is needed. This method allows cycle counters to rapidly verify inventory balances.

10. *Count items.* Count items when there is no significant activity in the warehouse, such as during a weekend. Elaborate cross-checking of the counts, as would be done during a year-end physical inventory count, is not necessary. It is more important to have the perpetual inventory system operational before the warehouse activity increases again; any errors in the data will be quickly detected during cycle counts and flushed out of the database. The initial counts must include a review of the part number, location, and quantity.

11. *Train the warehouse staff.* The warehouse staff should receive software training immediately before using the system, so they do not forget how to operate the software. Enter a set of test records into the software, and have the staff simulate all common inventory transactions, such as receipts, picks, and cycle count adjustments.

12. *Enter data into the computer.* Have an experienced data entry person input the location, part number, and quantity into the computer. Once the data has been input, another person should cross-check the entered data against the original data for errors.

13. *Quick-check the data.* Scan the data for errors. If all part numbers have the same number of digits, then look for items that are too long or short. Review location codes to see if inventory is stored in nonexistent racks. Look for units of measure that do not match the part being described. For example, is it logical to have a pint of steel in stock? Also, if item costs are available, print a list of extended costs. Excessive costs typically point to incorrect units of measure. For example, a cost of $1 per box of nails will become $500 in the inventory report if nails are incorrectly listed as individual units. All of these steps help warehouse personnel spot the most obvious inventory errors.

14. *Initiate cycle counts.* This topic is covered in considerable detail in the "Cycle Counting" section of this chapter. In brief, print out a portion of the inventory list, sorted by location. Using this report, have the warehouse staff count blocks of the inventory on a continuous basis. They should look for accurate part numbers, units of measure, locations, and quantities. The counts should concentrate on high-value or high-use items, although the entire stock should be reviewed regularly. The most important part of this step is to examine why mistakes occur. If a cycle counter finds an error, its cause must be investigated and then corrected, so that the mistake will not occur again. It is also useful to assign specific aisles to cycle counters, which tends to make them more familiar with their assigned inventory and the problems causing specific transactional errors.

15. *Initiate inventory audits.* The inventory should be audited frequently, perhaps as much as once a week. This allows the accountant to track changes in the inventory accuracy level and initiate changes if the accuracy drops below acceptable levels. In addition, frequent audits are an indirect means of telling the staff that inventory accuracy is important and must be maintained. The minimum ac-

ceptable accuracy level is 95%, with an error being a mistaken part number, unit of measure, quantity, or location. This accuracy level is needed to ensure accurate inventory costing, as well as to assist the materials department in planning future inventory purchases. In addition, establish a tolerance level when calculating the inventory accuracy. For example, if the computer record of a box of screws yields a quantity of 100 and the actual count results in 105 screws, then the record is accurate if the tolerance is at least 5% but inaccurate if the tolerance is reduced to 1%. The maximum allowable tolerance should be no higher than 5%, with tighter tolerances being used for high-value or high-use items.

16. *Post results.* Inventory accuracy is a team project, and the warehouse staff will feel more involved if the audit results are posted against the results of previous audits. Accuracy percentages should be broken out for the counting area assigned to each cycle counter, so that everyone can see who is doing the best job of reviewing and correcting inventory counts.

17. *Reward the staff.* Accurate inventories save a company thousands of dollars in many ways. This makes it cost-effective to encourage the staff to maintain and improve the accuracy level with periodic bonuses that are based on the attainment of higher levels of accuracy with tighter tolerances. Using rewards results in a significant improvement in inventory record accuracy.

The long list of requirements to fulfill before achieving an accurate perpetual inventory system makes it clear that this is not a project that yields immediate results. Unless the inventory is small or the conversion project is heavily staffed, it is likely that a company faces many months of work before it arrives at the nirvana of an extremely accurate inventory. Consequently, one should set expectations with management that project completion is a considerable ways down the road and that only by making a major investment of time and resources will it be completed.

Despite the major effort needed to implement this system, it is still a most worthwhile project. Once completed, the accounting staff can incorporate accurate inventory records into its inventory valuations, external auditors can review the system at any time, because there is no need to conduct a year-end physical inventory count, and the material planning staff can utilize the inventory database with confidence.

14-4 Taking the Physical Inventory[2]

Most companies still use a physical inventory system that only reconciles inventory to actual counts at the end of the fiscal year. The controllers of these companies need a reliable approach for organizing the inventory in preparation for a count, creating and managing counting teams, and properly using counting forms and inventory release teams to ensure that counts have been completed as accurately as possible. This section provides that information.

---

[2]Adapted with permission from pp. 56–57 of Bragg, *GAAP Implementation Guide*, John Wiley & Sons, 2004.

The following steps reveal how to conduct all phases of a physical inventory count and are grouped into activities that must be completed within specific time intervals. The specific steps follow:

One Week Before the Count

1. Appoint a team responsible for the physical count. This should include count teams, count supervisor, tag coordinator, and data entry clerks.

2. Contact the printing company and order a sufficient number of sequentially numbered count tags. The first tag number should always be 1000. The tags should include fields for the part number, description, quantity count, location, and the counter's signature. An example is shown in Exhibit 14-1; this is a two-part tag, with the lower section being collected for summarization. Space is provided on the reverse side for noting movements, so that slow-moving items can be counted in advance of the regular count.

3. Review the inventory and mark all items lacking a part number with a brightly colored piece of paper. Inform the warehouse manager that these items must be marked with a proper part number immediately.

4. Clearly mark the quantity on all sealed packages. Count all partial packages, seal them, and mark the quantity on the tape. This is a major labor saver during the counting process, although it requires a great deal of preparation.

Exhibit 14-1 *Inventory Tag*

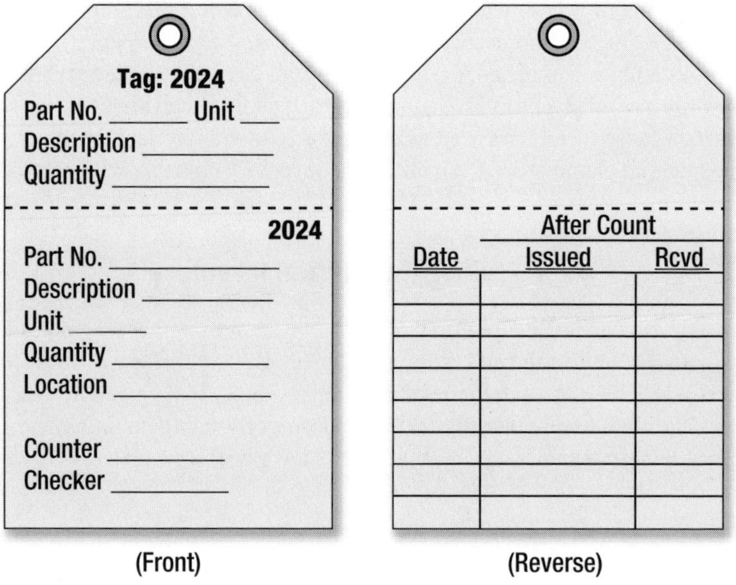

(Front)   (Reverse)

5. Consolidate parts stored in multiple locations, which eases the counting task. This requires the services of the most experienced warehouse staff, who have the best knowledge of part locations.

6. Prepare "Do Not Inventory" tags and use them to mark all items that should not be included in the physical inventory count.

7. Issue a list of count team members, with a notice regarding where and when they should appear for the inventory count.

8. Prepare counting instructions for the counting teams. The procedure will vary by company, but usually contains these basic steps:

   ▪ A team of two people is assigned a block of the warehouse for counting, with one person counting and the other recording the count information on an inventory tag.

   ▪ The person writing on the tag attaches one part of the tag to each lot that was counted and keeps the other copy.

   ▪ When the team completes its count of the assigned area, it sorts the tags into numerical order (they are numbered serially) and brings them to a data entry station, where the tags are reviewed for errors, entered into the computer system, and compared to database records for variances.

   ▪ The team then goes back to recount any variance items.

   ▪ Finally, a supervisor searches the count area for any items that may not have been counted, after which he signs off on the count area, and the counting team is released from duty.

One Day Before the Count

1. Remind all participants that they are expected to be counting the next day. All counters should be thoroughly familiar with the parts stored in the warehouse. The counts will be far more accurate if an experienced person correctly identifies the parts being counted. This is a common mistake that many companies make, by enrolling people from unrelated areas such as sales and accounting who have no idea of what a part looks like; these people make far more counting and part identification mistakes than experienced counters.

2. Notify the warehouse manager that all items received during the two days of physical counts must be segregated and marked with "Do Not Inventory" tags.

3. Notify the manager that no shipments are allowed for the duration of the physical count.

4. Notify the warehouse manager that all shipments for which the paperwork has not been sent to accounting by that evening will be included in the inventory count on the following day.

5. Notify the warehouse manager that all shipping and receiving documentation from the day before the count must be forwarded to the accounting department that day, for immediate data entry. Likewise, any pick information must be forwarded at the same time.

6. Notify all outside storage locations to fax in their inventory counts.

Morning of the Count

1. Enter all transactions from the previous day.

2. Assemble the count teams. Issue counting instructions to them, including a list of items not to count, such as tools, capital equipment, containers, supplies, consignment inventory, and anything marked with a "Do Not Inventory" tag. Also issue to the teams blocks of tags, for which they must sign a receipt. Give each team a map of the warehouse with a section highlighted on it that they are responsible for counting. Those teams with forklift experience will be assigned to count the top racks, while those without this experience will be assigned the lower racks. It may be useful to conduct a practice count of a small area to ensure that all count teams are familiar with the procedures to be used.

3. Call all outside storage warehouses and ask them to fax in their counts of company-owned inventory.

4. The count supervisor assigns additional count areas to those teams that finish counting their areas first.

5. A review team should check a few counts in each area, especially for expensive items, to see if there are obvious errors, such as incorrect part numbers, item numbers, or units of measure. This is also a good time to check on possibly fraudulent activity involving false counts, which can take several forms. One is empty or deliberately mislabeled boxes. Another is diluted liquid inventory (difficult to spot), as well as the presence of customer-owned inventory in counts. A classic problem is building squares of legitimately filled boxes to conceal an empty space in the middle that is counted as full. These problems require great diligence by the review team to spot.

6. The tag coordinator assigns blocks of tags to those count teams that run out of tags, tracks the receipt of tags, and follows up on missing tags. All tags should be accounted for by the end of the day. To do this, a group of reviewers should sort the cards into numerical sequence to ensure that there are no missing cards. The review should also include a check for missing part numbers, units of measure, or quantities. If any of these problems are present, the errors should be noted and the cards returned to the count teams for fixing.

7. Once the count supervisor is satisfied that everything has been counted in each inventory area and that variances have been accounted for, the supervisory group can sign off on the results of each counting area and send home the counting teams. Because the teams may finish their counts at widely scattered intervals, it is customary to complete the data entry work on the teams that are finished earliest, so those teams can resolve any problems and go home. This reduces a company's hourly payroll cost devoted to the inventory counting task.

8. The data entry person enters the information on the tags into a spreadsheet or computer database and then summarizes the quantities for each item and pencils the totals into the cycle count report that was run earlier in the day.

9. Review the test count with an auditor, if necessary. Give the auditor a complete printout of all tags, as well as the cycle counting spreadsheet, showing all variances.

The following job descriptions apply to the inventory counting procedure:

- *Count supervisor.* Supervises the count, which includes assigning count teams to specific areas and ensuring that all areas have been counted and tagged. This person also waits until all count tags have been compared to the quantities listed in the computer and then checks the counts on any items that appear to be incorrect. The count supervisor should also be available to provide advice to counting teams throughout the counting period on such topics as the unit of measure to use, whether to count something, and if an item is actually owned by the company and therefore to be included in the count.

- *Tag coordinator.* Tracks the blocks of count tags that have been issued and accounts for all tags that have been returned. When distributing tags, marks down the beginning and ending numbers of each block of tags on a tracking sheet, and obtains the signature of the person who receives the tags. When the tags are returned, puts them in numerical order and verifies that all tags are accounted for. Once the verification is complete, checks off the tags on the tracking sheet as having been received. Once returned tags have been properly accounted for, forwards them to the extension calculation clerk.

- *Extension calculation clerk.* Summarizes the amounts on the tags (if there are multiple quantities listed) to arrive at a total quantity count on each tag. This person also compares the part numbers and descriptions on each tag to see if there are any potential identification problems. This person forwards all completed tags to the data entry person.

- *Data entry person.* Enters the information on all count tags into the computer spreadsheet. When doing so, enters all of the information on each tag into a spreadsheet. Once a group of tags has been entered, stamps them as having been entered, clips them together, and stores them separately. Once all tags are entered into the spreadsheet, sorts the data by part number. Prints out the spreadsheet and summarizes the quantities by part number. Transfers the total quantities by part number to the cycle count report. If there are any significant variances between the counted and cycle count quantities, brings them to the attention of the count supervisor for review.

14-5 Ensuring a Proper Cutoff for the Physical Inventory Count[3]

The physical inventory counting process is highly dependent on a stationary inventory. This means that there can be no movement of inventory into or out of the warehouse area during the counting process, nor can there be a movement of any

---

[3]Adapted with permission from p. 1098 of Roehl-Anderson and Bragg, *Controllership 7E,* John Wiley & Sons, 2004.

related paperwork. If this basic rule is not followed, one will have great difficulty in determining the true value of the period-end inventory, because the quantities were in flux during the count. This section contains sample procedures that are applicable in most situations for ensuring a proper period-end cutoff of all inventory-related transfers. The following procedures cover receiving, central stores, and the finished goods storage area:

1. Receiving and receiving inspection
   - No paperwork or parts will be forwarded to the central stores area later than 11:00 a.m., October 26. This will allow paperwork to be processed and stock put away.
   - Beginning October 15, all receivers processed by receiving inspections must be stamped "Before Inventory."

2. Central stores
   - *Receipts.* All paperwork on parts received from receiving inspection must be transferred to data processing before 4:30 p.m., Friday, October 26.
   - *Issues.* The paperwork on all issues to open orders and jobs in process must be completed and sent to data processing before 4:30 p.m., Friday, October 26. On issues for sales orders, the issue documents and parts must be in the staging area or shipping area before 3:30 p.m., Friday, October 26.

3. Finished goods area
   - *Staging area.* If parts are not shipped before 3:30 p.m., Friday, October 26, they will be retained as part of the storeroom inventory.
   - *Receipts.* Receipts into the finished goods area must be received and the paperwork sent to data processing before 4:30 p.m., Friday, October 26. The warehouse manager must ensure that all finished units are properly stored and that all related paperwork is sent to data processing before the 11:00 a.m. cutoff.
   - *Issues.* On issues for sales orders, the issue card and parts must be in the staging or shipping areas before 11:00 a.m., Friday, October 26. For issues to orders and job numbers, all paperwork on issues to work-in-process must be in data processing before 4:30 p.m., Friday, October 26.

The preceding procedures are intended for those companies using traditional paper-based transactions that are centrally recorded in the inventory database. If a more advanced system is in place where the materials management staff enters transactions directly into the inventory database—either through local terminals in smaller batches or individually with radio-frequency scanners—then one can enter transactions until just a few moments before the beginning of the physical inventory count. Thus, advanced data entry systems allow a company to minimize the time period when inventory cannot be moved during a physical inventory count.

14-6   Reconciling Inventory Variances[4]

When a company uses a perpetual inventory system or a periodic physical count, it will find some variances between the quantity found in stock and the amount listed in the inventory database. These variances will occur in the best of companies and are caused by a myriad of problems, the most frequent of which is parts being physically added to or removed from the inventory without a corresponding adjustment to the underlying records. When these variances occur, one should follow the series of reconciliation steps noted in this section.

Each of the following steps is a filter that blocks out further action at the next step, thereby continually reducing the amount of items to review as one progresses to the next reconciliation step. The steps are as follows:

1. *Accept variances with small dollar values.* The bulk of all inaccuracies will be for large quantities of small and inexpensive items, such as fitting and fasteners. These are not worth the trouble of a further review, especially when there is a minimal change in the inventory cost, no matter what the outcome of a recount may be.

2. *Recount items with large dollar variances.* The obvious next step is to recheck the count to see if there was a counting error. If this does not resolve the problem, it is sometimes useful to recount the items in adjoining inventory locations in case there is a problem with a part having been incorrectly stored or counted in an adjacent space. The recount can also be extended to similar products to determine whether an item was mistaken for another part that looks the same.

3. *Check the identification.* Checking the part number that the counter marked down against the part number in the database for that location sometimes reveals the problem. This is because the part number on the physical part is missing, is mislabeled, or the code is smudged enough to alter its meaning.

4. *Check the ownership.* A company may have expensive parts in stock that are actually there on consignment and should not be valued. If these items were counted, there will be no corresponding record in the inventory database. One can then ignore the count, because the company does not own the item.

5. *Check receiving records.* If everyone thinks a part count is low, the answer may simply be that it was never received. Purchasing records may show that a part was due for receipt, but the supplier never sent it. If so, one can go back through earlier listings of the inventory to see when a part was listed as having been received and then compare the first date on which it appeared in the inventory database to the receiving records in that time period to see if there was a corresponding receipt.

---

[4]Adapted with permission from pp. 1099–1100 of Roehl-Anderson and Bragg, *Controllership 7E*, John Wiley & Sons, 2004.

6. *Review job cost records.* It is common for a part to be missing because it was used on product work but was never logged out. For this problem, the first place to look is the job cost records for any jobs that were open during the period when a part was recorded as missing. If the job cost records indicate an unusually high profit, it is likely that a part was not charged to it.

7. *Accept the variance.* When all else fails, one must conclude that there was either an earlier counting problem that created an initial inaccuracy in the inventory database or that a part is missing because of shrinkage. At this point, it is necessary to record the variance. However, one should keep track of part numbers for which there are unexplained variances on a continuing basis, to see if a pattern emerges that explains the problem.

The preceding investigation process is designed to reduce the inventory reconciliation work to a minimum while still ensuring an accurate inventory valuation. The first few steps either accept inventory counts or call for a quick review, which resolves the bulk of the variance analysis work. Subsequent steps narrow down the range of problems, so that by the time one is reduced to checking on the purchasing and job cost records for a missing part, there are few items for which this much work must be done. Thus, this system results in accurate inventory records while spending the smallest amount of time on inventory variance reconciliation.

14-7 Cycle Counting

There are two primary reasons for using cycle counting. The main one is to locate the underlying problems causing inventory record inaccuracy, while the second is to provide updated inventory balance information. The first reason typically results in a swarm of transactional errors that have to be fixed before the inventory tracking system will reliably produce accurate records. The second reason is useful for maintaining a sufficiently high level of record accuracy to run material requirements planning systems.

By finding and fixing problems causing inventory record errors, record accuracy will gradually improve over time, thereby solving the second reason for cycle counting. However, it is difficult to locate underlying problems, even if the computer system helpfully details the complete sequence of historical transactions and the identification of every person making an entry. The trouble is that there are usually so many transactions occurring that the person who originally caused the problem may have no idea why he or she made an entry, especially if a few days have passed and many other transactions have arisen in the interim. Consequently, only expect to locate the causes of a small percentage of errors, perhaps in the range of 10% to 20%.

Even if only a small percentage of the errors are determined, be sure to fix them right away. The reason is that fixing one transactional problem will impact not only the inventory item whose record was incorrect but also any other inventory items that are subject to the same type of transaction. Thus, correcting one problem could have a multiplier effect that prevents many identical transactional errors from occurring. Over time, as these problems are fixed, the cycle counters can commit more time to the resolution of a smaller number of problem areas, so the tough nuts can eventually be cracked and resolved.

One of the main reasons for record inaccuracy is the lack of responsibility for it. There are many positions in a company that can have a significant impact on record accuracy, such as engineers who create the bill of materials, the receiving staff, everyone in the warehouse, and the production staff who uses the parts. For example, a bill of material error will cause incorrect quantities or parts to be picked, while the receiving staff can incorrectly log a received quantity into the computer system. Thus, a cycle counter may track a record error to a stock picker, who shifts the blame to the engineering staff who created the bill. The best solution is for senior management to hold the entire group responsible for record accuracy, either with the carrot approach of offering a bonus for fixing the problem or with the stick approach of replacing those people who are not helping to solve the problem.

As the cycle counting team finds and fixes transactional problems, it is also necessary to formally document the problem and its resolution. By doing so, the company gradually compiles a valuable controls document that is exceedingly useful for revising inventory systems, both in terms of further streamlining systems and also to keep the company from making a systemic change for which there is a history of transaction errors.

The following steps show a simplified approach to ensure that a perpetual inventory database is properly cycle counted:

1. Print a portion of the inventory report, sorted by location. Block out a portion of the physical inventory locations shown on the report for cycle counting purposes. An example is shown in Exhibit 14-2.
2. Go to the first physical inventory location to be cycle counted and compare the quantity, location, and part number of each inventory item to what is described for that location in the inventory report. Mark on the report any discrepancies between the on-hand quantity, location, and description for each item.
3. Also use the reverse process to ensure that the same information listed for all items on the report match the items physically appearing in the warehouse location. Note any discrepancies on the report.
4. Verify that the noted discrepancies are not caused by recent inventory transactions that have not yet been logged into the computer system.
5. Correct the inventory database for all remaining errors noted.

Exhibit 14-2 *Cycle Counting Report*

Location	Item No.	Description	U/M	Quantity
A-10-C	Q1458	Switch, 120V, 20A	EA	
A-10-C	U1010	Bolt, Zinc, $3 \times \frac{1}{4}$		
A-10-C	M1458	Screw, Stainless Steel, $2 \times \frac{3}{8}$		

6. Calculate the inventory error rate and post it in the warehouse. An example of this report is shown in Exhibit 14-3.

7. Call up a history of inventory transactions for each of the items for which errors were noted, and try to determine the cause of the underlying problem. Investigate each issue and recommend corrective action to the warehouse or materials manager, so the problems do not arise again.

There are several variations on the basic cycle counting system that can be used to make it more efficient. For example, one can split the inventory into ABC categories based on part usage levels, and cycle count the highest-volume "A" category items the most frequently and "C" items the least. This approach targets the goal of improving record accuracy, rather than finding underlying transaction problems, which are more likely to be sprinkled throughout the inventory, regardless of each item's ABC designation. This approach can present problems if the cycle counting team is used to the more efficient approach of counting items within specific contiguous bins, which reduces travel time to a minimum. One can still use the ABC approach and minimize travel time if items are physically stored within the warehouse so that all A, B, and C items are stored in separate areas.

A variation on the ABC counting approach is to target only those items that are scheduled for use in the production system. By doing so, a company has a better chance of avoiding stockout conditions that will interfere with scheduled production. However, this ignores other inventory entirely, and so should be supplemented with scheduled counts of all inventory types.

Cycle counters consume a great deal of time tracking down inventory problems, so it is important from an efficiency perspective to set up error tolerance levels for categories of parts. For example, if one purchases large quantities of low-cost fittings that can be readily replenished within a short time period, it may be entirely acceptable to ignore large counting errors, because there is little impact on the company from either a cost perspective or based on its impact on production processes. Conversely, if an item is extremely expensive, is difficult to obtain, or could cripple the manufacturing process by its absence, the tolerance level may be zero. Generally, a tight tolerance is considered to be plus or minus 2%, whereas a loose toler-

Exhibit 14-3 *Inventory Accuracy Report*

Aisles	Responsible Person	2 Months Ago	Last Month	Week 1	Week 2	Week 3	Week 4
A-B	Fred P.	82%	86%	85%	84%	82%	87%
C-D	Alain Q.	70%	72%	74%	76%	78%	80%
E-F	Davis L.	61%	64%	67%	70%	73%	76%
G-H	Jeff R.	54%	58%	62%	66%	70%	74%
I-J	Alice R.	12%	17%	22%	27%	32%	37%
K-L	George W.	81%	80%	79%	78%	77%	76%
M-N	Robert T.	50%	60%	65%	70%	80%	90%

ance is closer to 5%. However, specific circumstances may mandate tolerances of 0% or well beyond 10%.

Another way to track down inventory errors most efficiently is to direct cycle counters to any item for which the computer system records a negative inventory balance, because there is obviously a correctable problem causing the error. However, some companies try to get away with *only* cycle counting negative or zero inventory balances on the grounds that low on-hand quantities are much easier to count and research; following this approach concentrates counting efforts on a tiny subset of the total inventory and ignores the rest, and so is not recommended.

Cycle counters may only perform counting work for a short period each day. If so, there is no particular need to schedule counting activities into a specific time block each day. Instead, consider scheduling it for slack periods throughout the shift, so it does not conflict with other activities that may be more time sensitive. However, this approach may not work if transactions are input into the computer system in batches; cycle counting should always be done immediately after a batch update, so the computer records will most closely match actual quantities.

Cycle counting work should be considered a privilege to which the warehouse staff aspires—it requires the best knowledge of parts, transaction flows, and probable errors. Thus, to obtain the best results from cycle counting activities, only assign these tasks to senior warehouse staff, consider paying extra for this type of work, and train cycle counters in the greatest depth of all the warehouse staff. Conversely, do not use inexperienced people for cycle counting, and absolutely never use people from outside the department who have no experience with inventory systems.

14-8   Reducing the Need for Inventory Tracking[5]

After reading the previous sections of this chapter, one should get the impression that a great deal of work goes into inventory tracking. This is a large burden on many employees, but it is necessary if a company has a significant inventory investment. However, if the investment were greatly reduced, there would be much less need to take such elaborate steps to ensure accuracy. This section describes the steps to follow to avoid any need for inventory counts.

There are two primary improvement areas if one wants to reduce inventory levels. One is a series of actions designed to reduce the amount of inventory currently in stock, and the other is to choke off the flow of incoming items. Most companies concentrate their attention on reducing what is already in stock, not realizing that what they are removing from inventory (usually at the cost of restocking fees or obsolescence write-offs) is just as rapidly being replaced by new parts coming into the warehouse. Consequently, it is better to work on choking off the incoming flow

---

[5]Adapted with permission from pp. 1101–1103 of Roehl-Anderson and Bragg, *Controllership 7E*, John Wiley & Sons, 2004.

of inventory, which takes a long time to complete, before beginning work on clearing out what is currently in stock. These steps are presented in that order:

1. *Choke off the flow of incoming inventory.* The following steps will reduce the inflow of parts to the warehouse to a trickle by forcing a company to purchase only what it requires for immediate production needs:
   - *Eliminate volume purchases.* The purchasing staff is accustomed to reducing its workload by purchasing parts in bulk, thereby reducing the number of purchase orders it must issue. Although this saves time for the purchasing staff, it entails more work by the warehouse staff to store the extra materials, as well as a larger investment in working capital to fund it. A better alternative is to continue issuing a small number of purchase orders, but only take delivery on incremental portions of each one as needed.
   - *Create accurate bills of material.* The purchasing staff must frequently make guesses about what to order for production. When they are wrong, the items purchased go into inventory, sometimes for a long time. By giving the purchasing staff better information about what to buy, it is possible to reduce or eliminate the number of items that are incorrectly purchased. The best format for this information is a bill of materials, which lists the quantity and part number for every item in a product. This bill of materials must be extremely accurate in order to reduce the inflow of parts to the warehouse, however. If the wrong parts or quantities are listed on the bill, the purchasing staff will mistakenly buy those items.
   - *Create an accurate production schedule.* The purchasing staff must know when to buy parts, as well as how many to purchase. An accurate production schedule that lists the exact quantities and numbers of products to be built is the information the purchasing staff needs to perform this job.
   - *Install a material requirements planning (MRP) system.* Even with bills of material and a purchasing schedule, the purchasing staff needs some way to combine the information into a schedule that tells it when to buy parts and how many to buy. An MRP system does this by using the bill of materials, the production schedule, and the inventory database to calculate the parts needed for production. It even tells the purchasing staff where to buy the parts and the necessary lead times for purchasing them. By using this system, a company avoids all unnecessary purchases and retains parts in the warehouse for only the briefest time periods. This is the capstone of the systems needed to avoid sending large quantities of inventory into the warehouse.
2. *Eliminate existing inventory.* The following steps will significantly reduce the size of any inventory, and in some cases will lead to the elimination of the warehouse area:
   - *Throw out inventory.* A large number of parts in any inventory are useless. They are old, they are no longer used in the company's products, or they have been superseded by new parts. Many of them are too inexpensive to be worth

the effort of returning to suppliers, so it is best to take a write-off and remove them from stock.

- *Return inventory.* A small number of parts are so expensive that they are worth the effort to attempt to return them to suppliers. This can be a protracted process involving many phone calls, so this step applies only to the most expensive parts. Also, there is usually a 15% or more restocking fee, so one should not expect full payment for the inventory. In addition, many suppliers will issue credits for returned inventory, but not cash payments. Nonetheless, this is an effective way to eliminate many of the most expensive items from the warehouse.

- *Use up inventory.* A difficult way to reduce the quantity of inventory is to use it up. This is not easy, because many of the inventory items may be parts that are no longer used and require special interference by management to force the production staff to add them to new products. This may also require extra design work by the engineering staff. Because of all this extra effort, it is generally best to focus on the typically small number of parts in stock that are actually usable. In short, this method tends to eliminate only a small fraction of the inventory in exchange for a large amount of staff effort.

- *Move inventory to the shop floor.* An excellent option is to pull inventory out of the warehouse and position it near the production areas. Once the inventory is moved out of the warehouse, the accounting staff usually charges it off to expense and no longer includes it in the inventory tracking system. This charge-off tends to be a small amount, because mostly fittings and fasteners, and other similar inexpensive items, are moved to the shop floor. This is a small dollar amount, but it can involve a large percentage of the parts in the warehouse, so it has a major favorable impact on the number of items to be cycle counted and audited. Moving the parts to production also avoids the effort and associated transactions needed to constantly move parts in and out of the warehouse, which also means that there are fewer chances to damage parts by moving them. This also makes it easier for the production staff, which no longer has to requisition parts from the warehouse.

The steps noted here to both choke off incoming inventory and reduce existing stocks require a great deal of time and effort, as well as the active cooperation of the materials management and production departments, so expect this project to require a considerable period of time to complete.

15

Inventory Best Practices[1]

15-1 Introduction

Controlling a company's investment in inventory requires a considerable knowledge of the ordering, receiving, storage, picking, production, and shipping processes. This chapter focuses on specific best practices within all of these areas that a controller can use to improve internal inventory-related systems. Please note that one should not use this chapter as a resource for making wholesale changes throughout a company; on the contrary, inventory levels are affected by interlocking systems, so each change must be planned in anticipation of what it will do to other parts of the company, such as machine utilization and customer service levels.

15-2 Inventory Purchasing

Key factors in the purchase of inventory arise well before the production date, extending back into the product design process. There are other key purchasing factors, involving communication levels, the distance to supplier locations, planning issues, and the frequency of deliveries, that all have a major impact on the level of inventory one must maintain within a company. This section addresses all of these issues.

By far the most common new-product design process is to design an entire product using an in-house design team and then ask suppliers to bid on portions of the resulting design. However, suppliers could have advised the design team to use different materials or components that would have resulted in the same performance specifications at a lower total price. Consequently, it is often worthwhile to include suppliers in the design process, which they will be willing to do as long as they are promised some portion of the resulting business.

Suppliers can also tell if some components are difficult to procure and can advise the design team to avoid these items if at all possible. Otherwise, the company's

---

[1]Adapted with permission from Chapter 28 of Bragg, *2004 Controllership Supplement*, John Wiley & Sons, 2004.

ability to manufacture the products at all, or at least within a reasonable price range, will be in doubt. If there are no suppliers available for this kind of advice, the design team should consult with the purchasing department to see if they will have problems obtaining certain items. If some items must be included in a design but are difficult to obtain, the purchasing department can at least be used to purchase supplier capacity in advance, thereby locking down key sources.

It may also be possible to reduce in-house safety stock levels simply by shrinking the delivery lead times assigned to suppliers. Safety stock is essentially designed to cover a company's interim needs while it places an order with a supplier and waits for the order to arrive. In many cases, suppliers have sufficient on-hand stocks of some goods to ship faster than is currently the case, or can work with the company's industrial engineers to find ways to hasten their delivery times. However, this approach does not work well when some final assembly or customization is required before a supplier can ship a product.

Some suppliers have order lead times of many days or weeks. If the company alters an order inside that time frame, the supplier may have a difficult time filling the order in a timely manner. To avoid this problem, consider freezing the short-term production schedule for a sufficient duration to give suppliers adequate notice to make changes outside of their minimum lead times. This can be difficult if suppliers have extremely long lead times, possibly necessitating the use of other suppliers with shorter lead times.

A major problem with obtaining goods from suppliers is when they are completely jammed with competing orders from multiple customers. In this situation, the company is forced to wait for its turn in the supplier's production process, and so must keep larger quantities of safety stock on hand until it receives replenishments. If the company requires large quantities of a predictable flow of goods, it can reduce this problem by purchasing blocks of supplier capacity. This essentially means that it buys the productive capacity of some portion of the supplier's manufacturing space, so that no one else can use it. This vastly improves the company's supply situation, resulting in far less need for safety stock. Also, in case the company's needs occasionally decline, one can even sell some of the capacity back to the supplier, who can then use it to service the needs of other customers.

Part of the time delay involved in ordering is the approval of orders within the company. If this requires multiple days, the inventory planning staff must plan for additional quantities of safety stock to ensure that supplies do not run out during this approval phase. Consequently, to reduce safety stock levels, consider either eliminating any form of approval for replenishment orders or at least creating a more streamlined approval process. The only acceptable reason to have an approval for a repeating purchase is to ensure that orders are not being issued for items that are scheduled for termination. This can more easily be achieved by turning on a product termination flag in the item master file in the computer system.

A good way to reduce safety stocks is to order from suppliers that are located as close to the company as possible. By doing so, delivery transit times become miniscule, allowing one to keep small safety stocks on hand to cover what may be just a few hours of production time until a replenishment arrives. This is a long-term approach to sourcing, because some fine suppliers may be located far away and will require considerable time to replace.

In-house inventory needs may decline even further by requiring suppliers to make multiple deliveries to the company each day. This drops the need for inventory to just a few hours' worth of stock. To avoid excessive paperwork, this approach works best if there is a long-term purchase order against which the company schedules a series of small product releases each day. At a more advanced level, one can even require suppliers to deliver directly into the production area, eliminating the need for any movement of inventory from the receiving dock to an intermediate storage area, and from there to the production floor. However, making this system work requires the presence of receiving docks close to the production area, the communication of a firm inventory requirements schedule to suppliers on a regular basis, high levels of product quality being delivered, and the presence of key suppliers just a short distance away. Given these requirements, obtaining multiple deliveries per day can be difficult to implement.

If a company wants to adopt multiple daily deliveries of products, it must switch to sole sourcing. Otherwise, it becomes extremely difficult to manage the flow of many deliveries of the same product from multiple suppliers. Also, this approach calls for the use of streamlined accounting, where suppliers are paid based on the total quantity of goods used in the production process; if there are several suppliers involved, it is impossible to tell whose goods were used, and therefore how much to pay which supplier.

It may be possible in limited situations for suppliers to retain ownership of their goods once they are shipped into the company's warehouse. The company only pays for them when they are extracted from the supplier's designated storage area on the premises, presumably to be sent to the production area. By using this approach, companies can reduce some working capital requirements by putting the onus of inventory storage on its suppliers. This approach is more attractive to suppliers when they are offered sole source status for the goods in question. However, suppliers must now increase their investment in inventory, while also spending more time monitoring and replenishing inventory levels, so they are likely to increase prices charged in order to compensate for these issues.

If there are a great many suppliers, it is possible that a company does not have enough purchasing expertise to deal with them all, or management feels that it can invest company funds more profitably in areas other than purchasing. If so, it may make sense to assign the role of lead supplier to a few suppliers, and have them handle the purchasing task for a large number of subcontractors. This approach works best for complex products requiring large subassemblies, for which lead suppliers can be assigned responsibility. Although lead suppliers are likely to charge extra for this service, they are also essentially guaranteed a larger proportion of the company's business, and so may be more willing to do it for only a modest price increase.

15-3 Inventory Receiving and Shipping

The shipping and receiving function requires the bulk of all warehouse staff time, as well as a great deal of warehouse space in which to break down and put away deliveries and marshal shipments for placement on trucks. Thus, receiving and shipping involve a considerable investment in both inventory and labor. This section describes ways to improve the efficiency of this key area.

A major receiving problem is the treatment of unplanned receipts. These are items for which someone in the company has placed a verbal purchase order, so there is no record in the computer system of its existence. Because the receiving staff has no idea what the order is, they park it to one side and send out a general notice, to which someone will hopefully respond in a few days, giving them some clue regarding where the order should be sent within the company. This approach consumes both storage space and the receiving staff's time. A better approach is to automatically reject all unplanned receipts at the point of delivery, with no exceptions. This will initially cause trouble within the company, because some of the verbal orders may be for critical items. Nonetheless, this is an appropriate action to take once a reasonable amount of warning has been given to the rest of the company.

The receiving area can become clogged with inventory, which not only requires more staff time to find needed items, but also calls for more warehouse space, and can result in damage to any items that are improperly stored out in the open. To avoid this problem, the warehouse manager can require supplier deliveries only during certain hours of the day, and then cluster most of the warehouse staff in the receiving area during that time, thereby focusing all attention on the putaway function for a brief period. It is also helpful to deepen the receiving area in front of the dock doors, so there is sufficient space for the receiving staff to sort through deliveries as they arrive. This approach calls for the presence of sufficient warehouse staff and material movement equipment to handle deliveries, which requires advance planning of received quantities, preferably several weeks in advance.

The efficient putaway of received goods can be accelerated through the use of advance shipping notices. Such notices can be a simple phone call from a shipper, as well as by fax, e-mail, or an electronic data interchange transmission. Whatever the communication medium, the intent is to forewarn the warehouse manager regarding the approximate arrival time of a delivery and the contents of the truck. This allows for much better putaway planning, where docks can be set aside for specific trailers based on the shortest in-house travel time to put away their contents. Competent shippers will generally comply with a request for advance shipping notices, although smaller shippers will require considerably more training.

When items arrive at the receiving dock, the warehouse staff is not under a specific deadline to put away all of the items, although it may be under considerable time pressure to pick and deliver items once they are ordered. Given this disparity, it may make sense to take somewhat more time in the receiving area to repackage received items into the quantities that are most commonly ordered by customers. By doing so, it will take much less time to fill orders. This approach works best if there is a great deal of excess space in the receiving area in which repackaging can be done.

An advanced form of an efficient putaway function is to stage received goods for putaway within designated zones. Under this approach, the receiving staff uses more space in the receiving area to break down deliveries into clusters small enough to be put away in a specific warehouse area (zone), which cuts down on the travel time of the putaway staff, allowing them to return to the receiving area more quickly to pick up another load. This approach is most cost-effective when the warehouse is so large that travel times are long.

Less efficient receiving operations will pile up all of the documentation related to items that have just been put away and enter them all into the receiving computer in one large batch at the end of the day. The problem is that some of the goods may already have been sent to the production area or shipped back out to suppliers, while pickers are already attempting to find newly received items on the warehouse shelves. Furthermore, it is impossible for cycle counters to make accurate inventory counts if some of the items they are counting are not yet present in the computer system. For all of these reasons, it is best to log in all items as soon as they are received. This data entry effort is much easier if the warehouse staff is equipped with radio-frequency terminals that allow them to complete data entry tasks from anywhere in the warehouse.

The ultimate goal in improving receiving efficiency is to have no receiving function at all. To do so, the engineering department must have precertified the quality level of every supplier, while the purchasing department has arranged with them to make inventory deliveries directly to the production area for immediate use. This implies extremely low inventory levels, just-in-time deliveries, and the complete elimination of the warehouse area. All of these preexisting conditions make it extremely rare to achieve complete elimination of the receiving function. More commonly, a few suppliers are certified to bypass the receiving function, while a reduced receiving staff is still available to handle a smaller volume of incoming goods.

Shipped items are typically loaded onto pallets by hand, shrink-wrapped, and loaded onto a truck for delivery. The packaging involved in a shipment may not be necessary if the customer breaks open the pallets before the putaway step. If so, consider contacting the customer to see if a reusable container system might make more sense, such as returnable wheeled containers. Although there may be a considerable upfront expense associated with the containers, the elimination of all other packaging materials may make this a cost-effective option.

The shipping function does not end at the dock door. The shipping manager should also be responsible for finding those freight companies with the best performance, both in terms of minimal damage to shipments and the ability to make deliveries on time. This may result in a reorientation away from using the lowest-cost shippers, instead requiring the use of a shipper evaluation system to determine which shippers are to be used. Otherwise, customers may require inventory on very short notice to replace either damaged goods or goods that have not arrived by the required due dates; this last-minute shipping can severely impact a company's shipment schedule and its freight costs.

15-4   Inventory Storage

There are many ways to improve the storage of inventory, beginning with the complete bypassing of the warehouse area and proceeding through better warehouse organization to zone storage and the use of special racking systems. This section discusses multiple options in each of these areas.

The best inventory storage option is not to store it at all. This can be done through the use of drop shipping, whereby the company contacts a supplier and requests that it send goods straight to a customer, thereby completely bypassing the corporate storage facility. This approach requires the cooperation of the supplier, who may only like to ship in large quantities and so is less than enthusiastic about odd-sized shipments or deliveries that must be repackaged to appear to have come from the company instead. Also, the company's accounting department must have a system in place to obtain shipping notice from the supplier and issue a billing to a customer at that time, rather than the more common process of having the in-house shipping department trigger an invoice. Furthermore, this approach only works if the goods being shipped require no additional transformation by the company through its own production process. A final complication is that a multiline order by a customer may call for deliveries from multiple suppliers, resulting in many deliveries to the customer, who may not appreciate the lack of a consolidated shipment. For all of these reasons, one can rarely obtain the full benefits of drop shipping.

If drop shipping is not possible, consider cross-docking shipments instead. Under this approach, supplier deliveries come into the warehouse through one dock door and are immediately shifted across the warehouse to an outbound truck for delivery to a customer. This approach calls for no on-site storage in a formal racking system at all and results in fast inventory turnover. However, the warehouse function must be extremely well organized to match inbound and outbound deliveries within short time periods. It may also require the repackaging of delivery quantities to match the outbound requirement, as well as the relabeling of goods that have just arrived from a supplier. In addition, a great many dock doors may be needed to support the large number of trailers that may sit at the warehouse, waiting to be filled. Nonetheless, many companies have achieved considerable success with the cross-docking concept.

Another way to eliminate inventory from the warehouse is to distribute it to floor stock locations in the production area. This approach tends to involve fittings and fasteners, which are the most labor-intensive inventory items to track and replenish. The production staff loves this approach, because they no longer have to requisition these items from the warehouse. The primary difficulty with the use of floor stock is that they are no longer covered by the formal inventory tracking system, so there is no computerized way to automatically determine when an item should be reordered. Instead, someone must be assigned the task of manually reviewing floor stock levels and placing orders with suppliers. It may be possible to assign this task to suppliers, who must visit the company frequently to replenish goods.

A key element of inventory storage is reducing the complexity of the storage system, so it is as easy as possible to find an item within the warehouse. The most basic way to do this is to assign a unique bin code to every bin in the warehouse, and to record in a computer system which inventory items are stored within each bin. A way to further streamline the system is to periodically review the inventory storage records and consolidate inventory items into the smallest possible number of adjacent bins. This typically results in a modest number of inventory items in a readily accessible bin near the front of the warehouse and an overflow quantity stored in a less accessible area. This concept of bin tracking is the most fundamental and necessary of all inventory storage requirements. Although bin tracking requires plenty of staff time to update, it is impossible to operate a warehouse without it.

The theoretically correct approach to storing inventory is to park it in any open bin, thereby maximizing the use of all available bins. However, this can result in high-usage items being stored in a distant corner of the warehouse, which lengthens the travel time of inventory pickers. To avoid this problem, consider assigning fixed inventory locations at the front of the warehouse to the most heavily used inventory, forcing less-used items into the nether regions of the warehouse. If this system is used, be sure to periodically review inventory usage levels, because the demand for a high-usage item may decline over time, reducing the need for a fixed location. For example, a company dealing in the sale of seasonal goods must completely reshuffle its warehouse once sales shift into a new season, because the demand for items will change at easily predictable times of the year.

The allocation of selected inventory to specific locations can be much more formally structured into the ABC storage system. Under this approach, the 20% most heavily used inventory items (the "A" items) are stored in the most readily accessible locations in the warehouse, while the 30% to 40% next most heavily used items (the "B" items) are stored in the next most accessible areas, and all remaining items (the "C" items) are stored in the rear of the warehouse. This approach is extremely useful for cutting down on the travel time of the warehouse staff, who usually end up spending nearly all of their time in the A area. Also, one can alter the storage rack system so that A items are stored in the most easily accessible storage systems, such as carousels, while less frequently used items are stored in less-expensive bulk storage systems.

If customers send the company some of their inventory for inclusion in finished goods, it can easily become mixed in with regular corporate inventory, resulting in excess inventory valuations associated with items that the company does not really own. To keep this problem from occurring, consider creating a segregated warehouse area for customer-owned inventory. Also, use different inventory item codes for this inventory to which zero costs are assigned, thereby ensuring that the inventory will not be accidentally overvalued.

Some companies take the concept of customer inventory segregation a step farther and block out large chunks of the warehouse for the storage of all inventory that a specific customer may use, no matter who owns it. Although this approach tends to waste space, it has the advantage of imposing tighter controls over inventory intended for the use of the most important customers. This is a useful technique only for the largest customers with whom a company does a significant proportion of its total business.

A company should alter its inventory storage systems to meet the requirements of its inventory, as well as the type of picking system in use. For example, if inventory is perishable, the racking system should allow for putaways on one side and picking from the other, so the oldest items must be picked first; gravity flow and pallet flow racks work best in this situation. Alternately, if large quantities of items are stored on pallets, it may be possible to avoid excess aisle space by storing them in double-deep racks, push-back racks, or stacking lanes. If inventory items are small, are not picked frequently, and space is at a premium, consider using movable racking systems that compress aisle space. For the same types of inventory but when there is plenty of vertical space available, an alternative is to install a multi-story manual picking system. If pickers must pick large quantities of items as rapidly as possible, it may make sense to install a carousel system that brings parts to them at a central picking station; this is an expensive storage alternative, so be sure to conduct a cost-benefit analysis before implementing it. Finally, in a limited number of situations, one can remove cross-braces from storage racks, so the warehouse staff can more efficiently access the racks from both sides. This option is only possible in low-weight storage situations where the structural integrity of the racks is not threatened.

Even the size of containers and their storage pattern can interfere with the effective storage of inventory. For example, if a storage bin is four feet high and each case stored in it is ten inches high, then eight inches of space at the top of each bin are going to waste. Depending on the contents of each container, it may make sense to alter their height to be either twelve inches (to fully store four stacked containers in the rack) or eight inches (to fully store six stacked containers). Also, the container stacking pattern on a pallet should match the dimensions of the pallet as closely as possible. Otherwise, the cubic volume of storage space may be underutilized. If the stacking pattern results in containers overhanging the edge of the pallet, those containers are more likely to be damaged in transit.

15-5 Inventory Picking

One of the highest-volume activities involving a large number of warehouse employees is inventory picking. Given its importance, one should consider all methods for arriving at the most cost-effective way to remove inventory from storage and transport it either to the customer or the production area. This section discusses several possible picking methods.

The least efficient picking method is to hand a single order to a stock picker, who walks all over the warehouse, searching for the required parts. At the most basic level, this picking ticket should include a column containing the inventory locations in which each inventory item is located, thereby reducing the search time. With the location available, pickers can now take a group of single-line orders, manually sort them by inventory location, and pick a large number of these orders during one picking tour of the warehouse. If there are multiline picking tickets, consider sorting each ticket by inventory location, so the picker can sequentially pick items within the ticket while walking down each aisle.

If pickers are handling multiple orders at once during a single picking tour, extra labor is required at the end of each tour to sort through all of the picked items and separate them into different kitting bins for order delivery. A better approach is to issue multibin kitting carts to the pickers, so they can pick into different bins on the spot, thereby eliminating further order sorting at the end of each tour. Although efficient, this approach will result in some order inaccuracy, because pickers may inadvertently place picked items in the wrong bin.

A kitting cart is also a useful platform for a portable scale. If a company has small parts in stock that pickers must manually count, portable battery-powered scales are an excellent way to streamline the picking process. However, these scales are expensive, so only procure them if a considerable amount of picking time is being wasted on small-part counting.

In more primitive picking environments where there is no computer system, customer orders are manually transferred to picking tickets, which introduces the risk that information will be incorrectly transferred from the order to the picking ticket. To avoid incorrect picks caused by this problem, consider using a photocopy of the original customer order as the picking ticket. If the customer order form's layout is not conducive to picking, consider altering the form.

Order pickers generally conduct picking tours based on the immediacy of an order due date. However, this may result in orders that could be concentrated into a full truck load delivery being broken into several more expensive partial truckloads. One can avoid this problem by summarizing orders to be shipped to the same general location in a single large picking tour. The main difficulty is that orders that would not normally be due yet are being picked in advance of orders for which the order date is more immediate.

Clustering orders into a single large picking tour is certainly a better use of picker time, but pickers may not have a thorough knowledge of the entire warehouse, and so conduct inefficient tours during which they spend extra time verifying that picked items are correct. An alternative is zone picking, whereby pickers are assigned small portions of the warehouse. A zone picker is usually responsible for maintaining a specific warehouse area, and so not only has an excellent knowledge of its contents, but can slot items within the zone for maximum picking efficiency. By shifting partially completed orders from zone to zone, the overall efficiency and accuracy of the picking process tends to improve substantially. However, this usually calls for the use of some computerization and a conveyor belt to move orders from zone to zone.

In picking environments where inventory is hard to handle, pickers must remember to record each transaction after having used both hands to move the picked item, which tends to result in a great deal of missed pick transactions. To avoid this problem, consider using voice picking, whereby each picker wears a headset over which the computer system issues commands in a synthetic voice to pickers, telling them where to go for the next pick and what to remove from each bin. Pickers communicate back to the computer by voice, which is translated by the computer into electronic transactions. Voice picking works best in lower-volume picking environments without an excessive amount of background noise.

Where there is a high volume of picking transactions, consider using a pick-to-light system. Under this approach, an information display is attached to the front of each storage bin, with a direct linkage back to the picking module of one's inventory tracking system. When the system requires a pick, a light flashes on the display, as well as a number indicating the quantity to pick. When the pick is complete, the picker presses a button on the display unit to indicate completion of the task. This approach works well when item dimensions are small and where broken-case picking by hand is the norm. Although this is a good picking system with a low rate of transaction error, it is also expensive to install, and so is only used for items that are subject to a high picking rate.

Several picking methods have been noted that involve more efficient picking of multiple orders at once, but they do not allow for the rapid picking of specific customer orders. If a customer is in a rush to receive a specific order, these picking methods are not the best way to fill the order. Instead, have an experienced picker do nothing but pick emergency orders from stock. This approach improves customer service at the expense of greatly reduced picking efficiency, so one should strongly consider charging the customer a picking fee to offset the loss of efficiency.

No matter what picking method is used, it is difficult to do so effectively if there are both pickers and putaway staff clogging the warehouse aisles at the same time. There are two ways to avoid this problem. First, install gravity-feed flow-through racking, so the putaway staff load parts into one side of a rack and the inventory rolls downhill for access by pickers on the other side. Second, have the putaway staff work a different shift than the pickers.

It is much easier to pick high-volume items when they are concentrated in one section of the warehouse. However, usage patterns will change over time, so be sure to periodically schedule a review of item usage to determine which items should be moved into or out of the high-volume picking areas.

15-6 Production Issues Impacting Inventory

Certain facets of a company's production system can impact the amount of inventory needed to run it, such as pay systems, equipment maintenance, and the configuration of equipment within the factory. Careful attention to these factors, as explained in this section, can reduce the required inventory investment substantially.

A company's production bonus plan can result in too much inventory. This occurs when the incentive pay system has employees cranking out massive quantities of inventory in order to meet stretch bonus goals. This can be a problem if there is no room in which to store the excess inventory created by the workers, so consider using such bonus plans only for bottleneck operations where there is never enough inventory being produced. A further problem with bonus plans is the propensity of workers to reduce the quality of their work in favor of more production volume. If this becomes an issue, consider issuing bonus reductions for low quality levels. Finally, consider eliminating production-based bonus plans entirely and converting to a just-in-time production system, where the emphasis is on manufacturing only what is needed.

Having an imbalance between the number of shifts worked in different parts of a factory can increase the level of work-in-process inventory. For example, one area may have two shifts and all other areas just one shift, so the one multishift area piles up completed inventory for eight hours before the next downstream area arrives for work and can begin processing it. Even if the multishift area is working extra hours because it is a bottleneck operation, it may still be feasible to run smaller skeleton crews in other production areas in order to begin processing work-in-process as soon as it becomes available, thereby reducing the total level of work-in-process in the facility.

If a factory is built around a small number of high-volume machines, it is likely that it requires a substantial amount of work-in-process inventory. This problem arises because a single, expensive machine must be run at all times in order to justify the company's investment, resulting in a buffer of raw materials stored in front of it and partially processed inventory after it. Furthermore, large and complex machines tend to break down or require more maintenance, so the production scheduling staff tends to build up inventory buffers against the eventuality that the machine will go down. To avoid these problems, consider replacing a single large machine with several smaller and less complex ones. This approach yields less total maintenance downtime and also the flexibility to shift work among several machines.

Not only is it better to use smaller machines in the production area, but it is also better to schedule smaller production runs on those machines. A large and complex machine necessitates the use of infrequent, lengthy equipment setups, followed by long production runs to justify the setup time. This results in large amounts of finished goods that must be stored until sold. A better approach is to use smaller, inexpensive equipment that can be easily set up for new production runs, thereby making it cost-effective to have production runs of as little as one unit, which in turn reduces downstream inventory levels to a remarkable extent. Small production runs also allow downstream workstation operations sufficient time to inspect each incoming part and tell the upstream machine operator if they have just produced an item that is out of specification. This immediate quality review creates such a rapid feedback loop that little inventory must be scrapped during the production process.

Equipment downtime is a major reason why work-in-process inventory tends to build up. When a machine goes down for any length of time, the work-in-process scheduled to be processed through it sits either until repairs are completed or are routed to another machine whose capacity may not be sufficient to process it in the short term. The inventory planning staff may also build up an expectation of considerable machine downtime, and so always plans for more inventory than is really needed. There are several ways to reduce these issues. First, create and follow a detailed machine maintenance plan, where equipment is serviced during nonproduction periods. Also, implement a preventive maintenance program, so machines are less likely to fail. Next, purchase as many machines as possible from the same manufacturer, so the maintenance staff does not require as much knowledge of different machines in order to effect repairs. This may also result in less spare parts inventory if the supplier uses many of the same parts on different machines. Finally, train the production staff to take care of minor repairs on their own. All of these steps can reduce machine downtime.

Even machines that appear identical on the outside will require varying levels of fine-tuning before parts produced on them fall within specifications, because of varying levels of machine wear and tear. For this reason, the production setup staff tends to waste raw materials while it conducts lengthy test runs on new production runs. To avoid wasting inventory, consider scheduling production runs only on the same machines every time and storing the exact machine settings to create those parts. It then becomes easier to initially set up each machine with few or no subsequent alterations to create perfect parts.

A major cause of work-in-process inventory build-up within the production area is the presence of aisles. A machine operator on one side of an aisle must complete enough work to fill up a pallet, at which point a forklift operator shifts the pallet across the aisle to the next workstation. The pallet-load of stock can be eliminated simply by running a conveyor across the aisle, so the first machine operator can roll stock directly to the next machine. This approach can eliminate a large amount of inventory while also giving industrial engineers the opportunity to shrink the production area by eliminating aisles.

The most efficient use of inventory is achieved when a production planning staff schedules production levels to match either the in-house or expected quantity of inventory. However, when customers order items at the last possible minute, this throws off the scheduling process, resulting in too much on-hand inventory in some areas and the incurrence of overnight delivery charges to bring in other items needed to fulfill the rush orders. Furthermore, expeditors must walk orders through the production and warehouse areas, leaving a considerable disturbance in their wakes. To eliminate these problems, consider refusing customer orders that fall within the minimum scheduling period set by the production planning staff. If a customer is an important one and insists on immediate service, then charge such a stiff premium that the customer will at least scale back its demands for short-term service, while the company is well compensated for its expediting assistance.

15-7 Inventory Transactions

There can be an enormous number of inventory transactions—recording initial receipt, quality review, putaway, picking, and delivery either to customers or the shop floor, depending on the transaction. This area is rife with errors, especially if the staff must manually log all entries into a computer system. This section describes techniques for reducing the inventory transaction error rate.

One of the simplest improvements is to eliminate any data entry backlogs. When several transactions are not entered at once, the on-hand quantities of inventory can become inaccurate, making it difficult to plan purchasing and production activities, as well as cycle counting. To eliminate backlogs, management should emphasize its importance in the warehouse manager's job review. Also, consider additional data entry training for the warehouse staff, as well as dedicating one person to nothing but data entry (which also tends to reduce data entry errors).

Another simple error correction technique is to run an inventory on-hand quantity report every day and search it for negative inventory balances. When found, investigate the underlying transactions causing the negative balance, and correct these problems. This approach works best if there is easy access in the computer system to all inventory transactions, along with the date and time when they were created and who entered them. This additional information is critical for tracking down problems.

Another way to spot transaction problems is to cycle count the inventory, so that someone is constantly comparing on-hand to book inventory balances. The key activity here is not finding discrepancies but rather investigating why they occurred. Continuous cycle counts put ongoing emphasis on bomb-proofing transactions, so the number of errors should decline precipitously if this approach is followed.

A primary cause of inventory transaction errors is manual data entry. Given the sheer volume of transactions, it is almost impossible not to have errors. One way to avoid the problem is to use bar codes. Under this approach, a bar code is added to a product as soon as it arrives at the receiving dock, detailing the item description, quantity, and unit of measure. As long as the information contained in the bar code is correct, all subsequent scans of this information will be correct as well. The concept can be taken a step farther by bar coding all inventory locations. By doing so, one can eliminate nearly all manual entries from inventory transactions.

Even bar coding can cause problems if scanned information is being stored in handheld units carried by the warehouse staff and only downloaded to the central computer at the end of their shifts. Under this approach, information may be updated with as much as an eight-hour delay. A much better alternative is to issue radio-frequency scanners to the warehouse staff, so any scanned transactions are immediately transferred by radio transmission to a receiver that is linked to the central computer system. Wireless scanning units are expensive, but this is an excellent way to ensure real-time entry of inventory transactions.

If a wireless system is installed, one can consider shifting to the ultimate in warehouse systems—a warehouse management system. This computerized system runs all warehouse functions in the most efficient manner possible by issuing commands to the wireless terminals being carried by the warehouse staff. It tells them where to put away inventory items based on their usage patterns, where pickers should go to obtain inventory while walking the shortest possible distance, where incoming trailers should dock in order to shorten the putaway time from them to the warehouse racks, and so on. Warehouse management systems are expensive, so they are only cost effective for the largest warehouse systems.

15-8   Inventory Quantity Management

There are many ways to reduce inventory levels through the inventory planning process while still maintaining high levels of customer service. These techniques are scattered throughout a company, encompassing product design, sales forecasting, management of the planning function, distribution systems, and the treatment of obsolete inventory. This section covers many possibilities in these areas that can lead to inventory reduction.

A major cause of inventory inflation is the use of a multitude of product options, which requires a company to stock some quantity of each product variation. Although this approach certainly gives customers a wide product range from which to choose, it is extremely common to also see high product obsolescence caused by some product configurations not selling as well as others. Thus, part of the design process is reducing the number of product options to a more tolerable level that reduces a company's inventory investment. One way to retain a large number of product configurations while still having small inventory levels is to only build inventory to a semi-finished level, with all options added after customers place orders. This approach only works if the product design team is involved, because they must create products with "bolt-on" options.

Inventory levels can also be reduced by continually examining sales quantities for each product and eliminating those items whose sales have dropped below a minimum cutoff level. This approach is complex, because one must also consider retaining stock in sufficient quantities to cover expected replacements resulting from warranty claims or service issues. Also, some products may continue to be sold for longer than would normally be the case if this is the best way to eliminate some components from stock that are no longer being used in the manufacture of any other products.

Engineers like to design finely crafted products that operate properly only when high-tolerance components are used. However, components with tight tolerances may be difficult to produce or acquire, resulting in a great deal of scrap. Thus, it is better to work with the engineers to design products requiring lower-tolerance parts, so that a larger percentage of raw materials will work properly in their manufacture.

When customers order a product and it is not available, they make take their business elsewhere rather than wait for the company to produce more stock. However, if the company maintains a list of substitute products, it may be able to ship one of the other items to the customer, thereby reducing its finished goods inventory. This typically calls for an updated substitute product list to be maintained where the order entry staff can easily access it.

Senior management may have mandated a high level of customer service, which is represented in the warehouse area by the continued presence of on-hand inventory for any product a customer may wish to order. However, this calls for a high level of inventory investment, which may in turn result in significant obsolete inventory if some items are never bought by customers. Consequently, it makes sense to periodically review the mandated customer service level with senior management, including in the discussion the cost of this policy in terms of incremental inventory investment.

High customer service levels may mandate a large safety stock for each finished goods item. However, what if product demand is highly seasonal? Safety stock levels may still result in stock outs during high-demand periods and excessive inventory during low-demand periods. To avoid this problem, consider scheduling periodic adjustments to safety stock levels for those inventory items that are known to have seasonal demand.

If there is a management directive to reduce the total investment in inventory, the production planning staff may have little time to do so, especially if there are thousands of parts in stock to be reviewed. A simple alternative is to only reduce inventory levels for the subset of items with high usage levels. The turnover rates on these items is so rapid that any reduction actions taken will be reflected in an inventory reduction in a short period. Conversely, if inventory reduction actions were taken on slow-moving inventory, it could be months before there is any discernible impact on the total inventory investment. The planning staff can save more time in reducing inventory by using an in-house material requirements planning system to model the impact of changes in safety stock, lot sizes, or lead times on the total level of inventory investment.

A company may distribute inventory to customers from regional warehouses. If so, it must stock a sufficient inventory quantity in each location to meet expected customer demand. An alternative is to centralize the storage of smaller or expensive items, so a smaller quantity can be stored in one location for distribution to all customers. This approach circumvents regional warehouses and their primary reason for existence—rapid delivery to customers—so be sure to only centralize those inventory items that can reasonably be inexpensively shipped by overnight delivery services directly to customers. This usually calls for a cost-benefit analysis to determine which inventory items should be treated in this manner.

A warehouse network is designed to ship inventory in the most economical manner possible to regional customer clusters. Given this objective, warehouses must be carefully sited within each region for maximum effect. However, customers change over time, as does the quantity of their purchases, so one should occasionally rationalize the warehouse network through a regularly scheduled warehouse analysis. This is not a frequent event, because a warehouse location must be clearly inefficient before a company should undertake the considerable expense required to move to a new location.

16

Inventory Transfer Pricing[1]

16-1 Introduction

Many organizations sell their own products internally—from one division to another. This is especially common in vertically integrated situations, where a company has elected to control the key pieces of its supply chain, perhaps to "lock down" the supply of key components. Each division sells its products to a downstream division that includes those products in its own production processes. When this happens, management must determine the prices at which components will be sold between divisions. This is known as *transfer pricing*. The level of transfer price used is important, because the managers of each division use it to determine if they should sell to an internal division or externally, on the open market. If the transfer price is set too low, then the managers will have an incentive to sell outside of the company, even if the organization as a whole would benefit from a greater volume of internal transfers. Similarly, an excessively high transfer price will result in too many internal sales, when some external ones would have yielded a higher overall profit. Because of its great impact on the operational behavior of corporate divisions, great care must be taken in selecting the most appropriate transfer price.

This chapter covers a wide range of transfer pricing methods, as well as several special issues involving them. It concludes with a summary and comparison of all of the transfer pricing methods.

16-2 The Importance of Transfer Pricing

Transfer pricing levels are important in companies experiencing any of the following three transfer or operational characteristics:

- *High volumes of interdivisional sales.* This is most common in vertically integrated companies, where each division in succession produces a component that

---

[1]Adapted with permission from Chapter 30 of Bragg, *Cost Accounting: A Comprehensive Guide*, John Wiley & Sons, 2001.

is a necessary part of the product being created by the next division in line. Any incorrect transfer pricing in this scenario can cause considerable dysfunctional behavior, as will be noted later in this section.

- *High volumes of segment-specific sales.* Even if a company as a whole does not transfer much product among its divisions, this does not mean that specific departments or product lines within each division do not have a much higher dependence on the accuracy of transfer pricing for selected products.

- *High degree of organizational decentralization.* If an organization is arranged under the theory that divisions should operate as independently as possible, then they will have no incentive to work together unless the transfer prices used are set at levels that give them an economic incentive to do so.

Alternately, the theoretical foundation for the calculation of transfer prices is of little importance to those organizations with a high degree of centralization, because individual divisions will be ordered to produce and transfer products to other divisions by the headquarters staff, irrespective of the prices charged. This is also the case for companies that rarely transfer any products among their divisions, because such transfers, when they occur, are typically approved at the highest management levels if the transfers are large, or they are so small that their impact is minimal.

For those organizations falling into the first set of conditions noted, it is crucial to be aware of the key factors that will be influenced by the level of transfer pricing used. One is the overall level of corporate profitability, another is its use in determining the financial performance of each division, and yet another factor is the ease of use of the transfer pricing method selected. Each of these factors is discussed in the following paragraphs.

The chief issue for any corporation is how to maximize its overall level of profitability. To do so, it must set its transfer prices at levels that will result in the highest possible levels of profits, not for individual divisions, but rather for the entire organization. For example, if a transfer price is set at nothing more than its cost, the selling division would much rather not sell the product at all, even though the buying division can sell it externally for a huge profit that more than makes up for the lack of profit experienced by the division that originally sold it the product. The typical division manager will select the product sales that result in the highest level of profit only for his or her division, because the manager has no insight (or interest) in the financial results of the rest of the organization. Only by finding some way for the selling division to also realize a profit will it have an incentive to sell its products internally, thereby resulting in greater overall profits. An example of such a solution is when a selling division creates a by-product that it cannot sell, but that another division can use as an input for the products it manufactures. The selling division scraps the by-product, because it has no incentive to do anything else with it. However, by assigning the selling division a small profit on sale of the by-product, it now has an incentive to ship it to the buying division. Such a pricing strategy assists a company in deriving the greatest possible profit from all of its activities.

If such steps are not taken, then the situation noted in Exhibit 16-1 can arise. In the exhibit, a sawmill is currently selling its sawdust to an outside company for $50 per ton. It does this because the internal transfer price used to sell the sawdust to another internal division is only $20 per ton. The sawmill manager's actions in selling the sawdust externally are entirely rational, from the perspective of the sawmill. However, because the internal division that would otherwise be buying the sawdust could convert it into particle board and sell it for a total company profit of $60 per ton, the profits of the company as a whole are reduced by $10 per ton; this problem results entirely from the use of an incorrect transfer price.

Exhibit 16-1 *Example of an Incorrect Transfer Price*

Saw Mill

External Particleboard Processor ← Sell at $50/Ton — Decision — Sell at $20/Ton → Internal Particleboard Processor

Total Company Profit = $50/Ton ($50/Ton - $0/Ton)

Additional Processing: $20/ Ton Cost

Sell Externally at $80/Ton

Total Company Profit = $60/Ton ($80/Ton - $20/Ton)

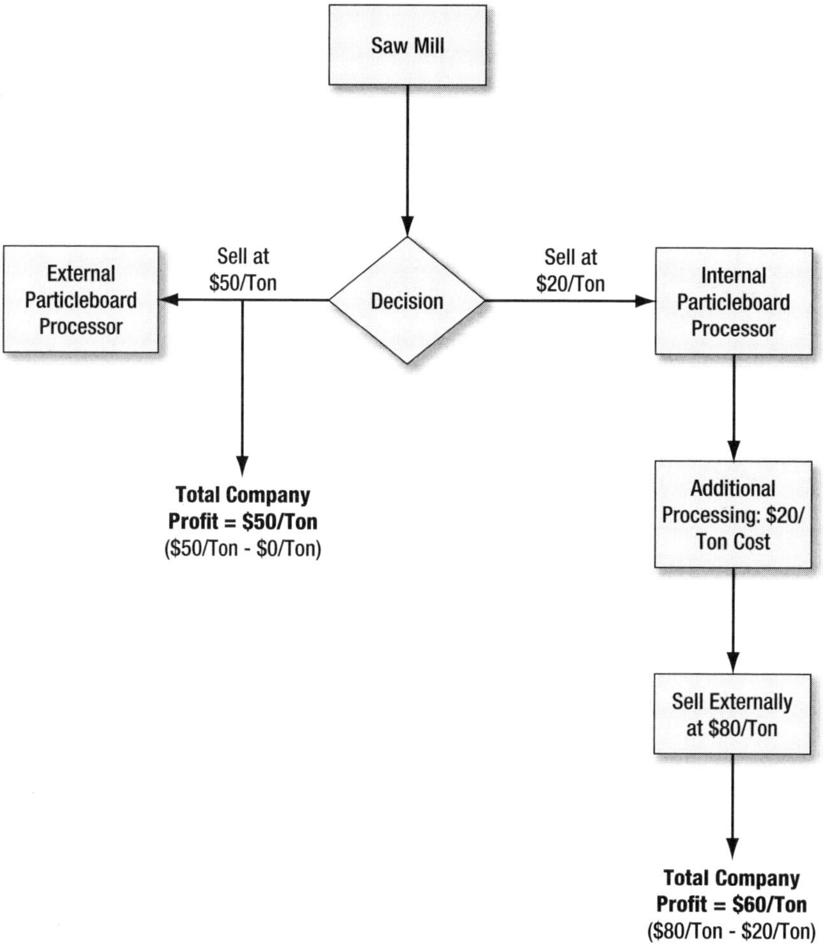

Another factor is that the amount of profit allocated to a division through the transfer pricing method used will impact its reported level of profitability and therefore the performance review for that division and its management team. If the management team is compensated in large part through performance-based bonuses, then its actions will be heavily influenced by the profit it can earn on intercompany transfers, especially if such transfers make up a large proportion of total divisional sales. If transfer prices are set at high levels, this can result in the manufacture of far more product than is needed, which may lock up so much production capacity that the selling division is no longer able to create other products that could otherwise have been sold for a profit. Conversely, an excessively low transfer price will result in no production at all, as long as the selling division has some other product available that it can sell for a greater profit. This later situation frequently results in late or small deliveries to buying divisions, because the managers of the selling divisions only see fit to produce low-price items if there is spare production capacity available that can be used in no other way. Thus, improper transfer prices will motivate division managers in accordance with how the prices impact their performance evaluations.

Yet another factor to consider is that the method used should be simple enough for easy calculation on a regular basis—some transfer pricing methods appear to yield elegant solutions, but require the use of such arcane accounting methods that their increased utility is more than outweighed by their level of formulation difficulty. This is a particularly thorny problem when the pricing method requires constant recalculation. For everyday use, a simple and easily understandable transfer pricing method is preferred.

Finally, altering the transfer price used can have a dramatic impact on the amount of income taxes a company pays, if it has divisions located in different countries that use different tax rates. All of these issues must be considered when selecting an appropriate transfer pricing method.

Companies that are frequent users of transfer pricing must create prices that are based on a proper balance of the goals of overall company profitability, divisional performance evaluation, simplicity of use, and (in some cases) the reduction of income taxes. The attainment of all these goals by using a single transfer pricing method is not common and should not be expected. Instead, managers must focus on the attainment of the most critical goals, while keeping the adverse affects of not meeting other goals at a minimum. This process may result in the use of several transfer pricing methods, depending on the circumstances surrounding each interdivisional transfer.

The following sections are divided into two main groups. The first cluster of topics cover those transfer prices that are either directly or indirectly related to transfer prices that are derived in some manner from market-based prices. The later group covers transfer prices that are instead based on product costs, usually because there is no reliable market price available. The advantages and disadvantages of each transfer pricing method are noted in the relevant sections, so that one can find the most appropriate method that will most closely mesh with his or her pricing requirements.

16-3   Transfer Pricing Based on Market Prices

The most commonly used transfer pricing technique is based on the existing external market price. Under this approach, the selling division matches its transfer price to the current market rate. By doing so, a company can achieve all of the goals outlined in the last section. First, it can achieve the highest possible corporate-wide profit. This happens because the selling division can earn just as much profit by selling all of its production outside of the company as it can by doing so internally; there is no reason for using a transfer price that results in incorrect behavior of either selling externally at an excessively low price or selling internally when a better deal could have been obtained by selling externally. Second, using the market price allows a division to earn a profit on its sales, no matter whether it sells internally or externally. By avoiding all transfers at cost, the senior management group can structure its divisions as profit centers, thereby allowing it to determine the performance of each division manager. Third, the market price is simple to obtain: it can be taken from regulated price sheets, posted prices, or quoted prices, and applied directly to all sales. No complicated calculations are required, and arguments over the correct price to charge between divisions are kept to a minimum. Fourth, a market-based transfer price allows both buying and selling divisions to shop anywhere they want to buy or sell their products. For example, a buying division will be indifferent as to where it obtains its supplies, because it can buy them at the same price, whether or not that source is a fellow company division. This leads to a minimum of incorrect buying and selling behavior that would otherwise be driven by transfer prices that do not reflect market conditions. For all of these reasons, companies are well advised to use market-based transfer prices whenever possible.

Unfortunately, many corporations do not use this type of pricing, not because they do not want to, but because no market prices are available. This happens when the products being transferred do not exactly match those sold on the market. For example, wheat is a product that exactly matches the wheat sold by other companies, but a dishwasher may not exactly match the dishwashers made elsewhere, because their features are sufficiently different that the market rate does not apply to the product. Also, many transfers are for intermediate-level products that have not yet been converted into final products, so no market price is available for them. When such situations arise, the transfer price must be obtained by other means, as noted in the following sections.

Another problem with using market prices is that there must truly be an alternative for a selling division to sell its entire production externally. This will not work if the market for the product is too small, because dumping an excessively large quantity of product on the market at one time will depress its price; when this happens, the selling division may find that it could have obtained a better price if it had sold its production internally. This is a common problem for specialty products, where the number of potential buyers is small and their annual buying needs are limited in size.

Another problem with market pricing is that the market price may not accurately reflect the somewhat reduced cost of selling a product to another division. A selling division may find that internal sales are slightly more profitable than external ones, because of reductions in selling costs, bad debt expenses, and a reduced investment in accounts receivable. With such incentives available, a selling division will ignore the possibility of selling externally and push as much of its production onto the buying division as possible, which may result in more shipments to the buyer than it needs. This issue is dealt with in more detail in the next section.

A final issue is that market-based pricing can work against the objectives of the senior management team, if it drives selling divisions to sell their production outside of the company. This problem arises in tight supply situations, where a buying division cannot obtain a sufficient amount of parts from a selling division because it is selling them externally, and outside manufacturers cannot produce sufficient quantities to make up the difference. In this case, the selling division is maximizing its own profit at the expense of divisions that need its output. This is particularly important when the buying division adds so much value to the product that it can then sell it externally at a much higher margin than could the selling division. These problems may require the corporate headquarters staff to require all or a specified portion of divisional output to be sold internally.

For all of the reasons noted here, most corporations will find that they cannot use a purely market-driven transfer pricing system. It is still the best approach for the limited number of situations in which it can be used, but other techniques must be considered if the problems with using market-based pricing outweigh their associated benefits. In the next section, we look at the applicability of adjusted market prices to the transfer pricing problem.

16-4   Transfer Pricing Based on Adjusted Market Prices

Although market pricing is generally the best way to derive a transfer price, there are many cases where such prices must be altered slightly to account for either slight anomalies in the external market prices or internal factors.

When market prices depend heavily on the volume of products purchased, there may be a wide array of prices, all of them valid, but only for a set range of product quantities. For example, a single car battery may sell for $60, but when sold by the trailer-load, the price drops to $45 per battery. Which price is a division to use when setting its transfer price? If it uses a wide range of transfer prices to reflect different sales volumes to buying divisions, it will achieve a reasonable correspondence between market prices and internal unit volumes. However, this may lead to a large number of transfer prices to keep track of, which can be difficult if a company transfers many products between its divisions. A simple approach is to determine the average shipment size once a year, and set transfer prices based on that volume, thereby allowing a division to use just one transfer price instead of many. If a buying division turns out to have purchased in significantly different quantities than the ones that were assumed at the time prices were set, then a company can retroactively adjust transfer prices at the end of the year, or it can leave the pricing alone and let the divisions do a better job of planning their interdivisional transfer volumes in the next year. The latter method is generally the better one to use, because the alternative of a multitiered transfer pricing formula tends to be difficult to calculate, not to mention mediate, because division managers like to argue over the correct pricing to use when they have several to choose from.

Several internal factors may also require a company to adjust its market-based transfer prices. One is the complete absence of bad debt. When a company sells externally, it reserves a small proportion of each sale for accounts receivable that will never be collected. However, when sales are made internally, there is no reason to believe that other divisions cannot pay their bills. Accordingly, this expense can be eliminated from the price charged to internal customers. Another such cost is for the sales staff. If sales arrangements have already been made between divisions, then the purchasing staffs and production planners from the selling and buying divisions (respectively) can bypass the sales staff of the selling division to place orders. Accordingly, the cost of the sales staff does not need to be apportioned to internal sales, which further reduces transfer prices. There may also be opportunities to reduce freight costs, if product shipments can be handled by a company's internal transportation fleet (assuming that this cost is less than what would be incurred by using a third-party shipper to deliver to an outside party). Finally, if divisions pay each other promptly, the cost required to support the selling division's investment in accounts receivable can be reduced. All of these factors can result in a respectable reduction in the transfer price charged to a buying division.

When the external sales price is adjusted downward to account for all of these factors, the difference may be sufficiently large that divisions will find themselves increasing their sales to one another to a considerable extent. This is just what the headquarters management team of an integrated corporation wants to see, as long as the adjusted prices are not so low that the internal transfer prices are resulting in behavior that is skewed in favor of sales transactions that are not resulting in optimal levels of corporate profitability.

A major issue to be aware of when using this pricing method is that there can be arguments between divisions over the exact reductions in external sale prices to be made. If aggressive managers are running each division, then those operating the selling divisions will mightily resist any reductions in the external sale price, while those managing the buying divisions will push hard for greater reductions. These squabbles can devolve into prolonged arguments that can seriously impact the management time available to each division's management team. Also, if the negotiations for price adjustments excessively favor one division over another, the "losing" division may either sell its production or purchase its components elsewhere, rather than conduct any further internal dealings. The corporate headquarters staff should watch out for and intervene in such situations to ensure that adjusted market pricing results in optimal internal transfer pricing levels.

16-5 Transfer Pricing Based on Negotiated Prices

Market-based pricing is generally the best way to structure transfer prices. However, there are many cases where external market prices are highly volatile, or where the volumes being transferred between divisions are so variable that it is difficult to determine the correct transfer price. In these special situations, many organizations use negotiated transfer pricing.

Under this technique, the managers of buying and selling divisions negotiate a transfer price between themselves, using a product's variable cost as the lower boundary of an acceptable negotiated price, and the market price (if one is available) as the upper boundary. The price that is agreed on, as long as it falls between these two boundaries, should give some profit to each division, with more profit going to the division with better negotiating skills. The method has the advantage of allowing division managers to operate their businesses more independently, not relying on preset pricing. It also results in better performance evaluations for those managers with greater negotiation skills.

Unfortunately, several issues relegate this approach to only a secondary role in most transfer pricing situations. First, if the negotiated price excessively favors one division over another, the losing division will search outside the company for a better deal on the open market and will direct its sales and purchases in that direction; this may result in suboptimal company-wide profitability levels. Also, the negotiation process can take up a substantial proportion of a manager's time, not leaving enough for other management activities. This is a particular problem if prices require constant renegotiation. Finally, the interdivisional conflicts over negotiated prices can become so severe that the problem is kicked up through the corporate chain of command to the president, who must step in and set prices that the divisions are incapable of determining by themselves. For all of these reasons, the negotiated transfer price is a method that is generally relegated to special or low-volume pricing situations.

16-6 Transfer Pricing Based on Contribution Margins

What is a company to do if there is no market price at all for a product? It has no basis for creating a transfer price from any external source of information, so it must use internal information instead. One approach is to create transfer prices based on a product's contribution margin.

Under the contribution margin pricing system, a company determines the total contribution margin earned after a product is sold externally, and then allocates this margin back to each division, based on their respective proportions of the total product cost. There are several good reasons for using this approach. They are as follows:

- *Converts a cost center into a profit center.* Without this profit allocation method, a company must resort to transfer pricing that is only based on product costs (as noted in later sections), which requires it to use cost centers. By using this method to assign profits to internal product sales, a company can force its divisional managers to pay stricter attention to their profitability, which helps the overall profitability of the organization. Also, when an organization has profit centers, it is easier to decentralize operations, because there is no longer a need for a large central bureaucracy to keep watch over divisional costs—the divisions are now in a position to do this work themselves.

■ *Encourages divisions to work together.* When every supplying division shares in the margin when a product is sold, it stands to reason that they will be much more anxious to work together to achieve profitable sales, rather than bickering over the transfer prices to be charged internally. Also, any profit improvements that can only be brought about by changes that span several divisions are much more likely to receive general approval and cooperation under this pricing method, because the changes will increase profits for all divisions.

These are powerful arguments, ones that make the contribution margin approach popular as a secondary transfer pricing method, after the market price approach. Despite this method's useful attributes, a company must guard against several issues in order to avoid behavior by divisions that will lead to suboptimal overall levels of profitability. They are as follows:

■ *Can increase assigned profits by increasing costs.* When the contribution margin is assigned based on a division's relative proportion of total product costs, it will not take long for the divisions to realize that they will receive a greater share of the profits if they can increase their overall proportion of costs. This problem can be counteracted by allocating based on a standard cost that is carefully reviewed and agreed on once a year, rather than an actual cost that requires constant oversight to avoid the loading of unrelated costs.

■ *Must share cost reductions.* If a division finds a way to reduce its costs, it will only receive an increased share of the resulting profits that is in proportion to its share of the total contribution margin distributed. For example, if Division A's costs are 20% of a product's total costs, and Division B's share is 80%, then 80% of a $1 cost reduction achieved by Division A will be allocated to Division B, even though it has done nothing to deserve the increase in margin. This problem can be avoided by basing the contribution margin allocation on standard costs once a year; this approach allows each division to reduce its costs below their standard cost levels and retain all of the resulting profit savings.

■ *Difficult to allocate among many divisions.* Some highly vertically integrated organizations have dozens of divisions selling each other products of various kinds. In these cases, it is difficult to determine the correct margin allocations, simply because of the number of transfers. The task can be achieved, but it requires a large accounting staff to calculate the distributions.

■ *Requires the involvement of the corporate headquarters staff.* The contribution margin allocation must be calculated by somebody, and because the divisions all have a profit motive to skew the allocation in their favor, the only party left that can make the allocation is the headquarters staff. This may require the addition of inventory accountants to the headquarters staff, which will increase corporate overhead.

- *Results in arguments.* When costs and profits can be skewed by the system, there will inevitably be arguments between the buying and selling divisions, which the corporate headquarters team may have to mediate. These issues detract from an organization's focus on profitability.

The contribution margin approach is not perfect, but it does give companies a reasonably understandable and workable method for determining transfer prices. It has more problems than market-based pricing, but it can be used as an alternative or as the primary approach if there is no way to obtain market pricing for transferred products.

16-7   Transfer Pricing Based on Marginal Cost

A transfer pricing technique that is supported more in the classroom than in corporations is based on marginal costs. Under this methodology, a company should continue to sell a product up until the point where the incremental increase in costs for each additional unit is exactly matched by the transfer price. By doing so, a division can earn the maximum amount of profit by selling the largest possible quantity of a product that still earns a profit. This concept is shown in Exhibit 16-2.

As noted in the exhibit, a cost that a company incurs to produce a product will gradually decline as it reaches optimum production volumes, which tend to be when a manufacturing facility is producing in the range of 50% to 80% of its total capac-

Exhibit 16-2   *Derivation of the Marginal Transfer Price*

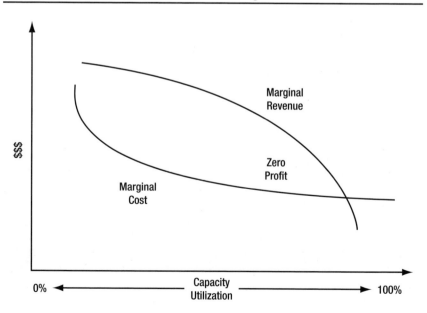

ity. In this zone, the production staff does not need to incur overtime hours, nor does the maintenance staff have to work during odd shifts to repair failed machinery, because there is enough slack time in the production schedule to complete any tasks during the normal work day. However, as production volumes rise past this optimum point and a company enters the upper reaches of its maximum capacity levels, it becomes more expensive to create each additional unit of product; the staff must work overtime or during late shifts that require a pay premium, and the machines require immediate repairs that may call for maintenance at any time of the day or night and the procurement of spare parts on a rush (and expensive) basis. For these reasons, the incremental cost to produce one additional unit of production gradually declines as production volumes go up, but then costs become more expensive as high levels of capacity utilization are reached.

As long as the transfer price is higher than the incremental cost required to make each additional unit of production, a division should continue to produce more parts (assuming that there is a willing buyer in the buying division for the extra units). However, once the marginal increase in costs forces a product's cost up to the point where there is no profit to be made on the sale of one more unit, then a division should sell no additional products. Although this approach works fine in theory, it is not at all simple to operate in practice. The following problems make it a difficult transfer pricing system to use:

- *Lack of marginal cost information.* Few organizations have such a fine-tuned knowledge of their marginal costs that they can determine the exact point where marginal costs equal the transfer price. Most organizations only operate their manufacturing facilities within a narrow band of capacity utilization (opting for production consistency), and so have no idea of what additional costs will be incurred if more capacity is used. Instead, the cost accounting staff can only specify a range of production volumes, somewhere within which the marginal cost will equal the transfer price. Because of this lack of precision, a division may find itself producing quite a few additional units at a loss.

- *Lack of marginal price information.* As production volumes increase, it is possible that so many units of the product will be available to buyers that they begin to bid the price downward. If so, the point at which the marginal increase in product cost matches the marginal decrease in prices may come much sooner than expected. Because it is difficult to predict how prices will change as volumes increase, this makes it difficult to predict the exact point at which additional production of a product will result in no further profits.

- *Impact of step costing.* In reality, costs do not increase by small amounts as each marginal unit of production is added. Instead, they tend to remain steady within certain ranges of production and then have sudden jumps in cost. These jumps are known as *step costs* and are caused by the acquisition of new assets or the need for additional activities that are required as soon as production levels reach a certain level of intensity. For example, if a production line cannot produce at a higher level without the addition of a band saw at a bottleneck operation, then the cost of acquiring this band saw is a step cost. Similarly, moving additional production to a weekend shift will require the payment of a shift premium that represents a permanent increase in costs at the higher level of production. It is difficult to estimate the size or timing of these step costs, which makes it more difficult to ascertain the exact increases in marginal costs as production volumes go up.

■ *Incentive problem.* As a division approaches the point at which its marginal costs nearly match its marginal revenue on the sale of each additional unit, its incentive to continue to churn out more products will decline, because its profit return approaches zero as it approaches this point. The manager of the selling division will see costs escalating and profits declining on additional sales, and so will prefer to stop production well short of the point where profits equal zero. The reason for stopping short is not based on just the diminishing size of profits per unit, but also the manager's uncertainty regarding the actual cost of each incremental unit; cost information is not exact, and the manager prefers to err on the side of caution.

The marginal cost concept appears to be a good one on paper, but it is difficult to calculate marginal costs, as well as estimate matching declines in marginal revenues. Also, as profits begin to decline, there is no incentive for selling divisions to produce additional product. For all of these reasons, basing transfer prices on marginal costs has found little real-world application.

16-8   Transfer Pricing Based on Cost Plus

In situations where a division cannot derive its transfer prices from the outside market—perhaps because there is no market for its products or it is a small one—the cost-plus approach may be a reasonable alternative.

The cost-plus approach is based on its name: just accumulate a product's full cost, add a standard margin percentage to the cost, and this becomes the transfer price. It has the singular advantage of being easy to understand and calculate, and it can convert a cost center into a profit center, which may be useful for evaluating the performance of a division manager.

Unfortunately, the cost-plus approach also has several serious flaws, as noted in the following list:

■ *Arbitrary margins.* The margin percentage added to a product's full cost may have no relationship to the margin that would actually be used if the product were to be sold externally. If several successive divisions were to add a standard margin to their products, the price paid by the final division in line—the one that must sell the completed product externally—may be so high that there is no room for its own margin, which gives it no incentive to sell the product (see the Impact of Profit Build-Up section later in this chapter).

■ *Incentive to increase costs.* If the selling division increases the cost of the product it is transferring, the margin assigned to it will be even larger (assuming that the margin is based on a percentage of costs, rather than a dollar amount).

This is a particularly dangerous incentive to give a division that sells some products externally, because it will shift reported costs away from its products that are meant for immediate external sale and toward costs that can be shifted to buying divisions. In this situation, not only is the buying division's cost increased (perhaps preventing it from later selling it at a reasonable profit), but the cost basis for external sales by the selling division is also artificially lowered (because the costs are shifted to internal sales), possibly resulting in the lowering of prices to external customers to a point below a product's variable cost. In short, changes in costs that are caused by the cost-plus system can result in reduced profits for a company as a whole.

Because of these issues, the cost-plus transfer pricing method is not recommended in most situations. However, if a company has only a small amount of internal transfers, the volume of internal sales may be so small that the method will engender no incorrect cost-shifting activity. Given its ease of use, the method may be applicable in this one case, despite its other flaws.

16-9   Transfer Pricing Based on Opportunity Costs

A completely unique approach to the formulation of transfer prices is based on opportunity costs. This method is not precisely based on either market prices or internal costs, because it is founded on the concept of foregone profits. It is best described with an example. If a selling division can earn a profit of $10,000 by selling widget A on the outside market, but is instead told to sell widget B to a buying division of the company, then it has lost the $10,000 that it would have earned on the sale of widget A. Its opportunity cost of producing widget B instead of A is therefore $10,000. If the selling division can add the foregone profit of $10,000 onto its variable cost to produce widget B, then it will be indifferent as to which product it sells, because it will earn the same profit on the sale of either product. Thus, transfer pricing based on opportunity cost is essentially the variable cost of the product being sold to another division, plus the opportunity cost of profits foregone in order to create the product being sold.

 This concept is most applicable in situations where a division is using all of its available production capacity. Otherwise, it would be capable of producing all products at the same time and would have no opportunity cost associated with not selling any particular item. To use the same example, if there were no market for widget A, on which there was initially a profit of $10,000, there would no longer be any possible profit, and consequently no reason to add an opportunity cost onto the sale price of widget B. The same principle applies if a company has specialized production equipment that can only be used for the production of a single product. In this case, there are no grounds for adding an opportunity cost onto the price of a product, because there are no other uses for the production equipment.

 A problem with this approach is that there must be a substantial external market for sale of the products for which an opportunity cost is being calculated. If not, then there is not really a viable alternative available under which a division can sell its products on the outside market. Thus, although a selling division may point to the current product pricing in a thin external market as an opportunity cost, further investigation may reveal that there is no way that the market can absorb the division's full production (or can only do so at a much lower price), thereby rendering the opportunity cost invalid.

Another issue is that the opportunity cost is subject to considerable alteration. For example, the selling division wants to show the highest possible opportunity cost on sale of a specific product, so that it can add this opportunity cost to its other transfer prices. Accordingly, it will skew its costing system by allocating fixed costs elsewhere, showing variable costs based on high unit production levels and the use of the highest possible prices, to result in a large profit for that product. This large profit will then be used as the opportunity cost that is foregone when any other products are sold to other divisions, thereby increasing the prices that other divisions must pay the selling division. Although this problem can be controlled with close oversight by the headquarters staff, the opportunity for a division manager to take advantage of this issue nonetheless exists.

This technique is also difficult for the accounting staff to support. Their problem is that the opportunity cost appears nowhere in the accounting system. It is not an incurred cost, because it never happened, and therefore does not appear in the general ledger. Without "hard" numbers that are readily locatable in the existing accounting system, accountants feel that they are working with "funny numbers." The level of understandability does not stop with accountants, either. Division managers have a hard time understanding that a transfer price is based on a product's variable cost plus a margin on a different product that was never produced. Accordingly, gaining company-wide support of this concept can be a difficult task to accomplish.

Another problem occurs when buying divisions have no other source of supply because the products made by the selling division are unique. In this instance, the managers of the buying divisions may appeal to the corporate headquarters staff to force the selling division to sell them product at a lower price, on the grounds that the selling division is in a monopoly situation, and therefore can charge any price it wants, and consequently must have its pricing forcibly controlled.

Despite these problems, this is a particularly elegant solution to the transfer pricing problem. It helps division managers select from among a variety of alternative types of product by setting the prices of *all* their products at levels that will uniformly earn them the same profit, as is illustrated in Exhibit 16-3. In the example, the profit margin on the 10-amp motor is $10, which is the highest profit earned by the division on any of its products. It now adds the same profit margin to its other two products, so that it is indifferent as to which products it sells—it will make the same profit in all cases. It is now up to the managers of the buying divisions to reject or accept the prices being charged by the selling division. If the price is too high, they can procure their motors elsewhere. If not, they can buy from the selling division, which not only allows the selling division to obtain a high profit on its operations, but also proves that the resulting price is still equal to or lower than the price at which the buying division would have obtained if it had purchased else-

Exhibit 16-3   *The Impact of Opportunity Costs on Transfer Pricing*

	10-Amp Motor	25-Amp Motor	50-Amp Motor
Variable Cost	$24.00	$27.00	$31.00
Profit Margin	10.00	10.00	10.00
Price	34.00	37.00	41.00

where. Under ideal conditions, this method should result in optimum company-wide levels of profitability.

Unfortunately, the key words here are "under ideal conditions." In reality, many of the preceding objections will come into play. For example, a selling division may find that its opportunity cost is a false one, because the external market for its products is too small. As a result, it sets a high opportunity cost on its products, only to see all of its interdivisional sales dry up because its prices are now too high. It then shifts all of its production to external sales, only to find that it either cannot sell all of its production, or that it can do so, but only at a reduced price. Given the various problems with transfer prices based on opportunity costs, it is not used much in practice, but it can be a reasonable alternative for selected situations.

We have come to the end of several sections that covered different types of transfer pricing. We now turn to a review of several ancillary issues pertaining to transfer pricing, including the uses of standard costs, fixed costs, and actual costs in the determination of transfer prices, as well as the impact of profit build-up on the selling activities of those company divisions that sell to the external market.

16-10   Types of Costs Used in Transfer Pricing Derivations

When creating a transfer price based on any type of cost, one should carefully consider the types of cost that are used to develop the price. An incorrectly considered cost can have a large and deleterious impact on the pricing structure that is developed. In this section, we cover the use of actual costs, standard costs, and fixed costs in the creation of transfer prices.

When *actual costs* are used as the foundation for transfer prices, a company will know that its prices reflect the most up-to-date costs, which allows it to avoid any uncertainty regarding sudden changes in costs that are not quickly reflected in prices. If such changes are significant, a company can find itself selling its products internally at price points that do not result in optimum levels of profitability. Nonetheless, the following problems keep most organizations from using actual costs to derive their transfer prices:

■ *Volume-based cost changes.* Actual costs may vary to such an extent that transfer prices must be altered constantly, which throws the buying divisions into confusion, because they never know what prices to expect. This is a particular problem when costs vary significantly with changes in volume. For example, if a buying division purchases in quantities of 10,000, the price it is charged will reflect that volume. However, if it places an order for a much smaller quantity, the fixed costs associated with the production of those units, such as machine setup costs that are spread over a much smaller quantity of shipped items, will drastically increase the cost, and therefore the price charged.

- *Transfer of inefficiencies.* By using actual cost as the basis for its transfer pricing, a selling division no longer has any incentive to improve its operating efficiencies, because it can allow its costs to increase and then shift the costs to the buying division. This is less of a problem when the bulk of all sales are external, because the division will find that only a small proportion of its sales can be loaded with these extra costs. However, a situation where most sales are internal will allow a division to shift nearly all of its inefficiencies elsewhere.

- *Shifting of costs.* When actual costs are used, the selling division will quickly realize that it can load the costs it is charging to the buying division, thereby making its remaining costs look lower, which improves the division manager's performance rating. By shifting these costs, the buying division's costs will look worse than they really are. Although this problem can be resolved by constant monitoring of costs by the relatively impartial headquarters staff, the monitoring process is a labor-intensive one. Also, there will be constant arguments between the divisions regarding what cost increases are justified.

In short, the use of actual costing as the basis for transfer prices is generally not a good idea, primarily because its use allows selling divisions to shift additional costs to buying divisions, which reduces their incentive to improve internal efficiencies.

A better approach is to use *standard costing* as the basis for a transfer price. This is done by having all parties agree at the beginning of the year to the standard costs that will be used for transfer pricing, with changes allowed during the year only for significant and permanent cost changes, the justification of which should be closely audited to ensure that the changes are valid. By using this approach, the buying divisions can easily plan the cost of incoming components from the selling divisions without having any concerns about unusual pricing variances arising. Meanwhile, the selling divisions no longer have an incentive to transfer costs to the buying divisions, as was the case with actual costing, and instead can now fully concentrate their attention on reducing their costs through improved efficiencies. If they can drop their costs below the standard cost levels at which transfer prices are set for the year, then they can report improved financial results that reflect well not only on the division manager's performance, but also on the performance of the company as a whole. Furthermore, there is no need for constant monitoring of costs by the corporate headquarters staff, because standard costs are fixed for the entire year. Instead, the headquarters staff can concentrate its attention on the annual setting of standard costs; this is the one time during the year when costs can be manipulated to favor the selling divisions, which requires in-depth cost reviews to avoid. As long as standard costs are set at reasonable levels, this approach is much superior to the use of transfer prices that are based on actual costs.

Yet another issue is the addition of fixed costs to variable costs when setting transfer prices. When these costs are combined, it is called *full costing.* When a selling division uses full costing, the buying division only knows that it cannot sell the purchased item for less than the price it paid. However, this may not be the correct selling strategy for the company as a whole. As noted in Exhibit 16-4, a series of divisions sell their products to a marketing division, which sells all products externally on behalf of the other divisions. The marketing division buys the products from the selling divisions at full cost. It does not know what proportions of the price it pays are based on fixed costs and which on variable costs. It can only assume that, from the marketing division's perspective, its variable cost is 100% of the amount it has paid for the products, and that it cannot sell for less than the amount it paid. In reality, as shown in the exhibit, only 51% of the transfer price it has paid consists of variable costs. If the marketing division were aware of this information, it could sell products at prices as low as the variable cost of $82.39. Although such a price would not cover fixed costs in the long run, it may be acceptable for selected pricing decisions where the marketing division has occasional opportunities to earn some extra margin on lower-priced sales.

The best way to ensure that the division making external sales is aware of both the fixed and variable costs that are included in a transfer price is to itemize them as such. When the selling division has full knowledge of the cumulate variable cost of any products it has bought internally, it can then make better pricing decisions. This separation of a transfer price into its component parts is not difficult and can be made on a cumulative basis for all products that have been transferred through multiple divisions.

Exhibit 16-4 *Impact of Full Costing on Selling Decisions*

	Division 1	Division 2	Division 3	Marketing Division	Cumulative Costs	Percent of Total
Transfered-in Cost	$ —	$ 41.58	$ 100.31	$ 171.98		
Division-Specific Variable Cost	$ 13.58	$ 41.02	$ 27.79	$ —	$ 82.39	51%
Division-Specific Fixed Cost	$ 22.58	$ 10.05	$ 34.53	$ 12.71	$ 79.87	49%
Total Division-Specific (15%)Cost	$ 36.16	$ 51.07	$ 62.32	$ 12.71	$ 162.26	100%
Margin On Division-Specific Cost	$ 5.42	$ 7.66	$ 9.35	$ 1.91		
Price Based on Division-Specific Cost	$ 41.58	$ 58.73	$ 71.67	$ 14.62		
Division Price + Transferred-In Price	$ 41.58	$ 100.31	$ 171.98	$ 186.60		

Another way to handle the pricing of fixed costs is to charge a budgeted amount of fixed cost to the buying division in each reporting period. By doing so, there is no need to run a calculation in each period to determine the amount of fixed cost to charge at different volume levels. Also, the budgeted charge reflects the cost of the selling division's capacity that the buying division is using, and so is a reasonable way for the buying division to justify its priority in product sales by the selling division over other potential sales—it has paid for the capacity, so it has first rights to production.

Another school of thought is that no fixed costs should be charged to the buying division at all. One reason is that the final price charged to an external customer is based on market rates, not internal costs, so there is no reason to account for the cost if it has no impact on the final price. Another reason is that the fixed cost typically charged to the buying division rarely includes all fixed costs, such as general and administrative expenses, so if the fixed cost cannot be accurately determined, why charge it at all? Also, the fixed costs of a division are not closely tied to the volume of units produced (otherwise, they would be variable costs), so it is not possible to accurately assign a fixed cost to each unit of production sold. In short, this viewpoint questions the reason for assigning any fixed cost to a product, because of the difficulty of measurement and its irrelevance to the ultimate price set for external sale.

Not including any fixed cost in the transfer price will reduce the price that the buying division pays, and makes its profits look abnormally high, because these costs will be absorbed by those upstream divisions that supplied the product. However, the profits of the division that sells the product externally can be allocated back to upstream divisions, in proportion to their costs included in the product, so there is a way to give these divisions a profit.

The arguments in favor of standard costing make it the clear choice over the use of actual costs in the derivation of transfer prices. However, the preceding arguments both in favor of and against the use of fixed costs are much less clear. A company can avoid the entire issue by simply basing intercompany transfers on market prices for each item transferred, but there is no outside market for many products, so managers cannot use this method to avoid the fixed-cost issue. The author's preferred approach is to assign a standard lump-sum fixed cost to the buying division in each period; this approach avoids the issue of how to determine the fixed cost per unit and also gives the buying division the right to reserve the production capacity of the selling division that is related to the fixed cost being paid by the buying division.

16-11   The Impact of Profit Build-Up

If an organization has many divisions that pass along products among themselves, it is possible that each successive division in the chain of product sales will tack on such a large profit margin that the last division in the chain will end up purchasing a product that is too expensive for it to make any profit when it is finally time to sell it externally. This problem is known as *profit build-up* and is illustrated in Exhibit 16-5. In the exhibit, the first three divisions add a preset profit margin to a product as each one adds value to it—the price accordingly increases as it advances through the chain of products. By the time the product reaches Division 4, the price is so high that it will lose $.25 upon sale of the product. Because it will lose money, the division has no incentive to sell the product, even though the company as a whole has earned a profit of $6.35 (net of the loss on sale) over the course of its manufacture in the various divisions. We arrive at the $6.35 figure by adding up all of the incremental margins added to the product in each division, less the loss that occurred at the time of sale.

The profit build-up problem is most common when a company sets up profit margins for each successive division to add to products, based on a final market price that is either no longer valid or that is reduced in the case of a special sale price.

In this situation, the final division in the chain has several alternatives. One is to purchase its component parts elsewhere. This option is the best when the supplying divisions can earn their standard profit markups by selling all of their production elsewhere, but is otherwise detrimental if the organization as a whole is not using excess production capacity to supply components to Division 4. Another option is to not sell the product at all, which may be acceptable if the division has other products it can sell that still earn a similar profit level; if not, however, the division will not optimize profitability by foregoing these sales. Yet another choice is to have the corporate headquarters staff review the margins added throughout the transfer process, to see if they should be reduced to reflect actual market rates. This approach may interfere with the normal transfer price-setting structure within the company, however, and may also require a great deal of corporate intervention if the final product price constantly fluctuates. The best alternative for Division 4 is to negotiate with downstream divisions for special transfer price breaks as the final sale price moves up or down; this approach keeps the headquarters staff out of the picture and allows the selling division to react more quickly to sudden downturns in the final price that may still result in an overall profit for the organization.

Exhibit 16-5   *Profit Build-Up Scenario*

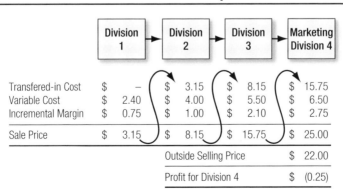

	Division 1	Division 2	Division 3	Marketing Division 4
Transfered-in Cost	$ —	$ 3.15	$ 8.15	$ 15.75
Variable Cost	$ 2.40	$ 4.00	$ 5.50	$ 6.50
Incremental Margin	$ 0.75	$ 1.00	$ 2.10	$ 2.75
Sale Price	$ 3.15	$ 8.15	$ 15.75	$ 25.00
Outside Selling Price				$ 22.00
Profit for Division 4				$ (0.25)

A helpful tool for determining the lowest price at which a company should sell its product is to divide the transfer price into two components: (1) the cumulative variable cost and (2) the cumulative margin that is added to the product at each transfer. By doing so, the selling division can see the size of the cumulative variable cost, which represents the point below which it cannot drop the selling price without incurring an overall loss on sale of the product. Without such a report, the selling division will not realize that some portion of the cost that has been transferred to it is only a margin that has been added internally.

16-12   Comparison of Transfer Pricing Methods

In the preceding sections, seven transfer pricing methods have been described, as well as the advantages and disadvantages of each one. The wide array of methods may be confusing to one who is attempting to select the method that best fits a company's particular circumstances. Accordingly, the summary table shown in Exhibit 16-6 may be of assistance. The table notes each transfer pricing method down the left side, in the order in which they were originally presented. Across the top are the three main criteria for selecting a transfer pricing method—profitability enhancement, performance review, and ease of use—as well as the problems that go along with each one.

Exhibit 16-6   *Comparison of Transfer Pricing Methods*

Type of Transfer Pricing Method	Profitability Enhancement	Performance Review	Ease of Use	Problems
Market Pricing	Creates highest level of profits for entire company	Creates profits centers for all divisions	Simple applicability	Market prices not always available; may not be large enough external market; does not reflect slight reduced internal selling costs; selling divisions may deny sales to other divisions in favor of outside sales
Adjusted Market Pricing	Creates highest level of profits for entire company	Creates profits centers for all divisions	Requires negotiation to determine reductions from market price	Possible arguments over size of reductions; may need headquarters intervention

Exhibit 16-6 *Continued*

Type of Transfer Pricing Method	Profitability Enhancement	Performance Review	Ease of Use	Problems
Negotiated Prices	Less optimal result than market-based pricing, especially if negotiated prices vary substantially from the market	May reflect more on manager negotiating skills than on division performance	Easy to understand, but requires substantial preparation for negotiations	May result in better deals for divisions if they buy or sell outside the company; negotiations are time-consuming; may require headquarters intervention
Contribution Margins	Allocates final profits among cost centers; divisions tend to work together to achieve large profit	Allows for some basis of measurement based on profits, where cost center performance is the only other alternative	Can be difficult to calculate if many divisions involved	A division can increase its share of the profit margin by increasing its costs; a cost reduction by one division must be shared among all divisions; requires headquarters involvement
Marginal Cost	Maximum profit levels for each division and in total	Can measure divisions based on profitability	Very difficult to calculate the point at which marginal costs equal revenues	Difficulty of cost and price measurement; reduced incentive to produce as marginal costs equate to margin prices
Cost Plus	May result in profit build-up problem, so that division selling externally has not incentive to do so	Poor for performance evaluation, because will earn a profit no matter what cost is incurred	Easy to calculate profit add-on	Margins assigned do not equate to market-driven profit margins; no incentive to reduce costs
Opportunity Cost	Good way to ensure profit maximization	Will drive managers to achieve company-wide goals	Difficult to calculate, and to obtain acceptance within the	Too arcane a calculation for ready acceptance; requires an organization outside market to determine the opportunity cost; the opportunity cost can be manipulated

When selecting from the list of transfer pricing methods, it is useful to follow a sequential list of yes/no rules that will gradually eliminate several methods, leaving one with just a few to choose from. Those decision rules are as follows:

1. *Is there an outside market for a selling division's products?*
   - If not, then throw out all market-based pricing methods and review cost-based methods instead.
   - If so, recommended methods are market pricing, adjusted market pricing, or negotiated pricing.
2. *Is the corporation highly centralized?*
   - If not, then avoid all cost allocation methods that require headquarters oversight.
   - If so, recommended methods are contribution margin or opportunity cost.
3. *Do the transferred items represent a large proportion of the selling division's sales?*
   - If not, it may be best to simply transfer products at cost and have all profits accrue to the division that sells completed products externally. This means that all divisions selling at cost probably have no external market for their products. They should be treated as cost centers, with management performance appraisals tied to reductions in per-unit costs.
   - If so, recommended methods are marginal cost or cost plus.

All of the transfer pricing methods noted in this chapter are based on the assumption that a company wants to treat all of its divisions as profit centers. However, as noted in the last item in the preceding set of decision rules, there will be some circumstances where it does not make sense to add any margin to a transferred product. In these cases, which usually involve the manufacture of products that cannot be sold outside of a company, and for which there is only one buyer—another company division—it is best to transfer at cost. Otherwise, a company creates a profit center that cannot be justified, because there is no way to prove, through comparisons to external market prices, that profit levels are reasonable.

The number of cost centers that a company allows should be kept to a minimum, for two reasons. First, the managers of a cost center are not concerned with the final price of a product, and so may not make a sufficient effort to reduce their costs to a level necessary for the company as a whole to sell a product to the external market at a reasonable profit margin. For example, the manager of a cost center may think that a 5% reduction in costs is a sufficient target to pursue for one year, even though the marketing division that must sell the final product is being faced with falling market prices that call for a 20% reduction in prices in order to stay competitive. Accordingly, the behavior of a cost center manager may not be tied closely enough to an organization's overall needs. The second problem is that, because the cost center is driven to keep its per-unit costs at the lowest possible level, it will resist any demands from buying divisions to increase its level of production to the point where its per-unit costs will increase. This typically happens when a production facility exceeds 60% to 70% of its theoretical production capacity level, requiring it to spend more on overtime and maintenance costs. Such behavior by the selling division does not maximize overall company profits, as long as the marginal increase in costs does not exceed the profit to be gained by producing each additional unit.

In short, market-based transfer prices are to be preferred over all other methods, because they result in the best level of conformance to a company's overall profitability, performance measurement, and ease-of-use goals. Other cost-based measures can also be used, but only as secondary measures in the event that market-based pricing is not possible.

APPENDIX A

Dictionary of Inventory Terms[1]

ABC inventory classification. A method for dividing inventory into classifications, either by transaction volume or cost. Typically, category A includes that 20% of inventory involving 60% of all costs or transactions, while category B includes the next 20% of inventory involving 20% of all costs or transactions, and category C includes the remaining 60% of inventory involving 20% of all costs or transactions.

Accumulation bin. A location in which components destined for the shop floor are accumulated before delivery.

Advance material request. Very early orders for materials before the completion of a product design, given the long lead times required to supply some items.

Aggregate planning. A budgeting process using summary-level information to derive various budget models, usually at the product family level.

Automated storage/retrieval system. A racking system using automated systems to load and unload the racks.

Back flush. The subsequent subtraction from inventory records of those parts used to assemble a product, based on the number of finished goods produced.

Bar code. Information encoded into a series of bar and spaces of varying widths, which can be automatically read and converted to text by a scanning device.

Batch picking. Picking for several summarized orders at the same time, thereby reducing the total number of required picks. The combined picks must still be separated into their constituent orders, typically at some central location.

Bill of materials. A listing of all parts and subassemblies required to produce one unit of a finished product, including the required number of units of each part and subassembly.

Bin. A storage area, typically a subdivision of a single level of a storage rack.

Bin transfer. A transaction to move inventory from one storage bin to another.

Blend off. The reintroduction of a faulty product into a process production flow by adding it back in small increments.

[1]Copied with permission from Appendix B of Bragg, *Inventory Best Practices*, John Wiley & Sons, 2004.

Bottleneck. A resource whose capacity is unable to match or exceed that of the demand volume required of it.

Breeder bill of materials. A bill of material that accounts for the generation and cost implications of byproducts as a result of manufacturing the parent item.

By-product. A material created incidental to a production process, which can be sold for value.

Carrying cost. The cost of holding inventory, which can include insurance, spoilage, rent, and other expenses.

Component. Raw materials or subassemblies used to make either finished goods or higher levels of subassembly.

Configuration audit. A review of all engineering documentation used as the basis for a manufactured product to see if the documentation accurately represents the finished product.

Configuration control. Verifying that a delivered product matches authorizing engineering documentation. This also refers to engineering changes made subsequent to the initial product release.

Consigned stocks. Inventories owned by a company, but located on the premises of its agents or distributors.

Cost of goods sold. The charge to expense of the direct materials, direct labor, and allocated overhead costs associated with products sold during a defined accounting period.

Cutoff control. A procedure for ensuring that transaction processing is completed before the commencement of cycle counting.

Cycle counting. The frequent, scheduled counting of a subset of all inventories, with the intent of spotting inventory record inaccuracies, investigating root causes, and correcting those problems.

Delivery policy. A company's stated goal for how soon a customer order will be shipped following receipt of that order.

Departmental stocks. The informal and frequently unauthorized retention of excess inventory on the shop floor, which is used as buffer safety stock.

Discrete order picking. A picking method requiring the sequential completion of each order before one begins picking the next order.

Distribution center. A branch warehouse containing finished goods and service items intended for distribution directly to customers.

Distribution inventory. Inventory intended for shipment to customers, usually comprised of finished goods and service items.

Earmarked material. Inventory that has been physically marked as being for a specific purpose.

Ending inventory. The dollar value or unit total of goods on hand at the end of an accounting period.

Engineering change. A change to a product's specifications as issued by the engineering department.

Enterprise resource planning system. A computer system used to manage all company resources in the receipt, completion, and delivery of customer orders.

Expedite. To artificially accelerate an order ahead of its regularly scheduled counterparts.

Explode. The multiplication of component requirements itemized on a bill of material by the number of parent items required to determine total parts usage.

Failure analysis. The examination of failure incidents to identify components with poor performance profiles.

Field warehouse. A warehouse into which service parts and finished goods are stocked, and from which deliveries are made directly to customers.

Finished goods inventory. Completed inventory items ready for shipment to customers.

First-in, first-out. An inventory valuation method under which one assumes that the first inventory item to be stored in a bin is the first one to be used, irrespective of actual usage.

Fixed-location storage. An inventory storage technique under which permanent locations are assigned to at least some inventory items.

Floor stocks. Low-cost, high-usage inventory items stored near the shop floor, which the production staff can use at will without a requisition and which are expensed at the time of receipt, rather than being accounted for through a formal inventory database.

Fluctuation inventory. Excess inventory kept on hand to provide a buffer against forecasting errors.

Forward buying. The purchase of items exceeding the quantity levels indicated by current manufacturing requirements.

Hedge inventory. Excess inventories kept on hand as a buffer against contingent events.

Inactive inventory. Parts with no recent prior or forecasted usage.

Indented bill of material. A bill of material reporting format under which successively lower levels of components are indented farther away from the left margin.

Interplant transfer. The movement of inventory from one company location to another, usually requiring a transfer transaction.

In-transit inventory. Inventory currently situated between its shipment and delivery locations.

Inventory. Those items included categorized as either raw materials, work-in-process, or finished goods, and involved in either the creation of products or service supplies for customers.

Inventory adjustment. A transaction used to adjust the book balance of an inventory record to the amount actually on hand.

Inventory diversion. The redirection of parts or finished goods away from their intended goal.

Inventory issue. A transaction used to record the reduction in inventory from a location, because of its release for processing or transfer to another location.

Inventory receipt. The arrival of an inventory delivery from a supplier or other company location.

Inventory returns. Inventory returned from a customer for any reason. This receipt is handled differently from a standard inventory receipt, typically into an inspection area, from which it may be returned to stock, reworked, or scrapped.

Inventory turnover. The number of times per year that an entire inventory or a subset thereof is used.

Item master file. A file containing all item-specific information about a component, such as its weight, cubic volume, and unit of measure.

Item number. A number uniquely identifying a product or component.

Just-in-time. A cluster of manufacturing, design, and delivery practices designed to continually reduce all types of waste, thereby improving production efficiency.

Kit. A group of components needed to assemble a finished product that has been clustered together for delivery to the shop floor.

Last-in, first-out. An inventory valuation method under which one assumes that the last inventory item to be stored in a bin is the first one to be used, irrespective of actual usage.

Lean production. The technique of stripping all non-value-added activities from the production process, thereby using the minimum possible amount of resources to accomplish manufacturing goals.

Locator file. A file identifying where inventory items are situated, by bin location.

Make-to-order. A production scheduling system under which products are only manufactured once a customer order has been received.

Make-to-stock. A production scheduling system under which products are completed before the receipt of customer orders, which are filled from stock.

Manufacturing resource planning. An integrated, computerized system for planning all manufacturing resources.

Mass customization. High-volume production runs of a product, while still offering high variability in the end product offered to customers.

Material requirements planning. A computerized system used to calculate material requirements for a manufacturing operation.

Material review board. A company committee typically comprising members representing multiple departments, which determines the disposition of inventory items that will not be used in the normal manufacturing or distribution process.

Materials requisition. A document listing the quantities of specific parts to be withdrawn from inventory.

Matrix bill of material. A bill of materials chart listing the bills for similar products, which is useful for determining common components.

Maximum inventory. An inventory item's budgeted maximum inventory level, comprising its preset safety stock level and planned lot size.

Minimum inventory. An inventory item's budgeted minimum inventory level.

Mix ticket. A list of the ingredients required for a blending operation.

Modular bill of material. A bill of material format in which components and subassemblies are clustered by product option, so one can more easily plan for the assembly of finished goods with different configurations.

Move. The movement of inventory among various locations within a company.

Multilevel bill of material. An itemization of all bill of material components, including a nested categorization of all components used for subassemblies.

Net inventory. The current inventory balance, less allocated or reserved items.

Nonconforming material. Any inventory item that does not match its original design specifications within approved tolerance levels.

Nonsignificant part number. An identifying number assigned to a part that conveys no other information.

Obsolete inventory. Parts not used in any current end product.

Offal material. The waste materials resulting from a production process.

On-hand balance. The quantity of inventory currently in stock, based on inventory records.

Order penetration point. The point in the production process when a product is reserved for a specific customer.

Order picking. The process of moving items from stock for shipment to customers.

Outbound stock point. A designated inventory location on the shop floor between operations where inventory is stockpiled until needed by the next operation.

Overrun. A manufactured or received quantity exceeding the planned amount.

Packing slip. A document attached to a customer shipment, describing the contents of the items shipped, as well as their part number and quantity.

Pallet ticket. A document attached to a pallet, showing the description, part number, and quantity of the item contained on the pallet.

Part. A specific component of a larger assembly.

Part number. A number uniquely identifying a product or component.

Parts requisition. An authorization to move a specific quantity of an item from stock.

Part standardization. The planned reduction of similar parts through the standardization of parts among multiple products.

Periodic inventory. A physical inventory count taken on a repetitive basis.

Perpetual inventory. A manual or automated inventory tracking system in which a new inventory balance is computed continuously whenever new transactions occur.

Phantom bill of material. A bill of materials for a subassembly that is not normally kept in stock, because it is used at once as part of a higher-level assembly or finished product.

Physical inventory. A manual count of the on-hand inventory.

Picking list. A document listing items to be removed from stock, either for delivery to the shop floor for production purposes or for delivery to a customer.

Picking transaction. Withdrawing parts or subassemblies from stock in order to manufacture subassemblies or finished products.

Point-of-use delivery. A delivery of stock to a location in or near the shop floor adjacent to its area of use.

Point-of-use storage. The storage of stock in a location in or near the shop floor adjacent to its area of use.

Primary location. A storage location labeled as the primary location for a specific inventory item.

Process flow production. A production configuration in which products are continually manufactured with minimal pauses or queuing.

Product. Any item intended for sale.

Projected available balance. The future planned balance of an inventory item, based on the current balance and adjusted for planned receipts and usage.

Pull system. A materials flow concept in which parts are only withdrawn after a request is made by the using operation for more parts.

Push system. A materials flow concept in which parts are issued based on planned material requirements.

Putaway. The process of moving received items to storage and recording the related transaction.

Rack. A vertical storage device in which pallets can be deposited, one over the other.

Random-location storage. The technique of storing incoming inventory in any available location, which is then tracked in a locator file.

Raw material. Base-level items used by the manufacturing process to create either subassemblies or finished goods.

Reconciling inventory. The process of comparing book to actual inventory balances, and adjusting for the difference in the book records.

Record accuracy. The variance between book and on-hand quantities, expressed as a percentage.

Remanufactured parts. Parts that have been reconstructed to render them capable of fulfilling their original function.

Repair bill of material. A special bill itemizing changes needed to refurbish an existing product.

Replacement parts. Parts requiring some modification before being substituted for another part.

Reprocessed material. Material that has been reworked and returned to stock.

Requirements explosion. The component-level requirements for a production run, derived by multiplying the number of parent-level requirements by the component requirements for each parent, as specified in the bill of materials.

Reserved material. Material that has been reserved for a specific purpose.

Rework. The refurbishment of a faulty part.

RFID. Acronym for Radio Frequency Identification. It is the basis for small radio transmitters that emit an RFID to receiver devices. The transmitter is a tiny tag, storing a unique product identification code that is transmitted and used for inventory tracking.

Safety stock. Extra inventory kept on hand to guard against requirements fluctuations.

Scrap. Faulty material that cannot be reworked.

Scrap factor. An anticipated loss percentage included in the bill of material and used to order extra materials for a production run, in anticipation of scrap losses.

Seasonal inventory. Very high inventory levels built up in anticipation of large seasonal sales.

Shelf life. The time period during which inventory can be retained in stock and beyond which it becomes unusable.

Shelf life control. Deliberate usage of the oldest items first, in order to avoid exceeding a component or product's shelf life.

Shrinkage. Any uncontrolled loss of inventory, such as through evaporation or theft.

Shrinkage factor. The expected loss of some proportion of an item during the production process, expressed as a percentage.

Significant part number. An identifying number assigned to an item that conveys additional embedded information.

Single-level bill of material. A list of all components used in a parent item.

Single sourcing. Using a single supplier as the only source of a part.

SKU. Acronym for *Stock Keeping Unit,* which is an item used at a single location.

Slow-moving item. An inventory item having a slower rate of turnover than the average turnover for the entire inventory.

Split delivery. The practice of ordering large quantities on a single purchase order, but separating the order into multiple smaller deliveries.

Stackability. The ability to safely stack multiple layers of the same SKU on top of each other.

Staging. Picking parts from stock for an order before they are needed, in order to determine parts shortages in advance.

Standard containers. Common-sized containers that are used to efficiently move, store, and count inventory.

Stock. Any item held in inventory.

Stockless purchasing. The purchase of material for direct delivery to the production area, bypassing any warehouse storage.

Stockout. The absence of any form of inventory when needed.

Stockpoint. An inventory storage area used for short-term inventory staging.

Subassembly. A group of assembled components used in the assembly of a higher-level assembly.

Summarized bill of materials. A bill of materials format showing the grand total usage requirement for each component of a finished product.

Supplies. General supplies used throughout a company and expensed at the time of acquisition.

Surplus inventory. Parts for which the on-hand quantity exceeds forecasted requirements.

Traceability. The ability to track the components used in production through their inclusion in a finished product and from there to specific customers.

Two-bin system. A system in which parts are reordered when their supply in one storage bin is exhausted, requiring usage from a backup bin until the replenishment arrives.

Unit of measure. The summarization unit by which an item is tracked, such as a box of 100 or an each of 1.

Unplanned receipt. A stock receipt for which no order was placed or for which an excess quantity was received.

Vendor-managed inventory. The direct management and ownership of selected on-site inventory by suppliers.

Visual control. The visual inspection of inventory levels, enabled by the use of designated locations and standard containers.

Visual review system. Inventory reordering based on a visual inspection of on-hand quantities.

Warehouse demand. The demand for a part by an outlying warehouse.

Wave picking. The practice of grouping the priority of pick lists so that groups of picked orders can be delivered at the same time, such as a set of orders being delivered to a single customer on a single truck departing at a specific time.

Where-used report. A report listing every product whose bill of material calls for the use of a specific component.

Withdrawal. The release of items from storage.

Work-in-process. Any items being converted into finished goods or released from the warehouse in anticipation of beginning the conversion process.

Zone picking. The practice of picking by area of the warehouse, rather than by order, requiring an additional consolidation step from which picking by order is completed.

Index

ABC storage system, 199
Activity-based costing, 132–138
Activity driver, 136
Adjusted market pricing, 214–215
Affiliated group, 172–173
Aisles, elimination of, 204
Audit
  Inventory, 42, 45, 178–179
  Prices paid, 45–46
  Production set-up costs, 47
  Receiving dock, 50, 63
  Shipping log, 48

Backflushing, 13–14, 32–33, 49, 64–65
Backorder length measurement, 80–81
Bar coding, 2–4, 49, 205
Bill and hold fraud, 61
Bill of activities, 138–140
Bill of materials
  Accuracy, 47, 190
  Fraud, 53
  Measurement, 69–70
Billing
  Controls, 48
Budgeting
  Finished goods, 104–107
  Raw materials, 97–102
  Work-in-process, 103–104
By-products, 142–148

Containers, standardized, 41
Controls, inventory, 35–50
Cost
  Allocation in JIT environment, 30–31

Allocation shortcomings, 131–132
Fraud, 54–55
Pools, 128–129, 134, 137–138
Roll-up, 45–47
Cost-plus
  Contracts, 143–144
  Transfer pricing, 220–221
Cross-docking, 198
Cut-off date
  Fraud, 63–64
  Physical count, 183–184
Cycle counting, 50, 91, 176, 178, 186–189, 205

Dictionary, 233–240
Dock door utilization, 81
Document imaging, 7–9
Dollar-value LIFO, 114–116
Drop shipment notifications, 48

Electronic data interchange, 9–10
Engineering change orders, 38

FIFO
  Inventory valuation, 109–111
  Racking, 43
Finished goods
  Budgeting, 104–107
  Journal entries, 160
Floor stock, 198
Fraud, inventory, 51–66
Full costing, 224–225

In-transit inventory, 36–37, 159–160
Insurance reimbursement, 144